# THE LONGEST PUN WAR

by Adam Hill and Ryan Chapman

Groan Men Productions
www.dailypunwars.com

DAILY PUN WARS

PEW PEW

The Longest Pun War by Adam Hill and Ryan Chapman
Published by Groan Men Productions

www.dailypunwars.com



For permissions contact:

info@dailypunwars.com



Cover and interior design by Ryan Chapman

ISBN: 9781097511723

Dear Reader,

The book you hold in your hands holds the record for the longest pun war ever.

Actually, we have no idea if that's true, but it has to be, right? I mean, I can't imagine anyone else has ever spent the time to pun back and forth on text message for this long.

Of course, that is what makes this book unique. This book is literally one long text message string between the two of us. There are almost no changes from the actual text message string to what is printed in this book.

We literally got together one day and decided to do the longest pun war ever and then publish it. So, we opened a text message and started punning. We hardly ever prompted each other or planned our next pun. We just punned our hearts out.

We hope this book makes you love it in the way everyone loves a good pun (deep down, but never publicly).

Sincerely,
Ryan and Adam

To our families.
Thank you for putting up with our puns.

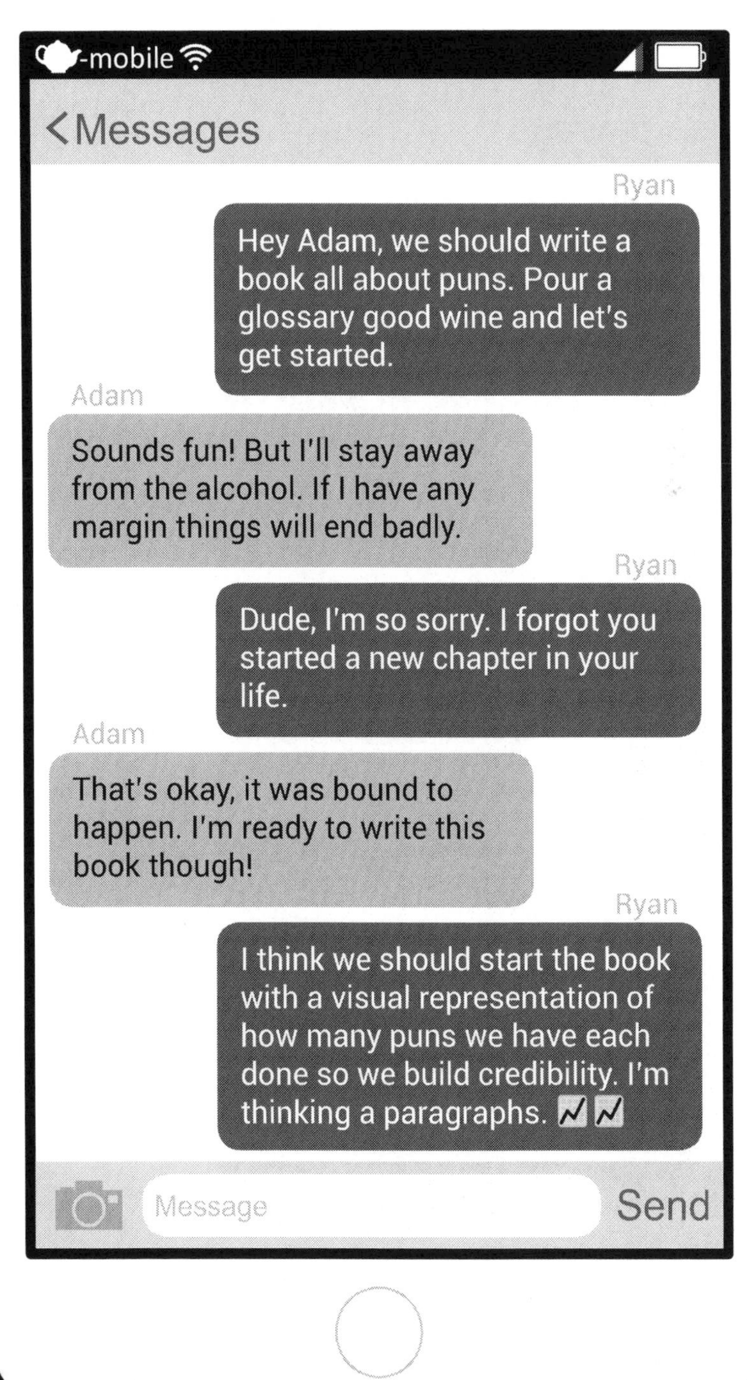
-mobile
Messages
Ryan
Hey Adam, we should write a book all about puns. Pour a glossary good wine and let's get started.
Adam
Sounds fun! But I'll stay away from the alcohol. If I have any margin things will end badly.
Ryan
Dude, I'm so sorry. I forgot you started a new chapter in your life.
Adam
That's okay, it was bound to happen. I'm ready to write this book though!
Ryan
I think we should start the book with a visual representation of how many puns we have each done so we build credibility. I'm thinking a paragraphs.
Message
Send

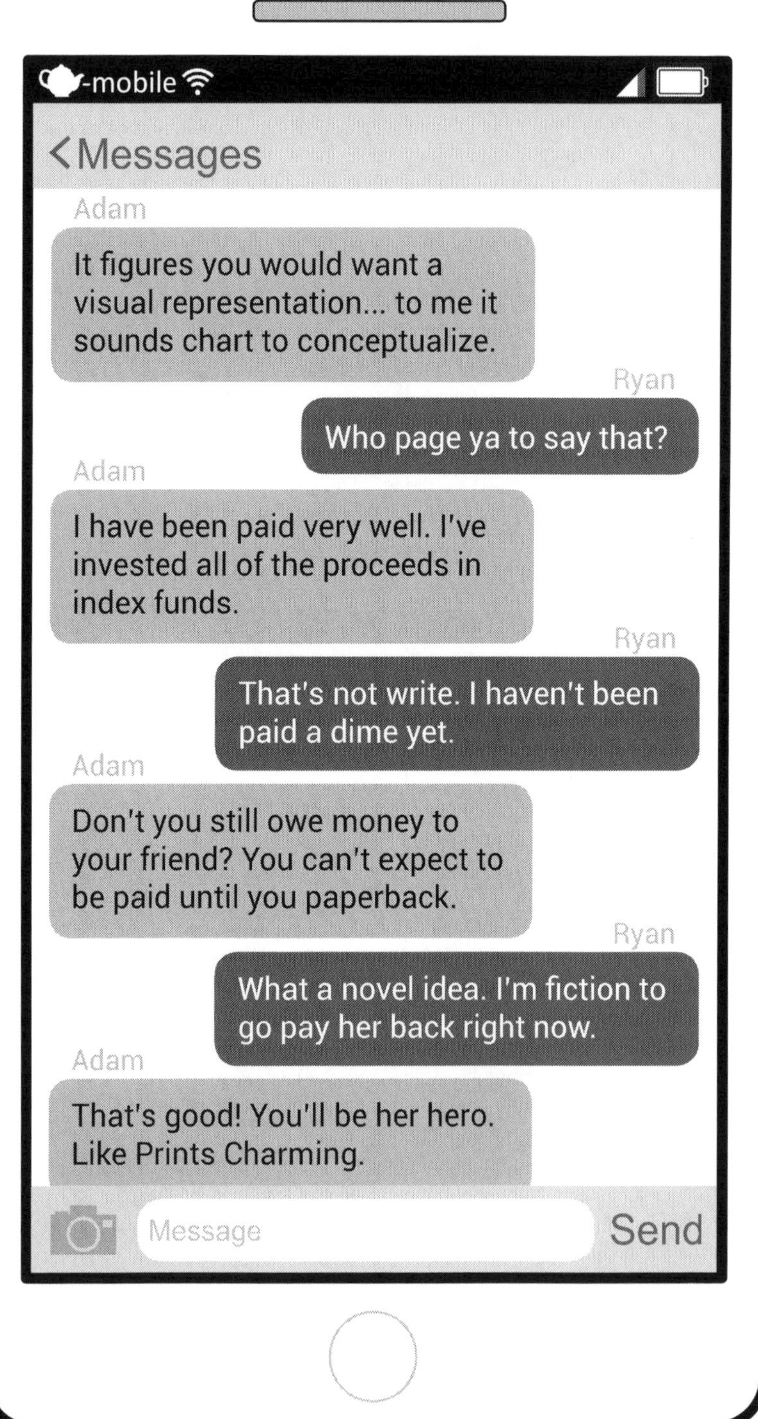
-mobile
Messages
Adam
It figures you would want a visual representation... to me it sounds chart to conceptualize.
Ryan
Who page ya to say that?
Adam
I have been paid very well. I've invested all of the proceeds in index funds.
Ryan
That's not write. I haven't been paid a dime yet.
Adam
Don't you still owe money to your friend? You can't expect to be paid until you paperback.
Ryan
What a novel idea. I'm fiction to go pay her back right now.
Adam
That's good! You'll be her hero. Like Prints Charming.
Message
Send

-mobile
Messages
Ryan
Like, literary.
Adam
Word.
Ryan
Speaking of that, can I just say...you really Excel at puns.
Adam
Aww thanks! I could use some advice on when to make a good pun. Can you let me know Windows times come up?
Ryan
Yes. I'll be on the Outlook for them.
Adam
Boy, I love making puns Visio. You make it lots of fun
Ryan
I am glad I can Access your puns as well.
Message
Send

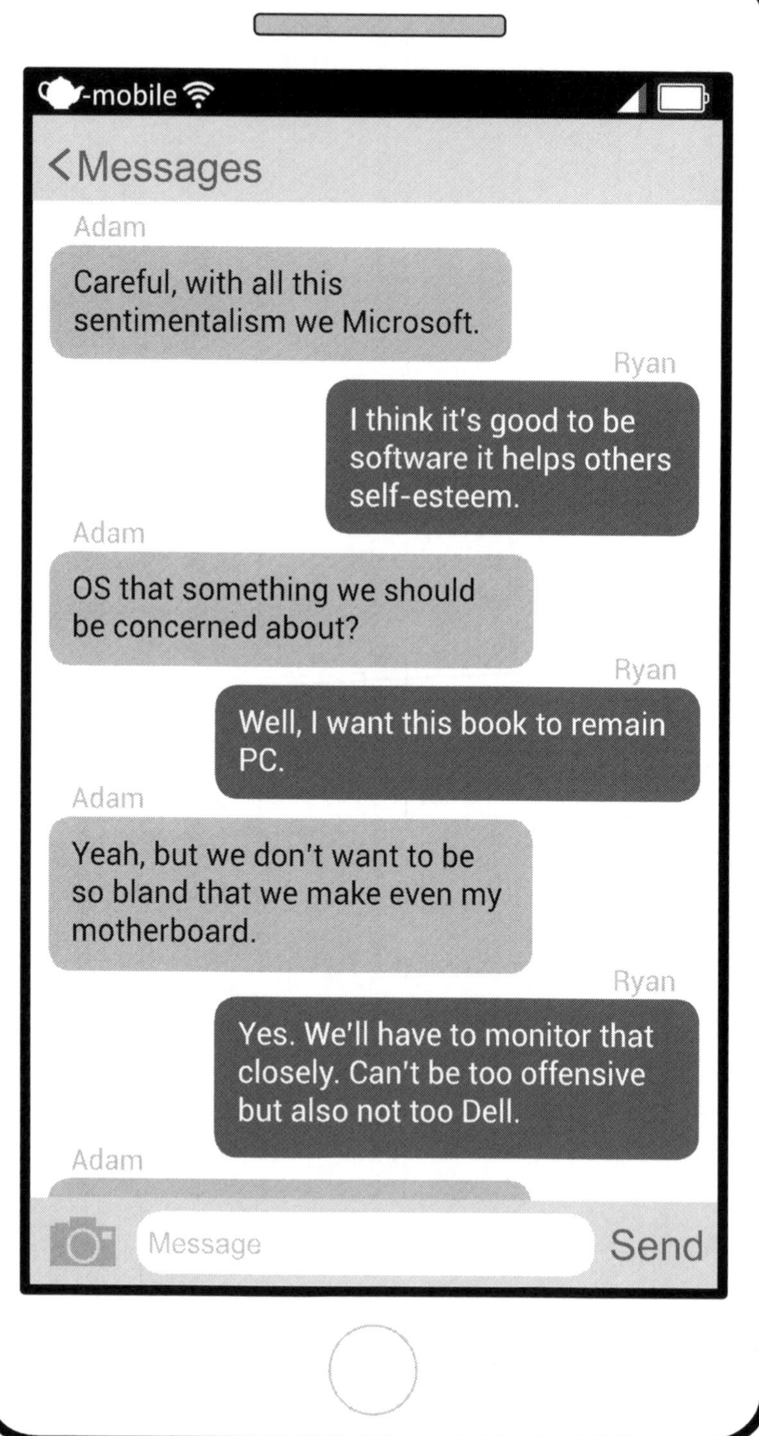
-mobile
Messages
Adam
Careful, with all this sentimentalism we Microsoft.
Ryan
I think it's good to be software it helps others self-esteem.
Adam
OS that something we should be concerned about?
Ryan
Well, I want this book to remain PC.
Adam
Yeah, but we don't want to be so bland that we make even my motherboard.
Ryan
Yes. We'll have to monitor that closely. Can't be too offensive but also not too Dell.
Adam
Message
Send

-mobile
Messages
If we do this right nobody will be as funny Asus.
Ryan
Nobody will Mac jokes as good as ours!
Adam
It's true. You and Apple really great jokes out of thin Air.
Ryan
Well, let's go ahead Intel some more then.
Adam
Yes we should tell a lot more. We'll Gateway more followers that way.
Ryan
Yes. My goal is Tandy 20 thousand followers this year.
Adam
Haha! I've already got 20,000 followers! Commodore me!
Message
Send

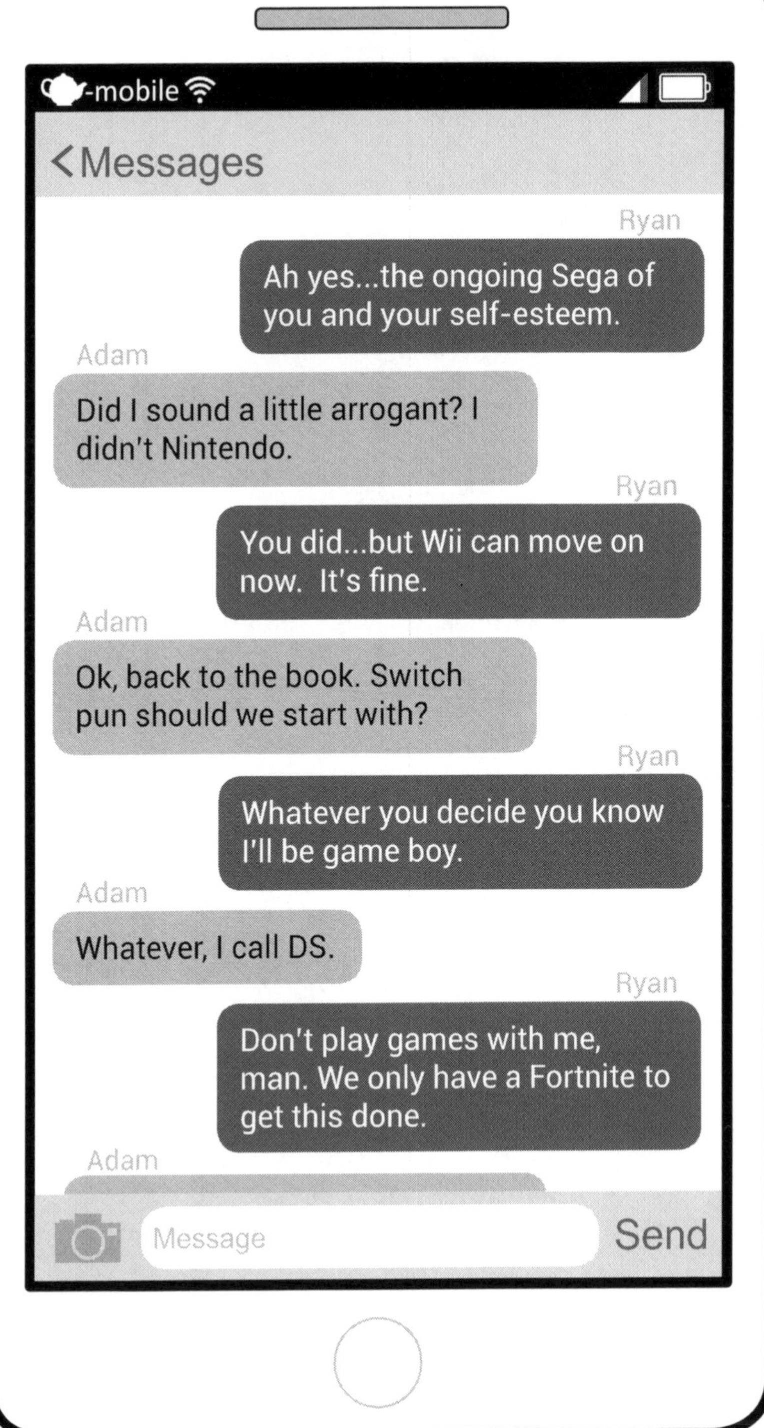
-mobile
<Messages
Ryan
Ah yes...the ongoing Sega of you and your self-esteem.
Adam
Did I sound a little arrogant? I didn't Nintendo.
Ryan
You did...but Wii can move on now. It's fine.
Adam
Ok, back to the book. Switch pun should we start with?
Ryan
Whatever you decide you know I'll be game boy.
Adam
Whatever, I call DS.
Ryan
Don't play games with me, man. We only have a Fortnite to get this done.
Adam
Message
Send

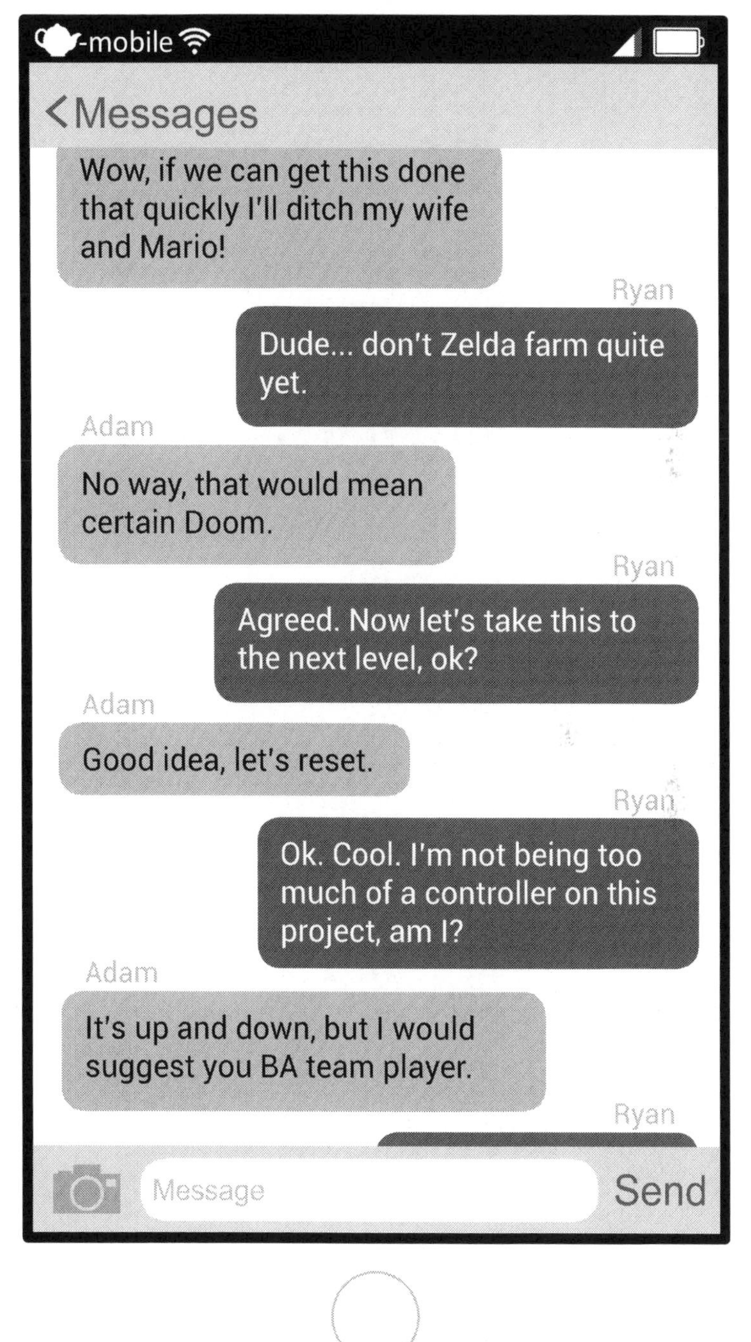
-mobile
Messages
Wow, if we can get this done that quickly I'll ditch my wife and Mario!
Ryan
Dude... don't Zelda farm quite yet.
Adam
No way, that would mean certain Doom.
Ryan
Agreed. Now let's take this to the next level, ok?
Adam
Good idea, let's reset.
Ryan
Ok. Cool. I'm not being too much of a controller on this project, am I?
Adam
It's up and down, but I would suggest you BA team player.
Ryan
Message
Send

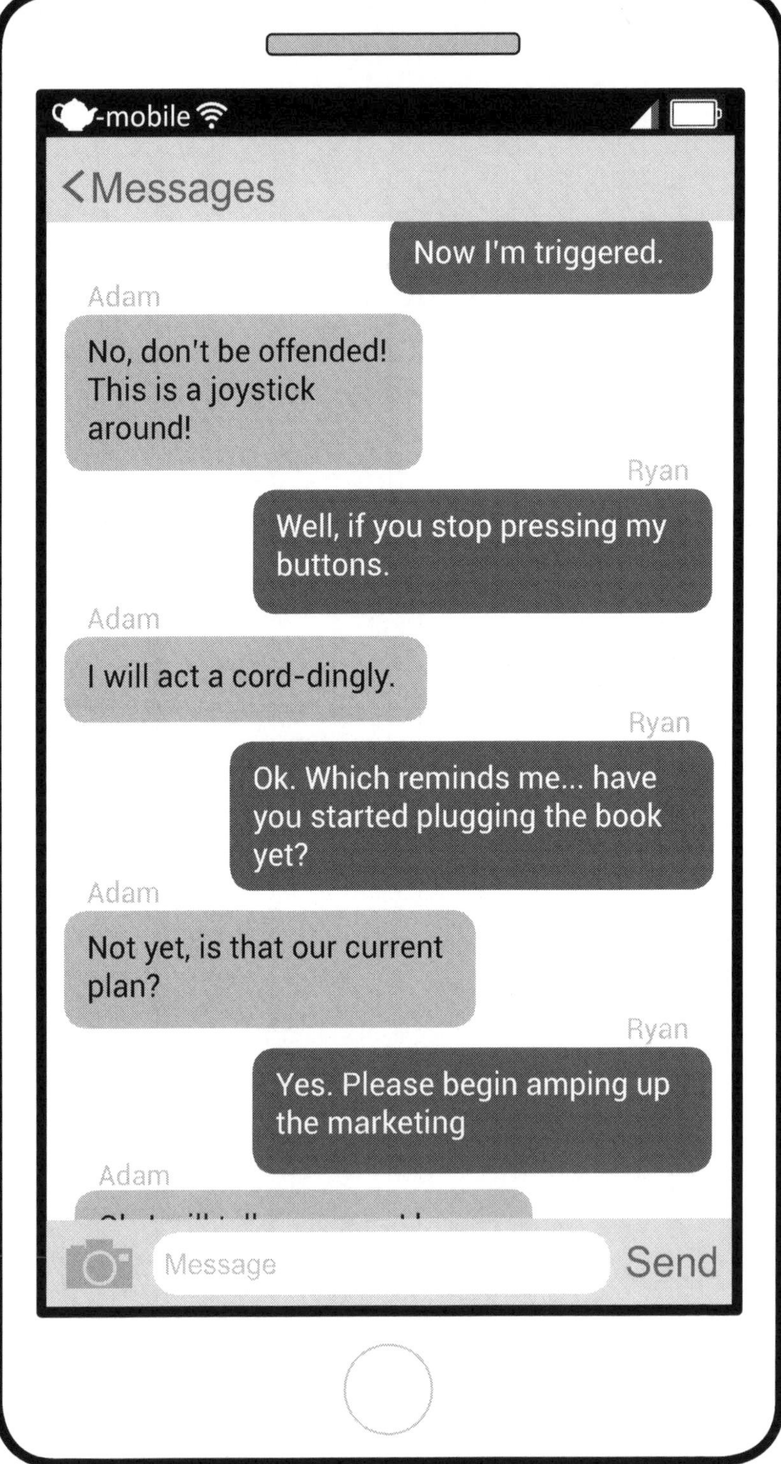
-mobile
Messages
Now I'm triggered.
Adam
No, don't be offended! This is a joystick around!
Ryan
Well, if you stop pressing my buttons.
Adam
I will act a cord-dingly.
Ryan
Ok. Which reminds me... have you started plugging the book yet?
Adam
Not yet, is that our current plan?
Ryan
Yes. Please begin amping up the marketing
Adam
Message
Send

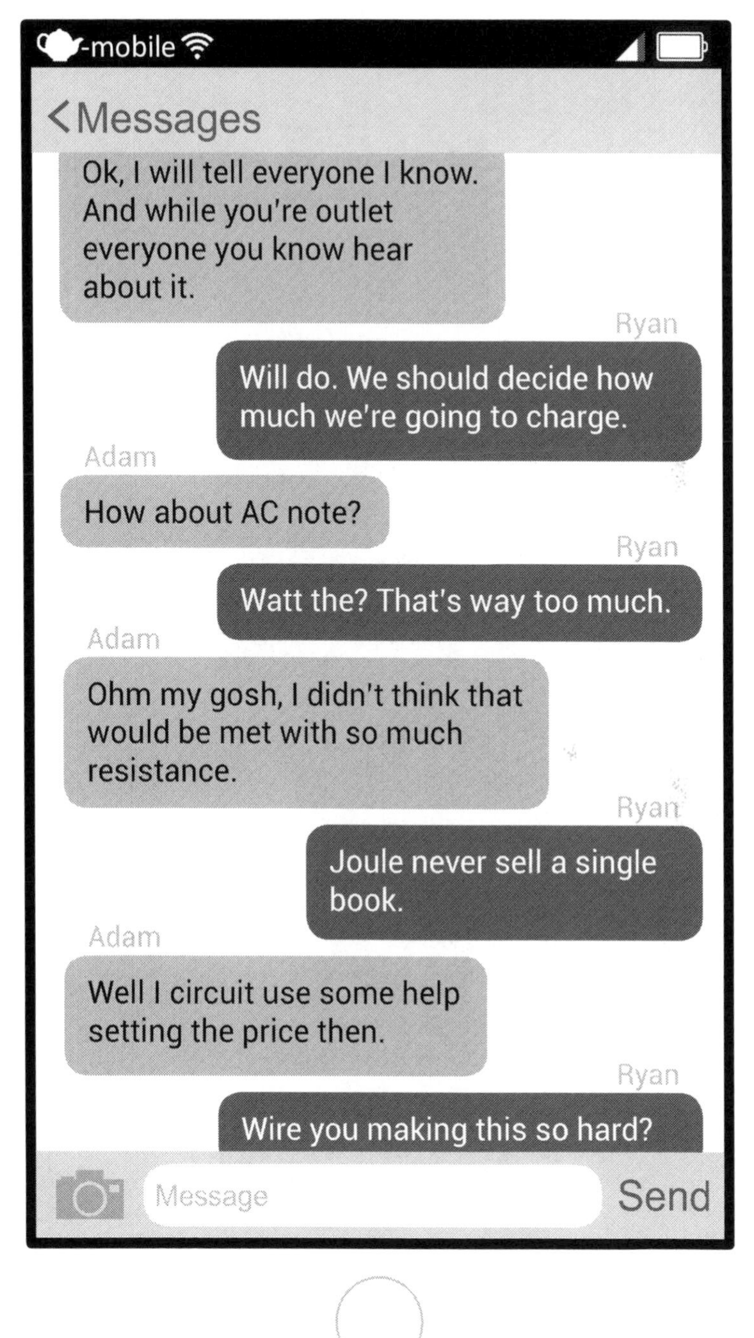
-mobile
<Messages
Ok, I will tell everyone I know. And while you're outlet everyone you know hear about it.
Ryan
Will do. We should decide how much we're going to charge.
Adam
How about AC note?
Ryan
Watt the? That's way too much.
Adam
Ohm my gosh, I didn't think that would be met with so much resistance.
Ryan
Joule never sell a single book.
Adam
Well I circuit use some help setting the price then.
Ryan
Wire you making this so hard?
Message
Send

-mobile
Messages
Adam
I'm just trying to be like one of the coil kids.
Ryan
Whoa....slow down thermistor.
Adam
But you said we have to hurry. I re fuse to slow down.
Ryan
You don't want to take a breaker anything? Ok.
Adam
GFI take a break, we'll never get this book finished.
Ryan
Maybe we need to put together a panel to help us decide. Or would that just trip us up?
Adam
I'd be shocked if it came to that.
Message
Send

-mobile
Messages
Ryan
Ok. We can figure it out. I guess I battery do my plans here. How about $30. That's Farads say.
Adam
I can go with that. Probably a good idea to Tesla market first.
Ryan
Right. I think most people can a Ford that though.
Adam
Last time we argued about money it Taurus apart.
Ryan
Yea, and here we are on Edge again.
Adam
I think we should continue to Explorer options frankly and with an open mind.
Ryan
Yea, that is a fact we can't Escape. Let's Focus.
Message
Send

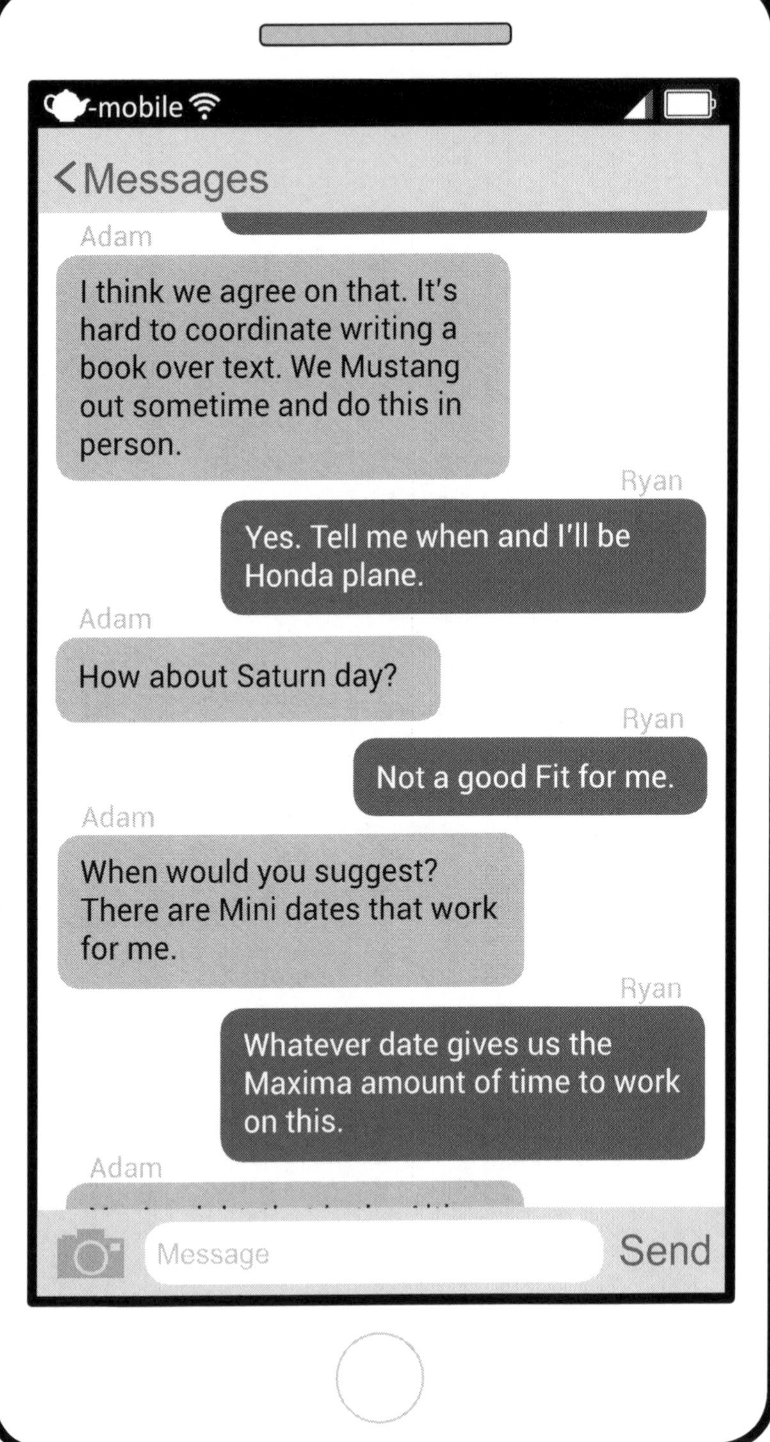
-mobile
Messages
Adam
I think we agree on that. It's hard to coordinate writing a book over text. We Mustang out sometime and do this in person.
Ryan
Yes. Tell me when and I'll be Honda plane.
Adam
How about Saturn day?
Ryan
Not a good Fit for me.
Adam
When would you suggest? There are Mini dates that work for me.
Ryan
Whatever date gives us the Maxima amount of time to work on this.
Adam
Message
Send

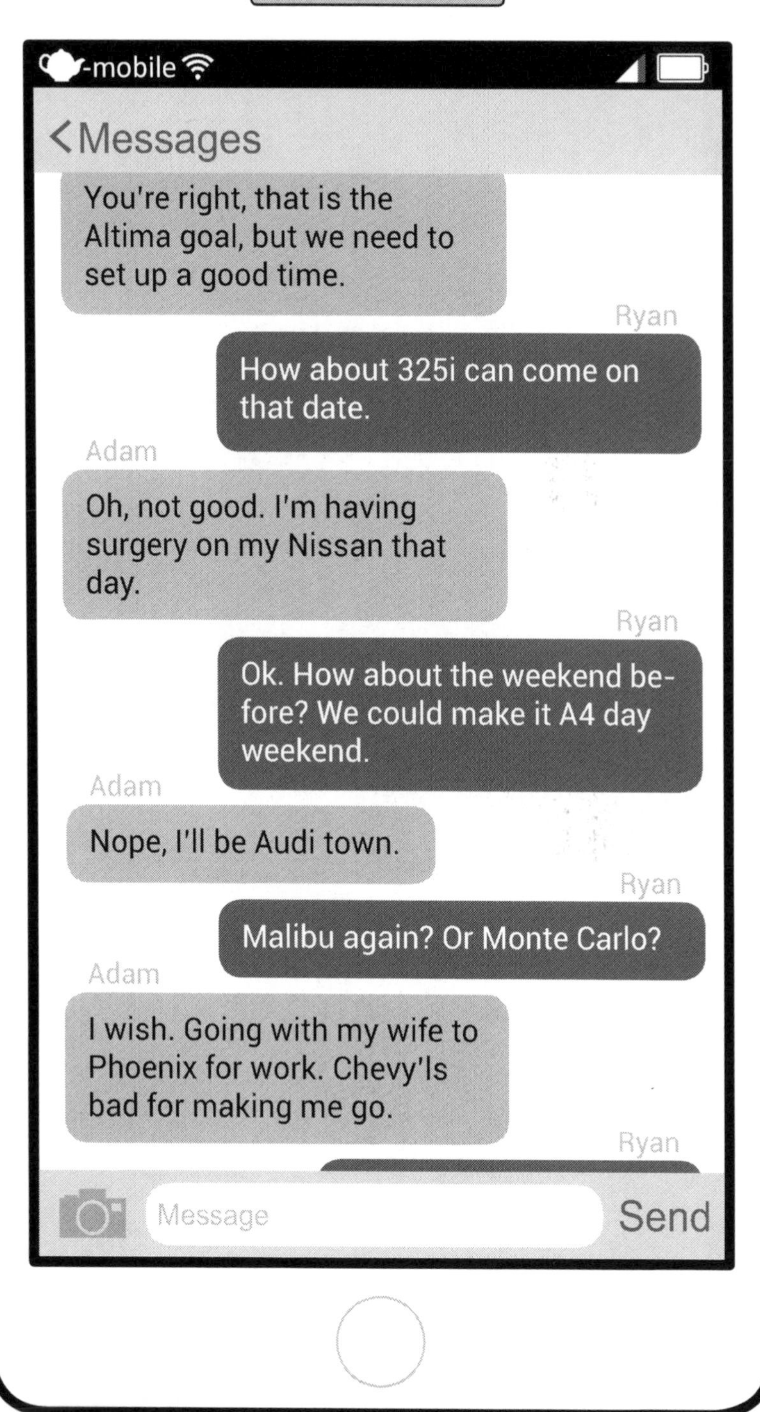
-mobile
Messages
You're right, that is the Altima goal, but we need to set up a good time.
Ryan
How about 325i can come on that date.
Adam
Oh, not good. I'm having surgery on my Nissan that day.
Ryan
Ok. How about the weekend be-fore? We could make it A4 day weekend.
Adam
Nope, I'll be Audi town.
Ryan
Malibu again? Or Monte Carlo?
Adam
I wish. Going with my wife to Phoenix for work. Chevy'ls bad for making me go.
Ryan
Message
Send

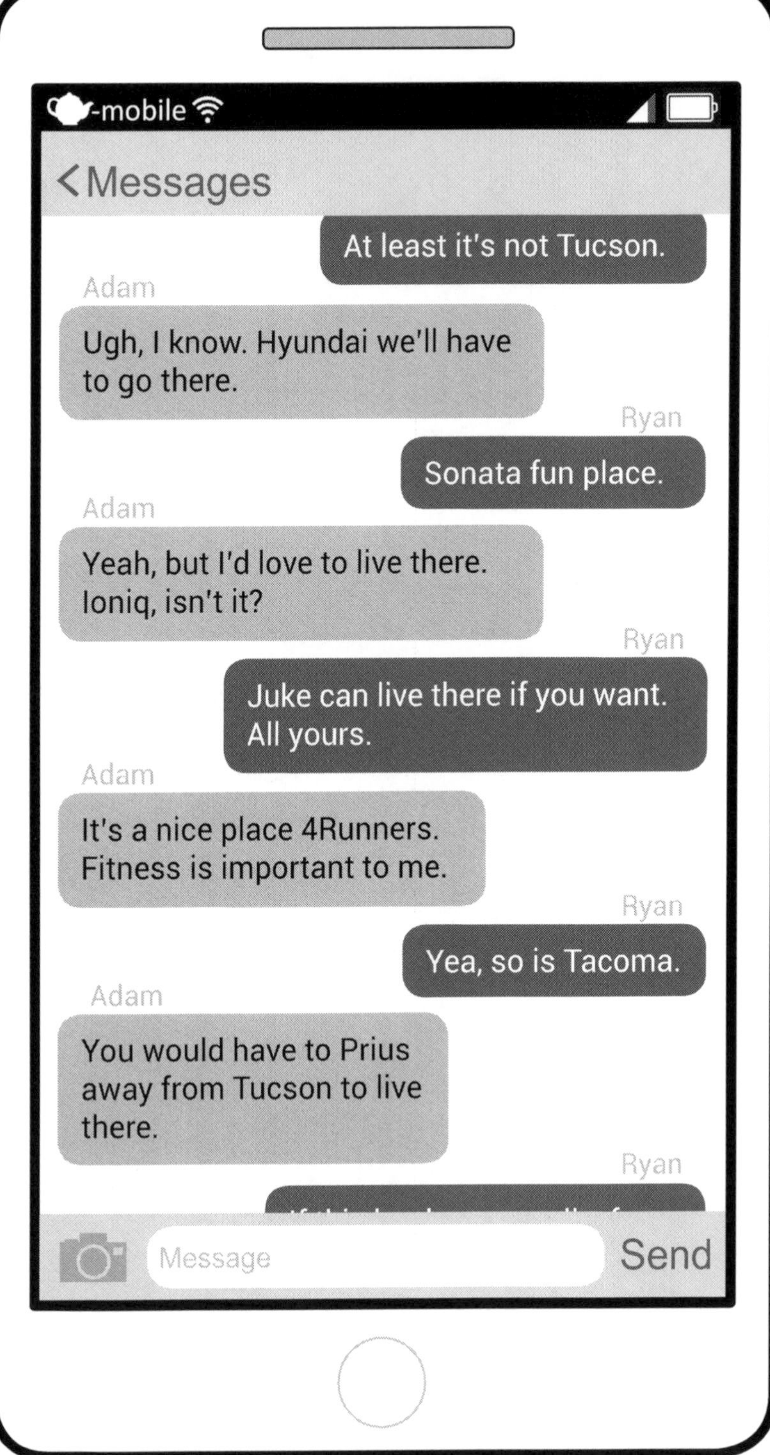
-mobile
<Messages
At least it's not Tucson.
Adam
Ugh, I know. Hyundai we'll have to go there.
Ryan
Sonata fun place.
Adam
Yeah, but I'd love to live there. Ioniq, isn't it?
Ryan
Juke can live there if you want. All yours.
Adam
It's a nice place 4Runners. Fitness is important to me.
Ryan
Yea, so is Tacoma.
Adam
You would have to Prius away from Tucson to live there.
Ryan
Message
Send

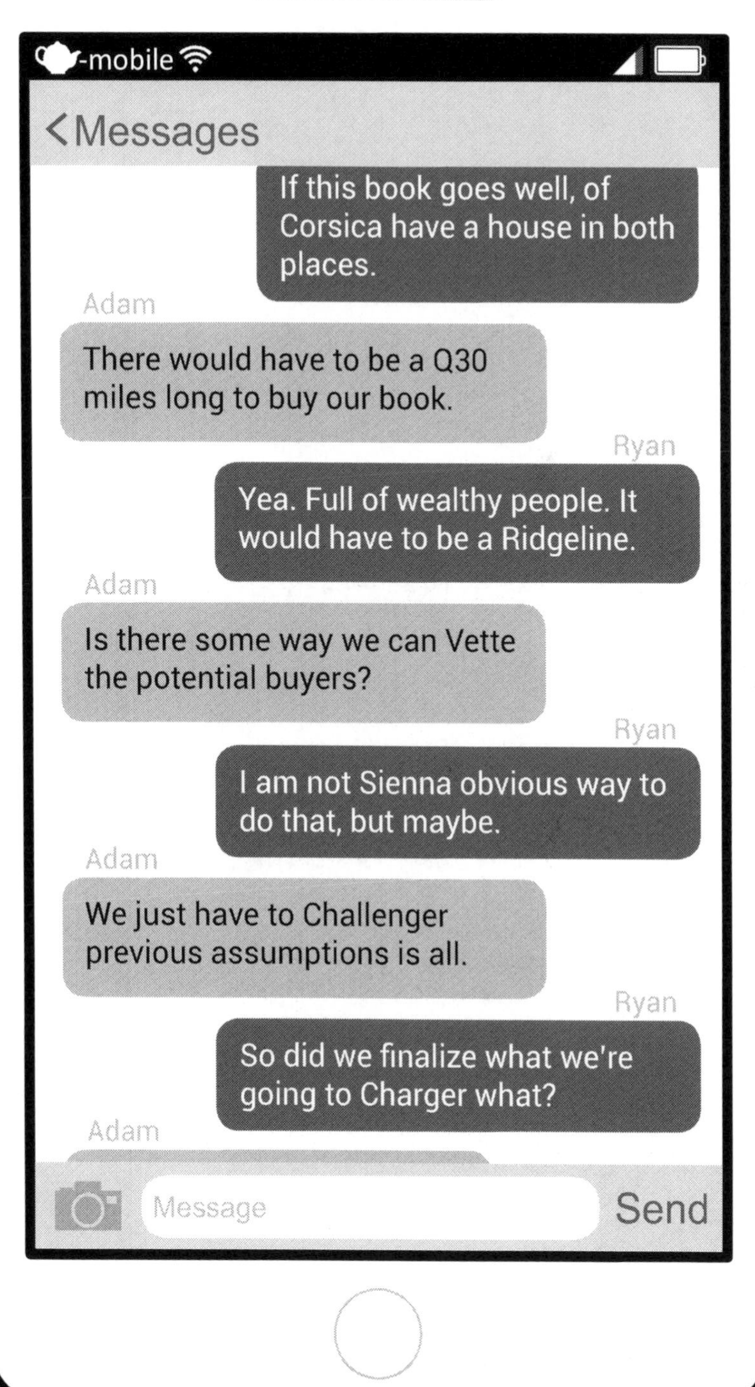
-mobile
Messages
If this book goes well, of Corsica have a house in both places.
Adam
There would have to be a Q30 miles long to buy our book.
Ryan
Yea. Full of wealthy people. It would have to be a Ridgeline.
Adam
Is there some way we can Vette the potential buyers?
Ryan
I am not Sienna obvious way to do that, but maybe.
Adam
We just have to Challenger previous assumptions is all.
Ryan
So did we finalize what we're going to Charger what?
Adam
Message
Send

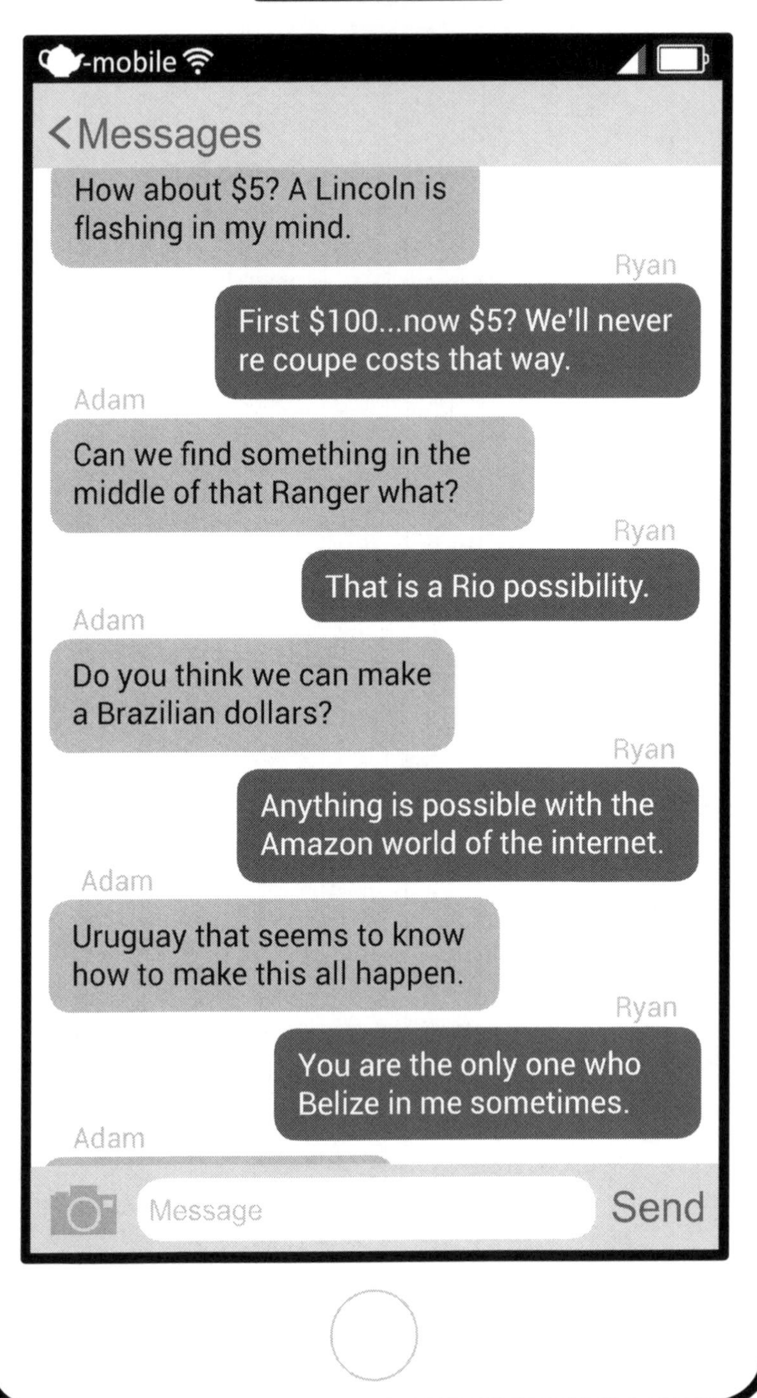
-mobile
< Messages
How about $5? A Lincoln is flashing in my mind.
Ryan
First $100...now $5? We'll never re coupe costs that way.
Adam
Can we find something in the middle of that Ranger what?
Ryan
That is a Rio possibility.
Adam
Do you think we can make a Brazilian dollars?
Ryan
Anything is possible with the Amazon world of the internet.
Adam
Uruguay that seems to know how to make this all happen.
Ryan
You are the only one who Belize in me sometimes.
Adam
Message
Send

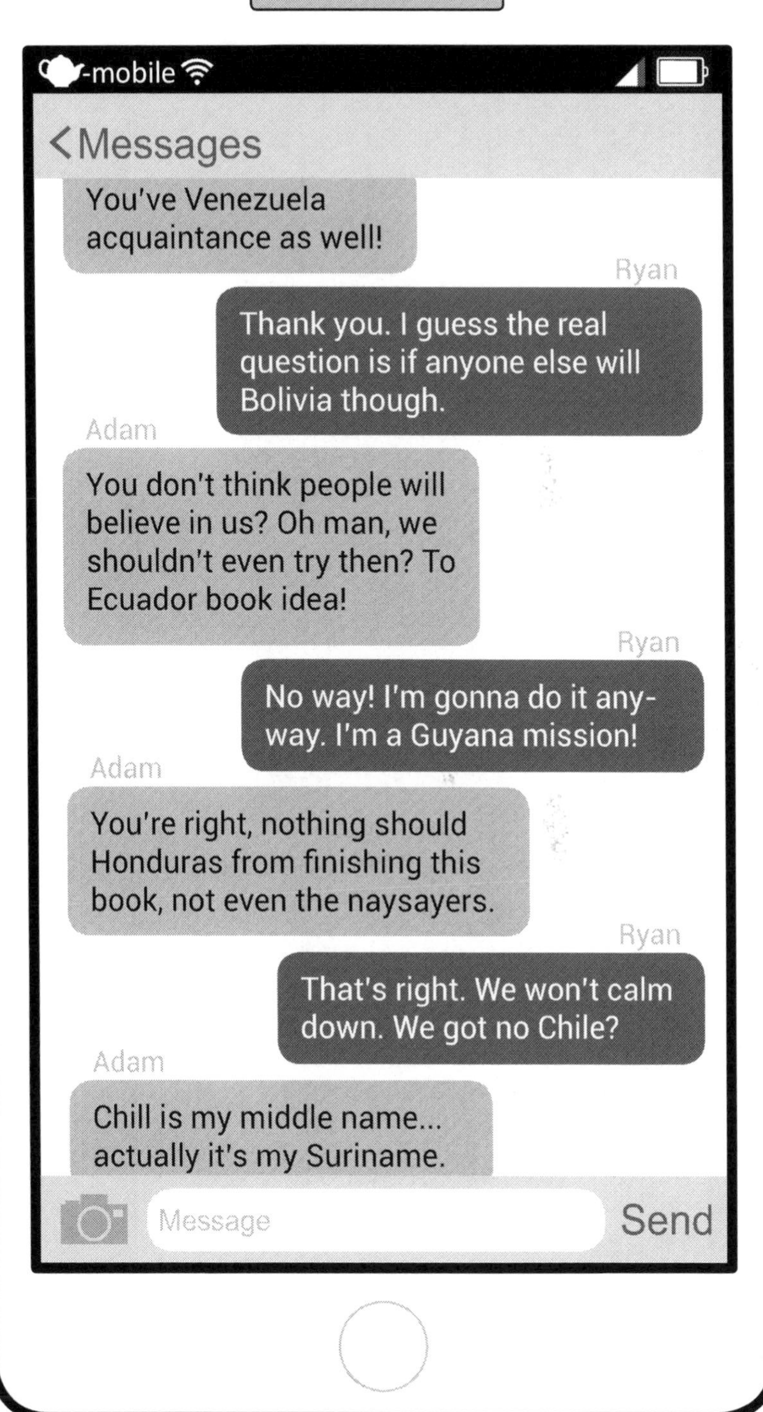
-mobile
Messages
You've Venezuela acquaintance as well!
Ryan
Thank you. I guess the real question is if anyone else will Bolivia though.
Adam
You don't think people will believe in us? Oh man, we shouldn't even try then? To Ecuador book idea!
Ryan
No way! I'm gonna do it any-way. I'm a Guyana mission!
Adam
You're right, nothing should Honduras from finishing this book, not even the naysayers.
Ryan
That's right. We won't calm down. We got no Chile?
Adam
Chill is my middle name... actually it's my Suriname.
Message
Send

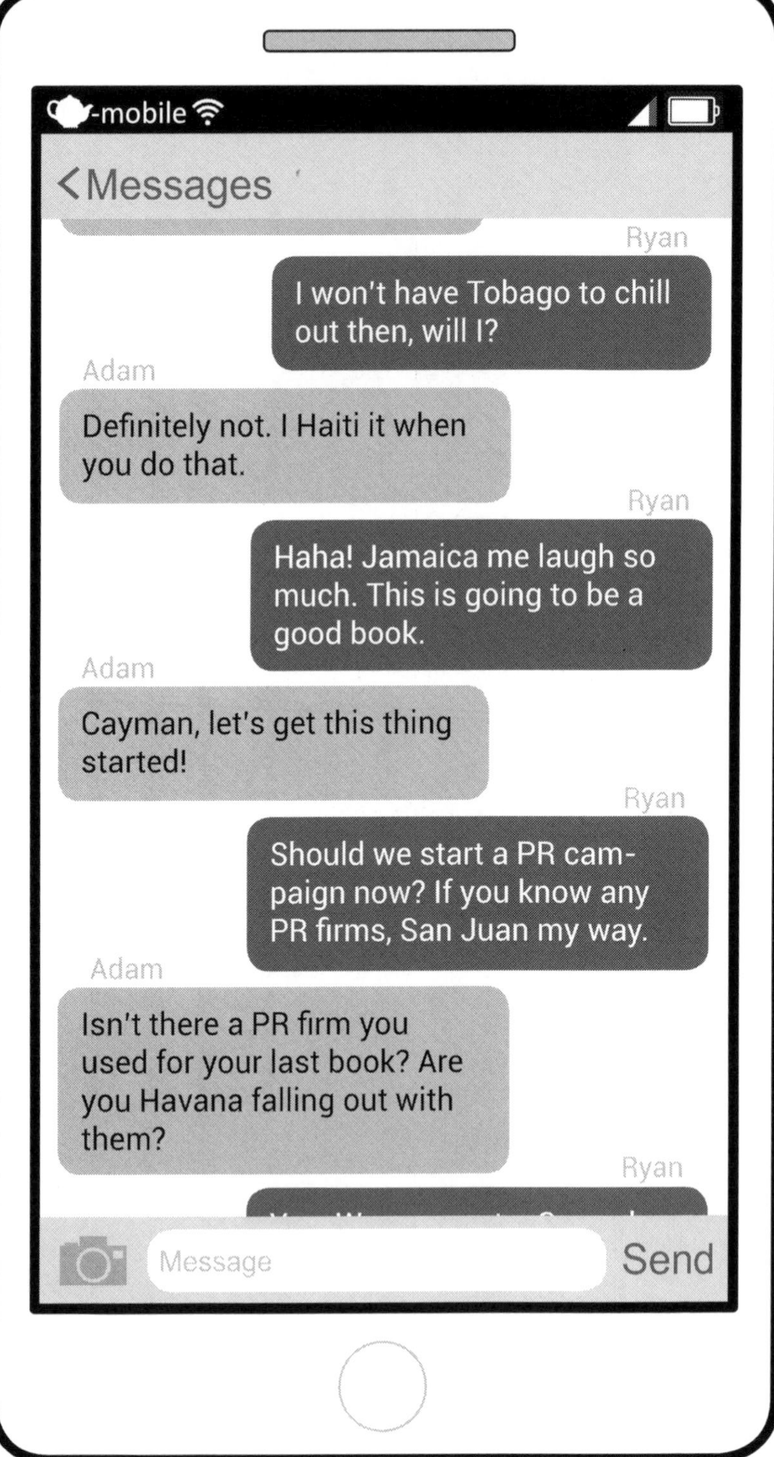
-mobile
Messages
Ryan
I won't have Tobago to chill out then, will I?
Adam
Definitely not. I Haiti it when you do that.
Ryan
Haha! Jamaica me laugh so much. This is going to be a good book.
Adam
Cayman, let's get this thing started!
Ryan
Should we start a PR campaign now? If you know any PR firms, San Juan my way.
Adam
Isn't there a PR firm you used for your last book? Are you Havana falling out with them?
Ryan
Message
Send

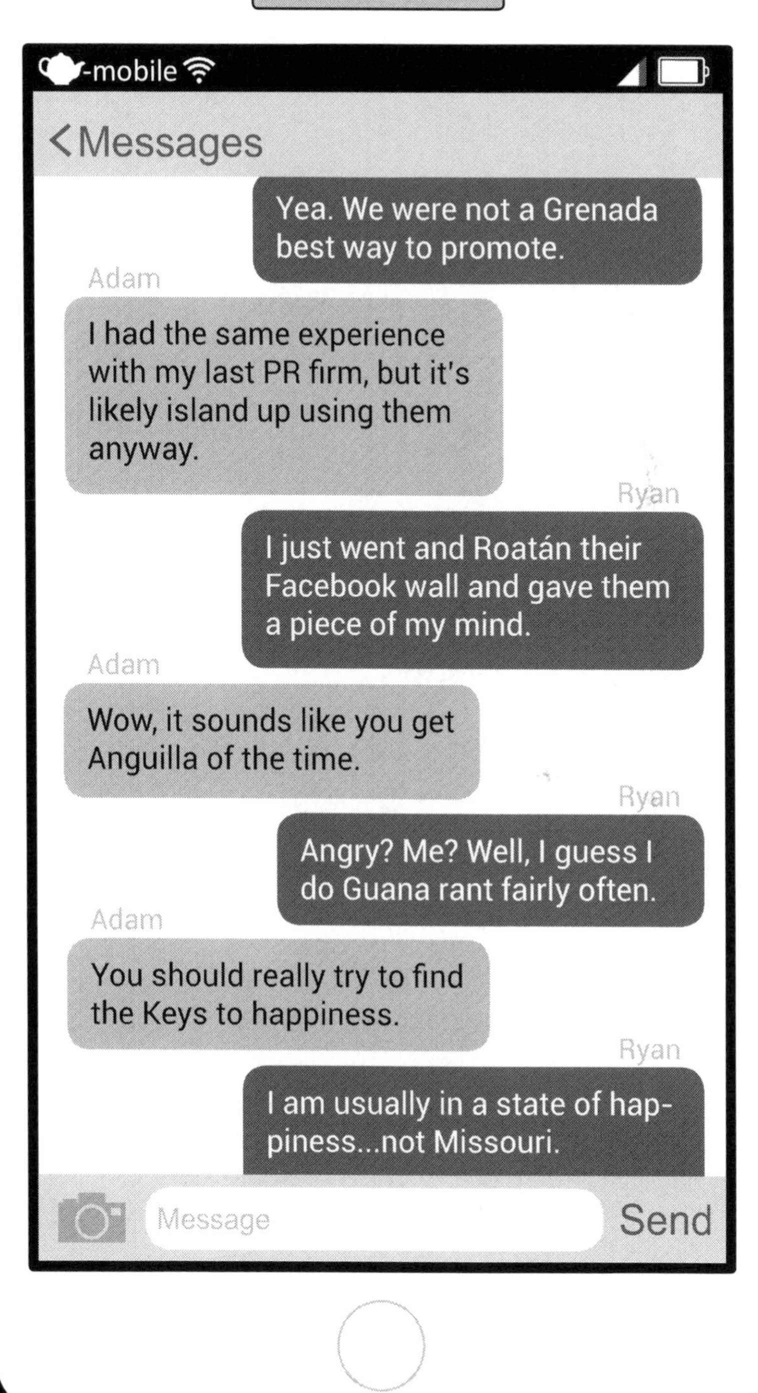
-mobile
Messages
Yea. We were not a Grenada best way to promote.
Adam
I had the same experience with my last PR firm, but it's likely island up using them anyway.
Ryan
I just went and Roatán their Facebook wall and gave them a piece of my mind.
Adam
Wow, it sounds like you get Anguilla of the time.
Ryan
Angry? Me? Well, I guess I do Guana rant fairly often.
Adam
You should really try to find the Keys to happiness.
Ryan
I am usually in a state of hap-piness...not Missouri.
Message
Send

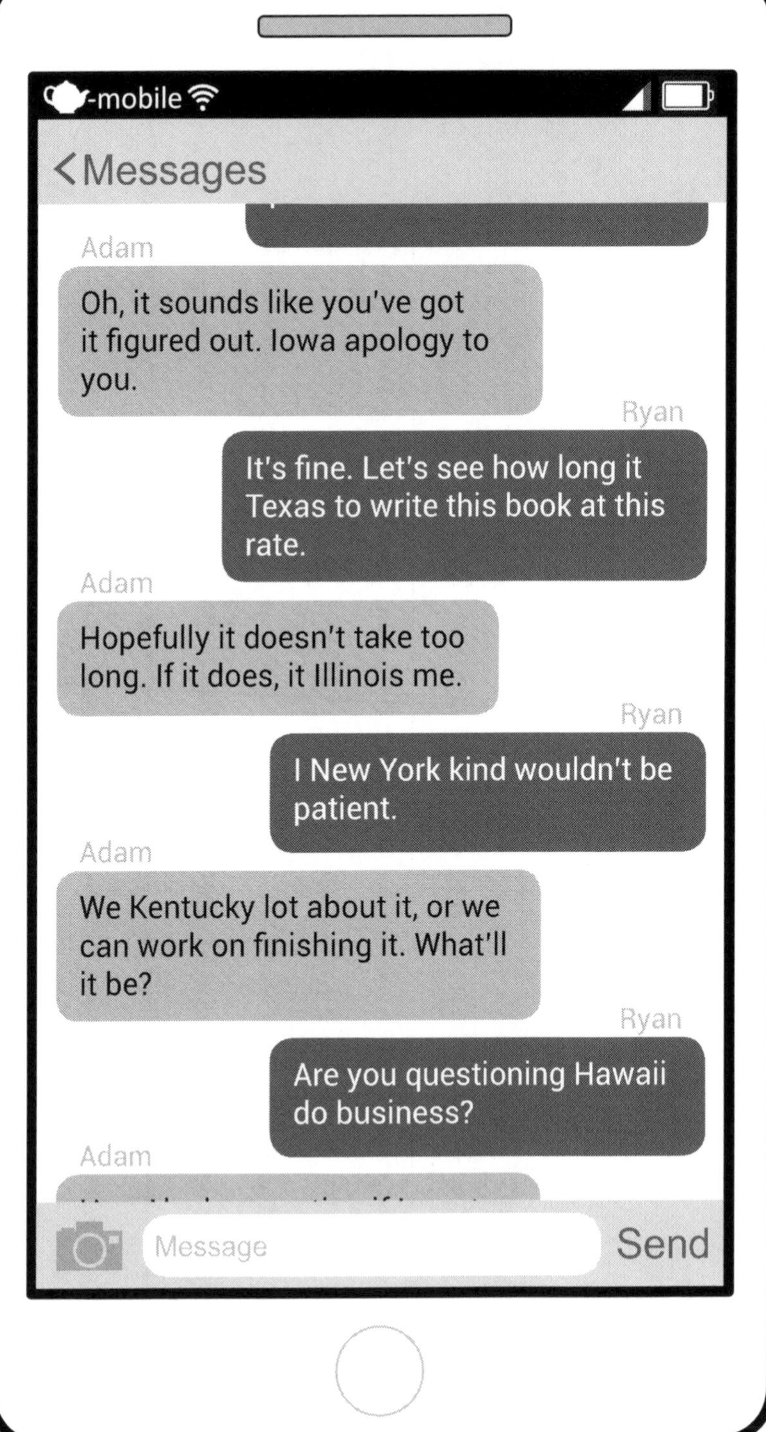
-mobile
Messages
Adam
Oh, it sounds like you've got it figured out. Iowa apology to you.
Ryan
It's fine. Let's see how long it Texas to write this book at this rate.
Adam
Hopefully it doesn't take too long. If it does, it Illinois me.
Ryan
I New York kind wouldn't be patient.
Adam
We Kentucky lot about it, or we can work on finishing it. What'll it be?
Ryan
Are you questioning Hawaii do business?
Adam
Message
Send

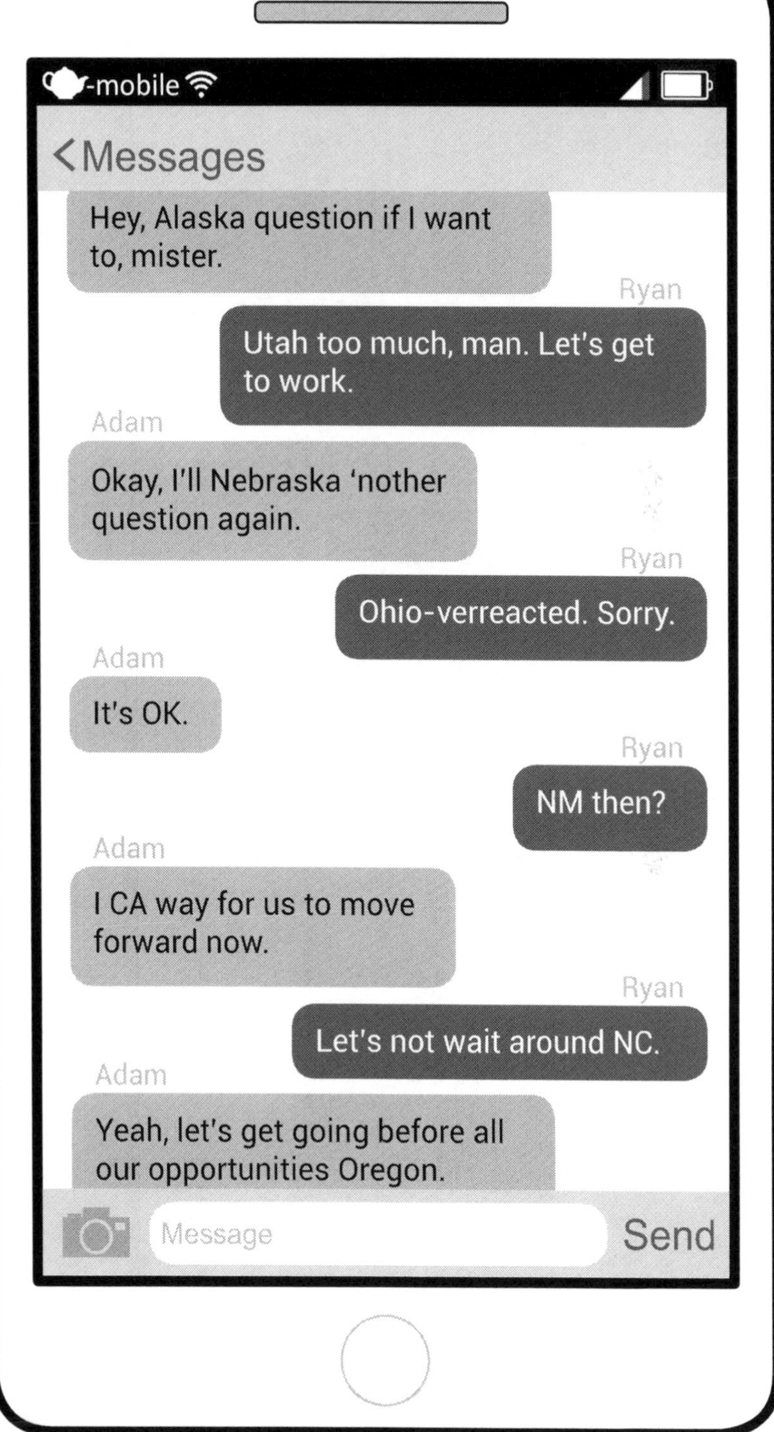

-mobile
Messages
Hey, Alaska question if I want to, mister.
Ryan
Utah too much, man. Let's get to work.
Adam
Okay, I'll Nebraska 'nother question again.
Ryan
Ohio-verreacted. Sorry.
Adam
It's OK.
Ryan
NM then?
Adam
I CA way for us to move forward now.
Ryan
Let's not wait around NC.
Adam
Yeah, let's get going before all our opportunities Oregon.
Message
Send

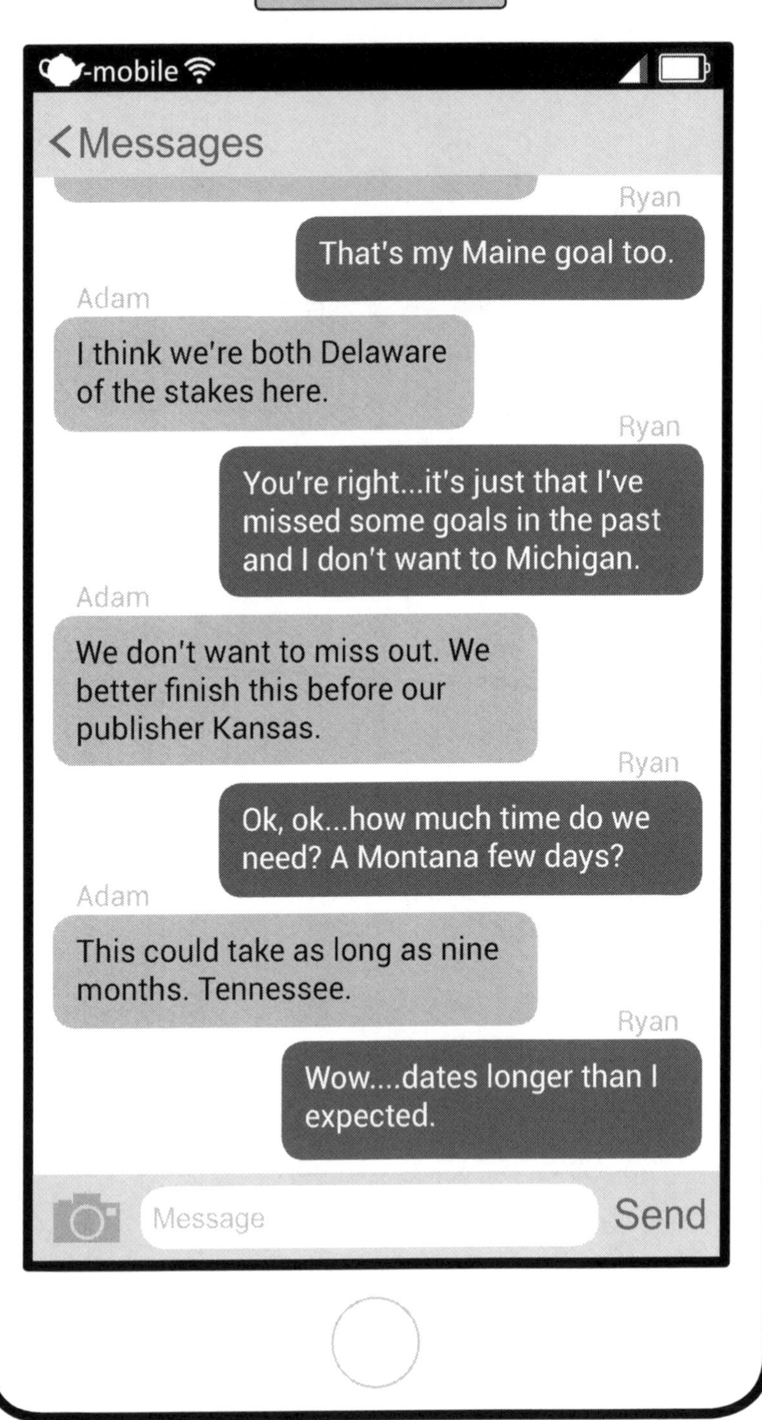
-mobile
<Messages
Ryan
That's my Maine goal too.
Adam
I think we're both Delaware of the stakes here.
Ryan
You're right...it's just that I've missed some goals in the past and I don't want to Michigan.
Adam
We don't want to miss out. We better finish this before our publisher Kansas.
Ryan
Ok, ok...how much time do we need? A Montana few days?
Adam
This could take as long as nine months. Tennessee.
Ryan
Wow....dates longer than I expected.
Message
Send

-mobile
Messages
Adam
Books take a long time. And day are costly.
Ryan
Week can do it.
Adam
Yes, let's keep hour motivation level high.
Ryan
If I said anything mean recently, I didn't minute that way.
Adam
That's the second time you've apologized to me.
Ryan
I know. Anyway, can't get a hold of that PR firm. Been calendar number all day.
Adam
Well, August they don't want to talk to you either.
Ryan
Message
Send

-mobile
Messages
Yes. We March forward without them then.
Adam
Great! May I join you?
Ryan
June know it!
Adam
July, you won't let me join you.
Ryan
Are you having a bad day or something? I know summer better than others but....
Adam
You autumn mind your own business, buddy.
Ryan
When I season thing wrong, I have to ask. We need to be able to talk if we're going to be in business together.
Adam
Message
Send

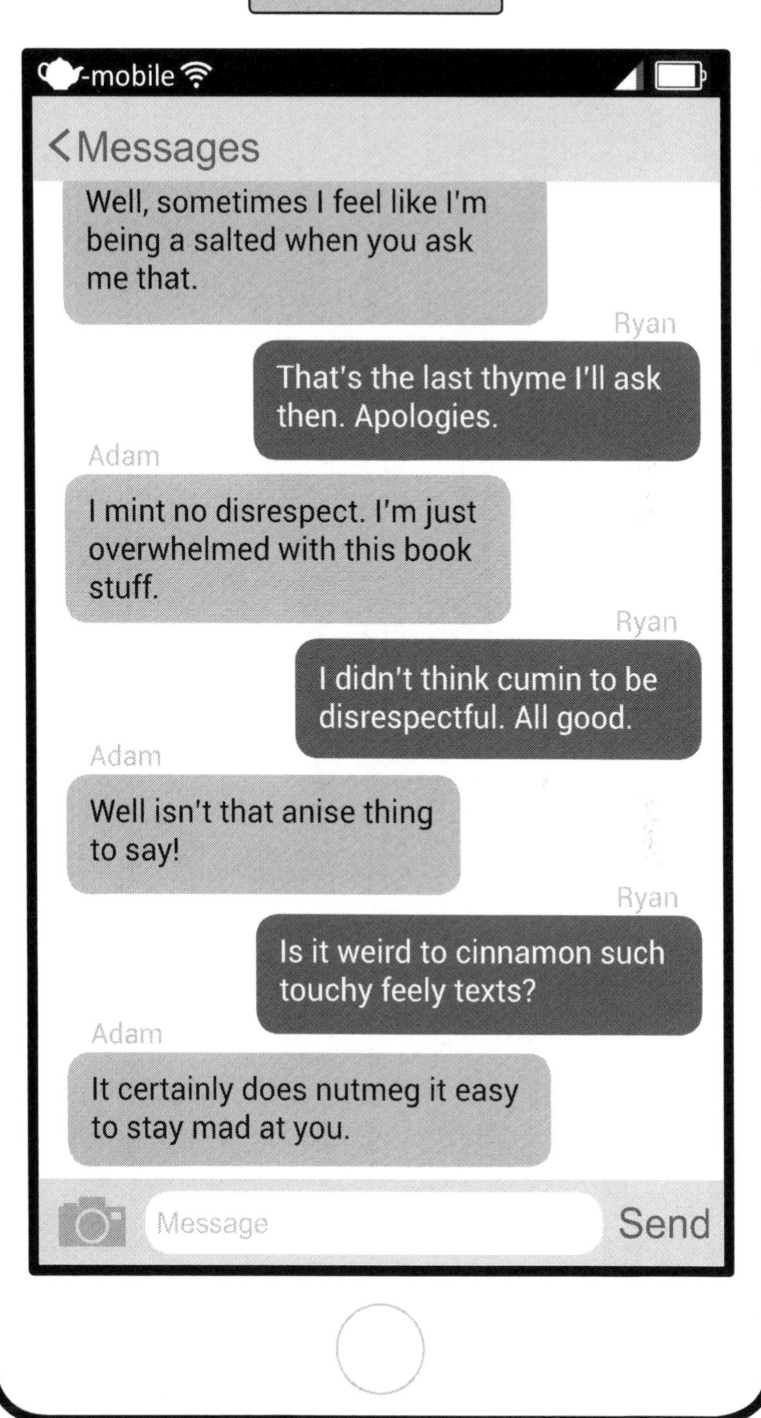
-mobile
Messages
Well, sometimes I feel like I'm being a salted when you ask me that.
Ryan
That's the last thyme I'll ask then. Apologies.
Adam
I mint no disrespect. I'm just overwhelmed with this book stuff.
Ryan
I didn't think cumin to be disrespectful. All good.
Adam
Well isn't that anise thing to say!
Ryan
Is it weird to cinnamon such touchy feely texts?
Adam
It certainly does nutmeg it easy to stay mad at you.
Message
Send

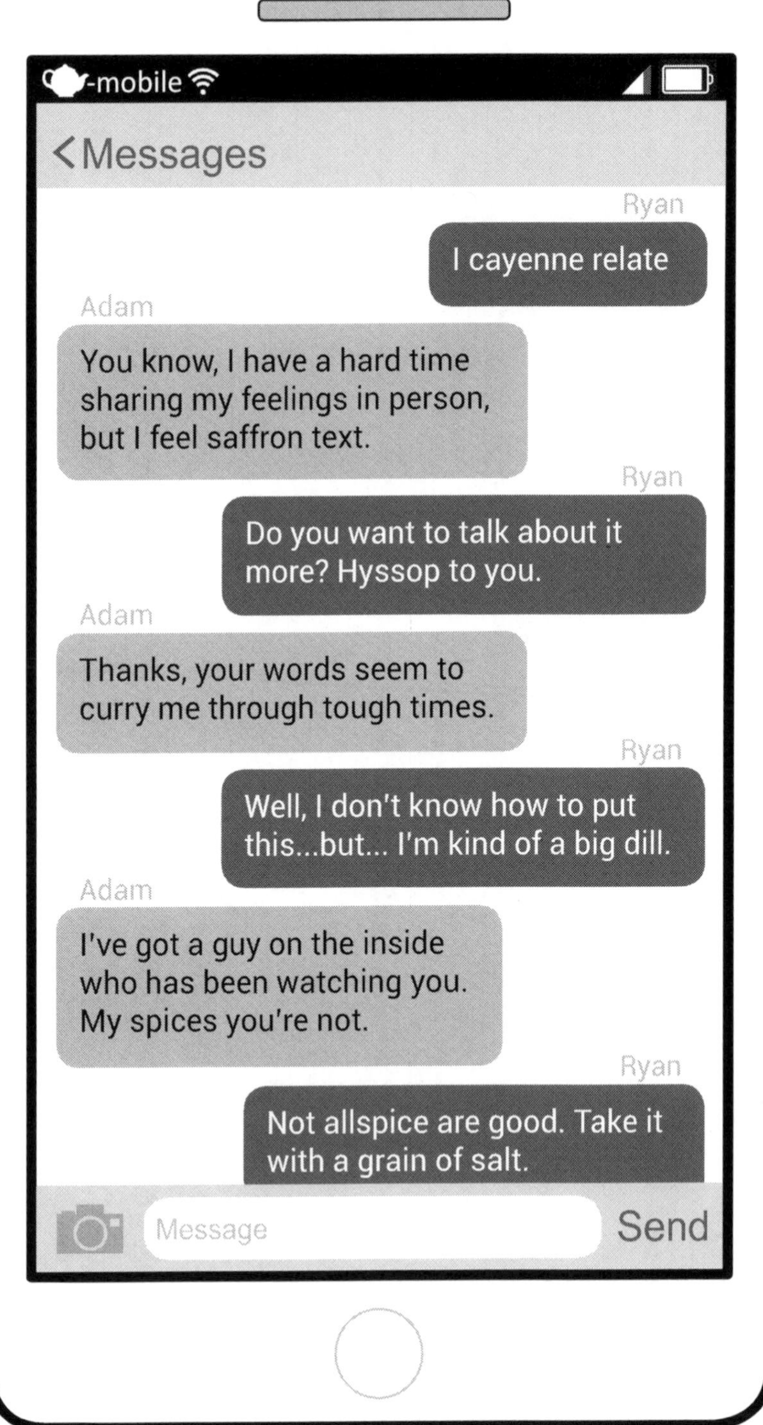
-mobile
<Messages
Ryan
I cayenne relate
Adam
You know, I have a hard time sharing my feelings in person, but I feel saffron text.
Ryan
Do you want to talk about it more? Hyssop to you.
Adam
Thanks, your words seem to curry me through tough times.
Ryan
Well, I don't know how to put this...but... I'm kind of a big dill.
Adam
I've got a guy on the inside who has been watching you. My spices you're not.
Ryan
Not allspice are good. Take it with a grain of salt.
Message
Send

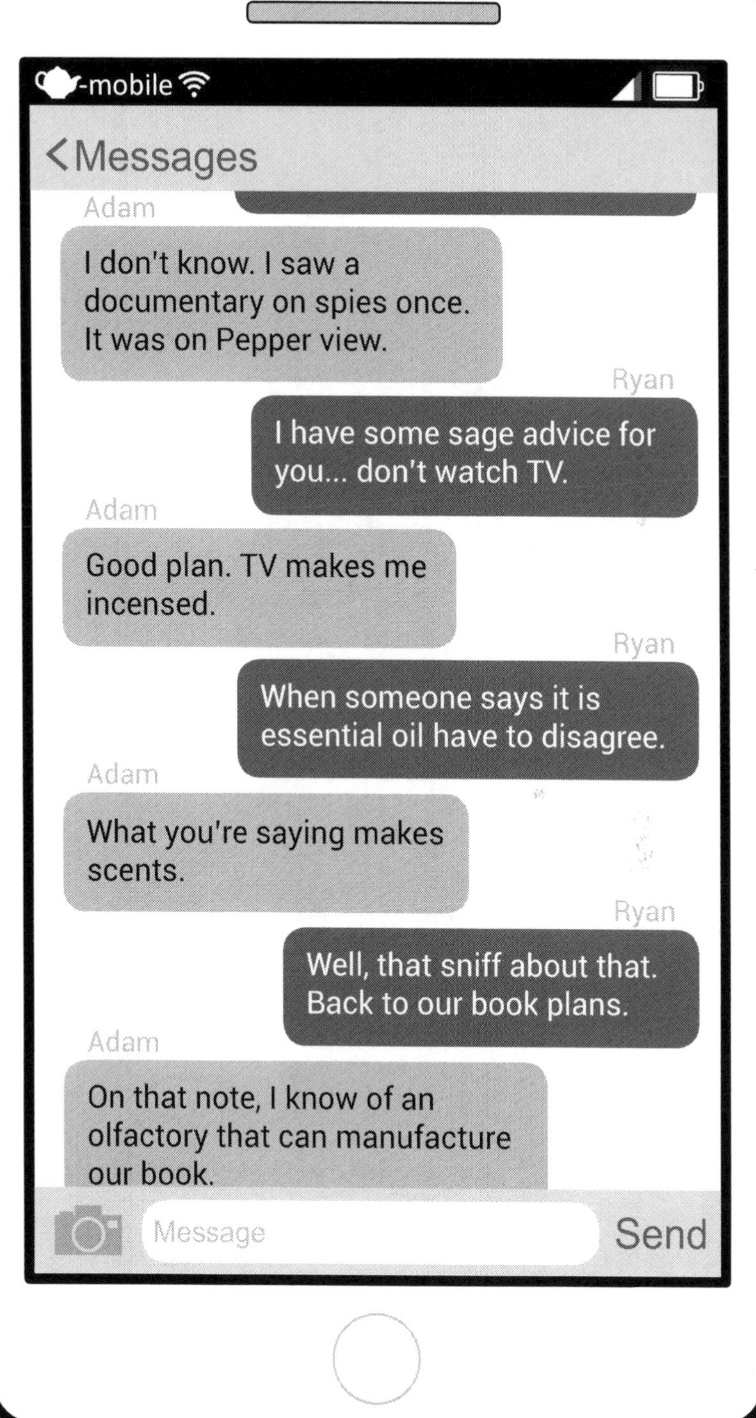
-mobile
Messages
Adam
I don't know. I saw a documentary on spies once. It was on Pepper view.
Ryan
I have some sage advice for you... don't watch TV.
Adam
Good plan. TV makes me incensed.
Ryan
When someone says it is essential oil have to disagree.
Adam
What you're saying makes scents.
Ryan
Well, that sniff about that. Back to our book plans.
Adam
On that note, I know of an olfactory that can manufacture our book.
Message
Send

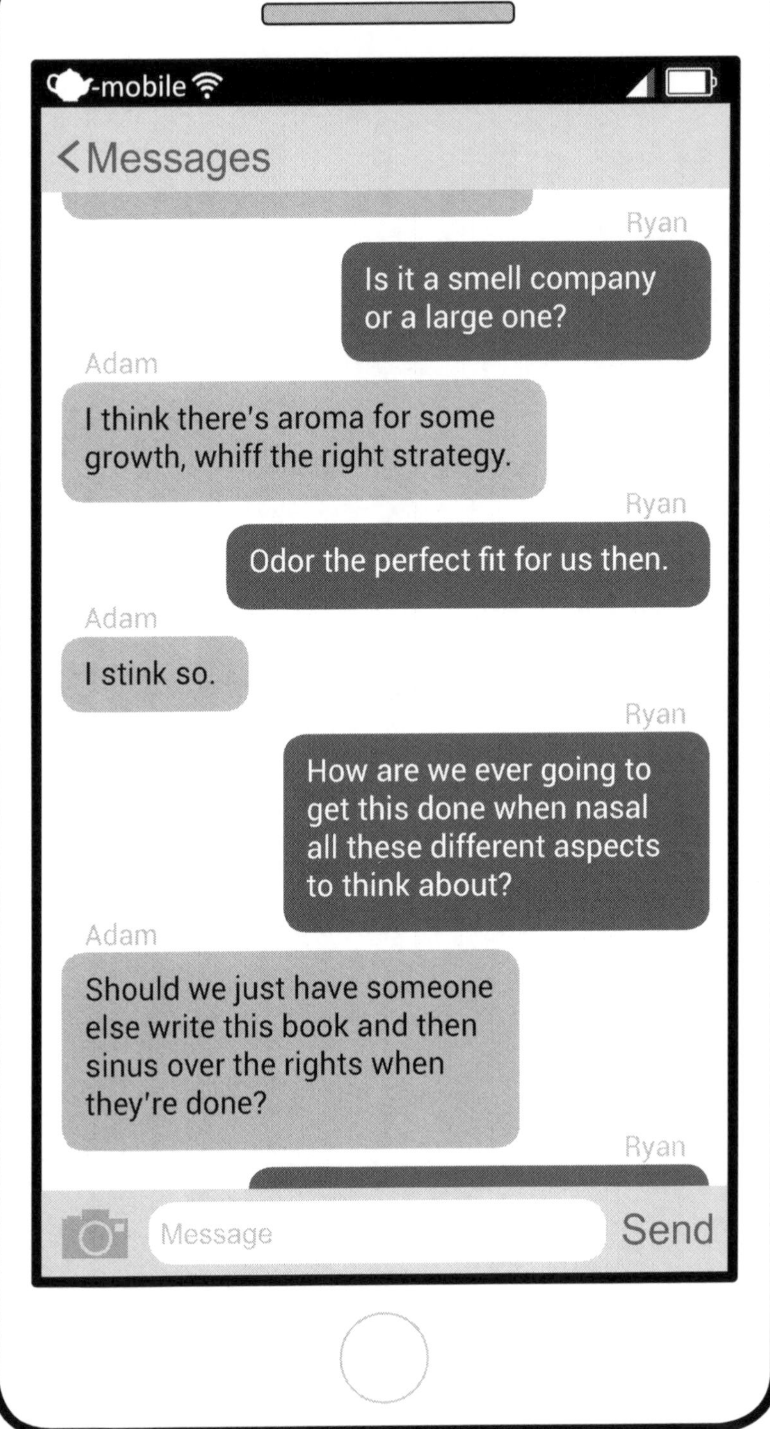
-mobile
Messages
Ryan
Is it a smell company or a large one?
Adam
I think there's aroma for some growth, whiff the right strategy.
Ryan
Odor the perfect fit for us then.
Adam
I stink so.
Ryan
How are we ever going to get this done when nasal all these different aspects to think about?
Adam
Should we just have someone else write this book and then sinus over the rights when they're done?
Ryan
Message
Send

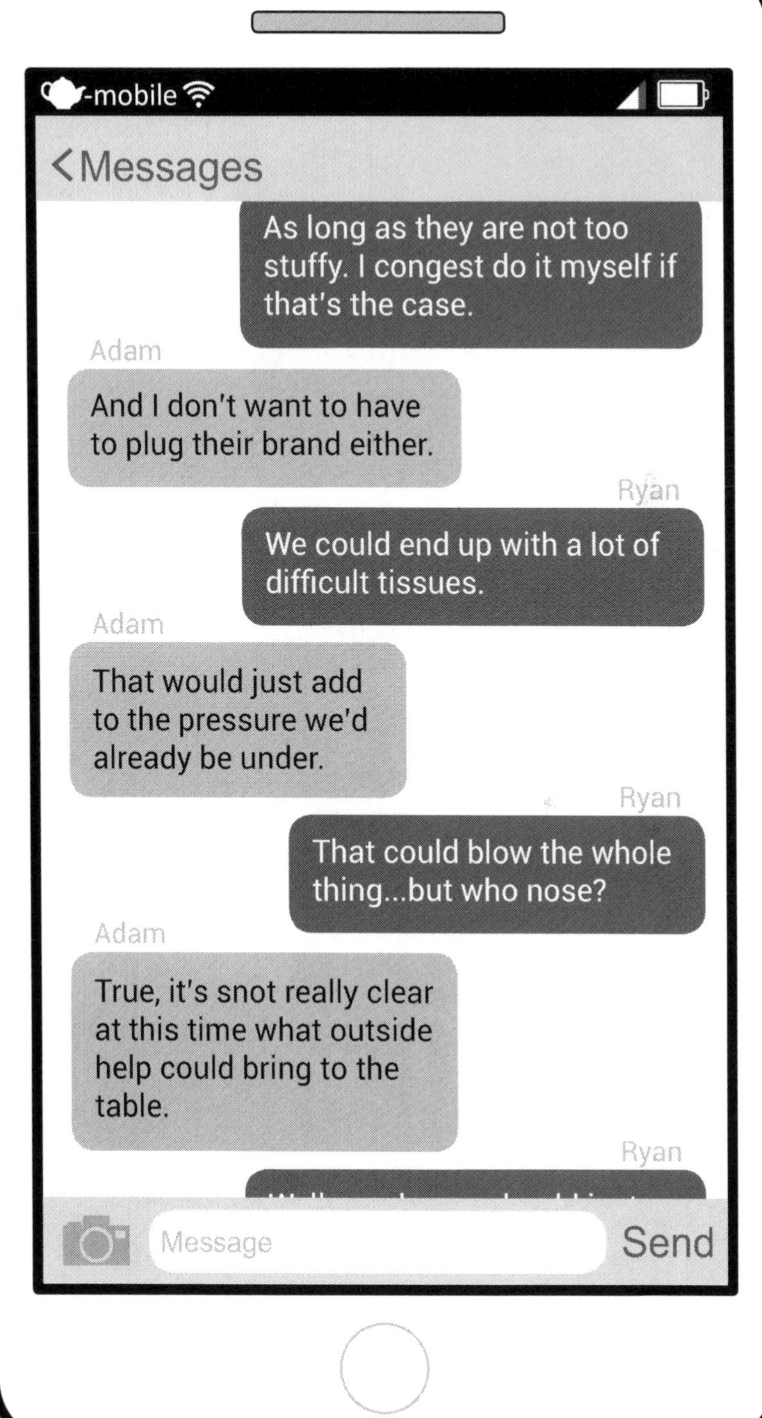
-mobile
Messages
As long as they are not too stuffy. I congest do it myself if that's the case.
Adam
And I don't want to have to plug their brand either.
Ryan
We could end up with a lot of difficult tissues.
Adam
That would just add to the pressure we'd already be under.
Ryan
That could blow the whole thing...but who nose?
Adam
True, it's snot really clear at this time what outside help could bring to the table.
Ryan
Message
Send

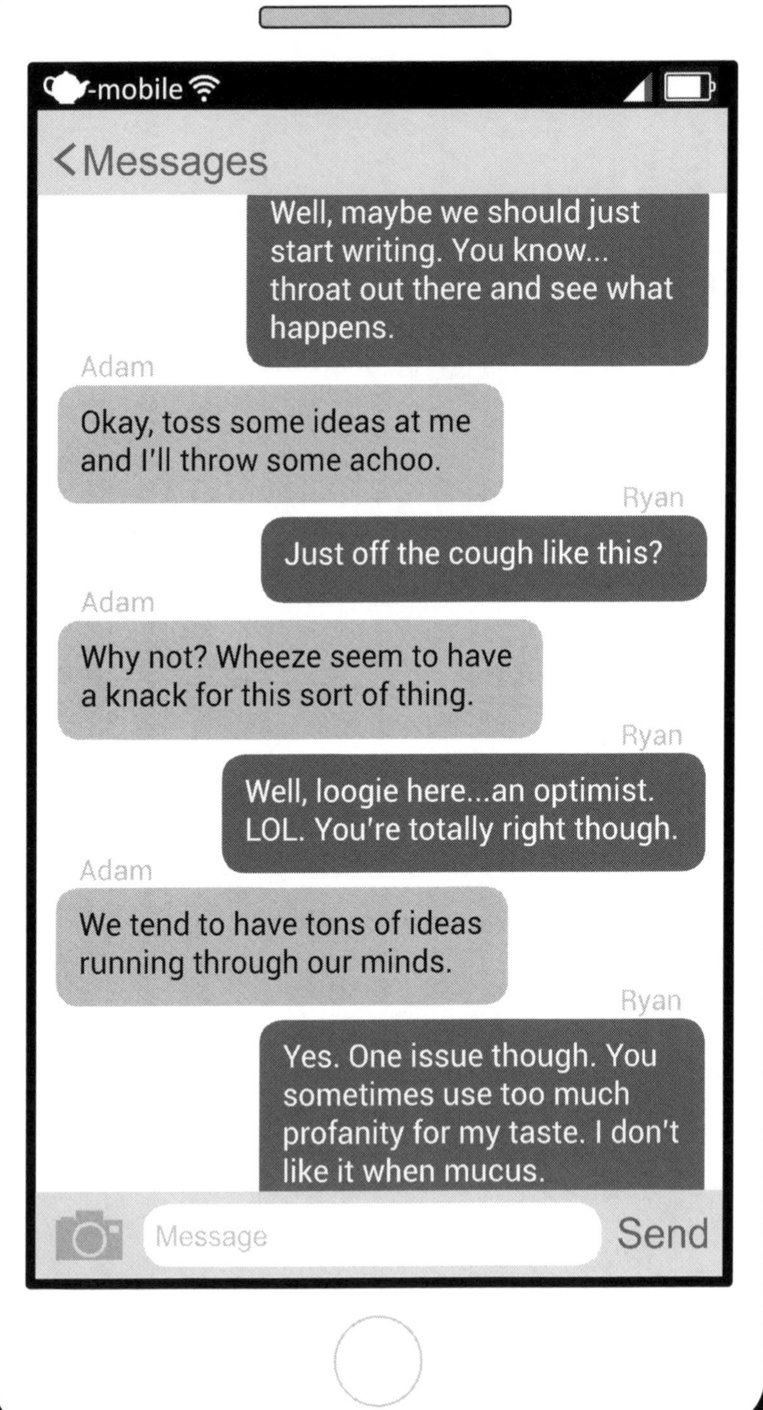
-mobile
Messages
Well, maybe we should just start writing. You know... throat out there and see what happens.
Adam
Okay, toss some ideas at me and I'll throw some achoo.
Ryan
Just off the cough like this?
Adam
Why not? Wheeze seem to have a knack for this sort of thing.
Ryan
Well, loogie here...an optimist. LOL. You're totally right though.
Adam
We tend to have tons of ideas running through our minds.
Ryan
Yes. One issue though. You sometimes use too much profanity for my taste. I don't like it when mucus.
Message
Send

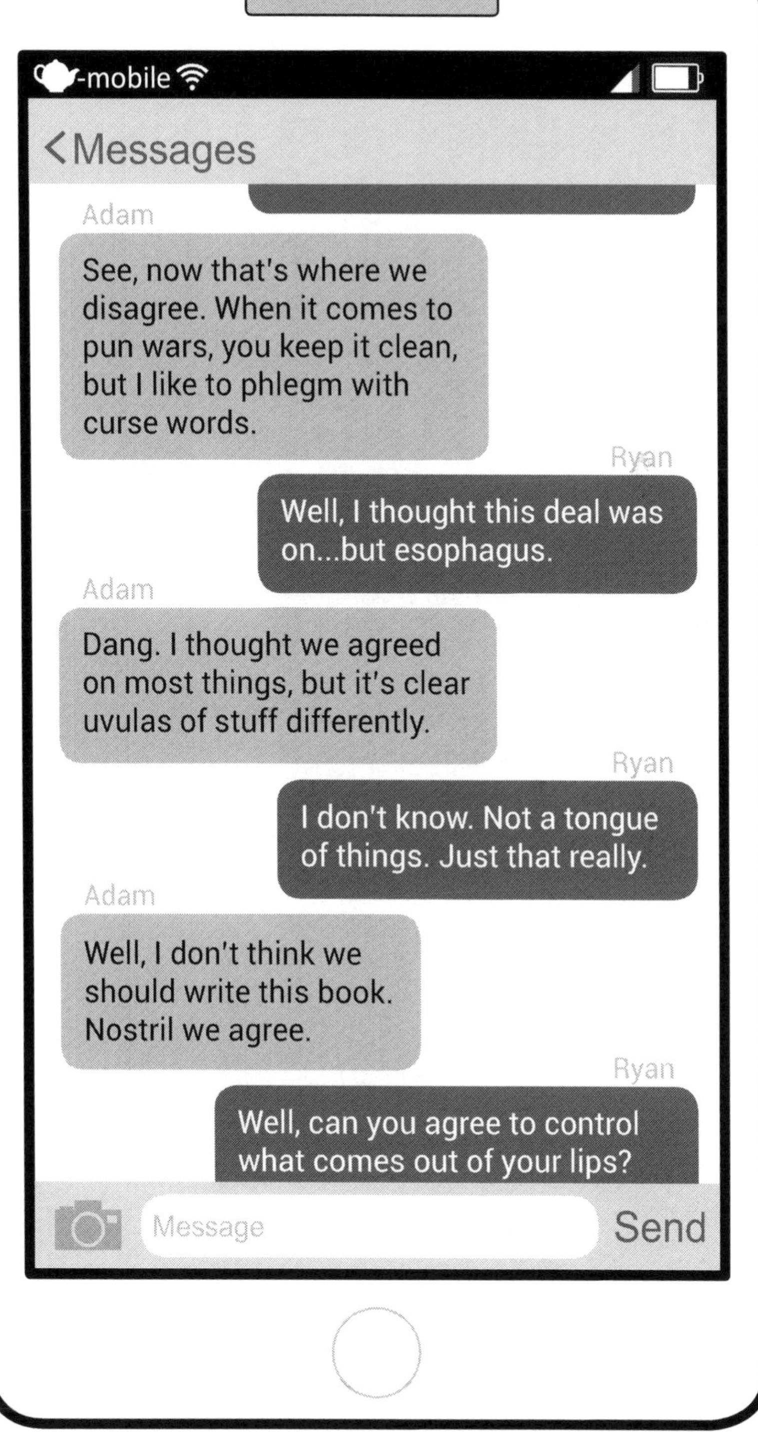
-mobile
Messages
Adam
See, now that's where we disagree. When it comes to pun wars, you keep it clean, but I like to phlegm with curse words.
Ryan
Well, I thought this deal was on...but esophagus.
Adam
Dang. I thought we agreed on most things, but it's clear uvulas of stuff differently.
Ryan
I don't know. Not a tongue of things. Just that really.
Adam
Well, I don't think we should write this book. Nostril we agree.
Ryan
Well, can you agree to control what comes out of your lips?
Message
Send

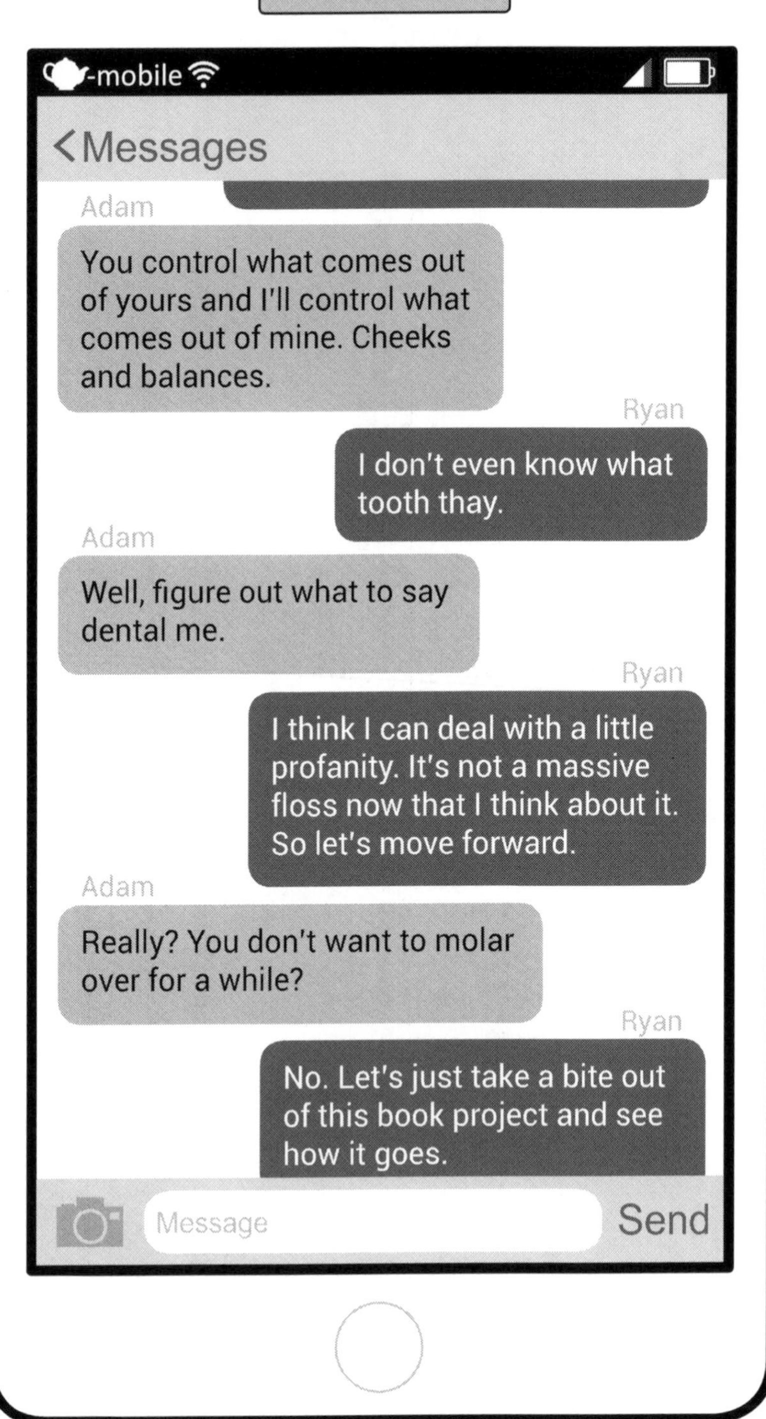
-mobile
Messages
Adam
You control what comes out of yours and I'll control what comes out of mine. Cheeks and balances.
Ryan
I don't even know what tooth thay.
Adam
Well, figure out what to say dental me.
Ryan
I think I can deal with a little profanity. It's not a massive floss now that I think about it. So let's move forward.
Adam
Really? You don't want to molar over for a while?
Ryan
No. Let's just take a bite out of this book project and see how it goes.
Message
Send

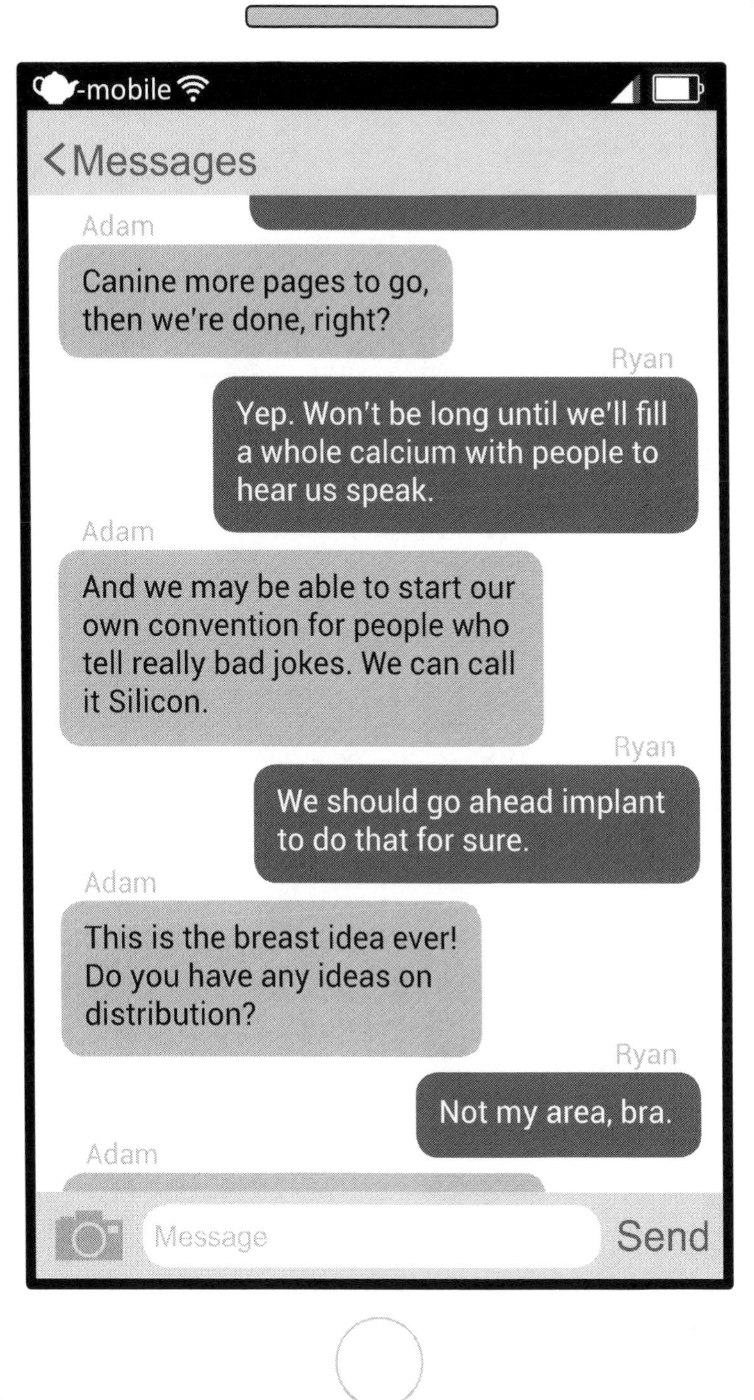
-mobile
Messages
Adam
Canine more pages to go, then we're done, right?
Ryan
Yep. Won't be long until we'll fill a whole calcium with people to hear us speak.
Adam
And we may be able to start our own convention for people who tell really bad jokes. We can call it Silicon.
Ryan
We should go ahead implant to do that for sure.
Adam
This is the breast idea ever! Do you have any ideas on distribution?
Ryan
Not my area, bra.
Adam
Message
Send

-mobile
Messages
You wanna try something else? Knockers self out.
Ryan
No, I'm saying I totally support it. I chest don't have ideas for distribution. Not my department.
Adam
I don't want you to support something just B Cups I said so.
Ryan
Well, I guess this idea is a bust.
Adam
We need more ideas. I'll rack my brain.
Ryan
I nude dats what you'd say.
Adam
Maybe we can feature our puns in a show, like an exhibitionist what I'm thinking.
Message
Send

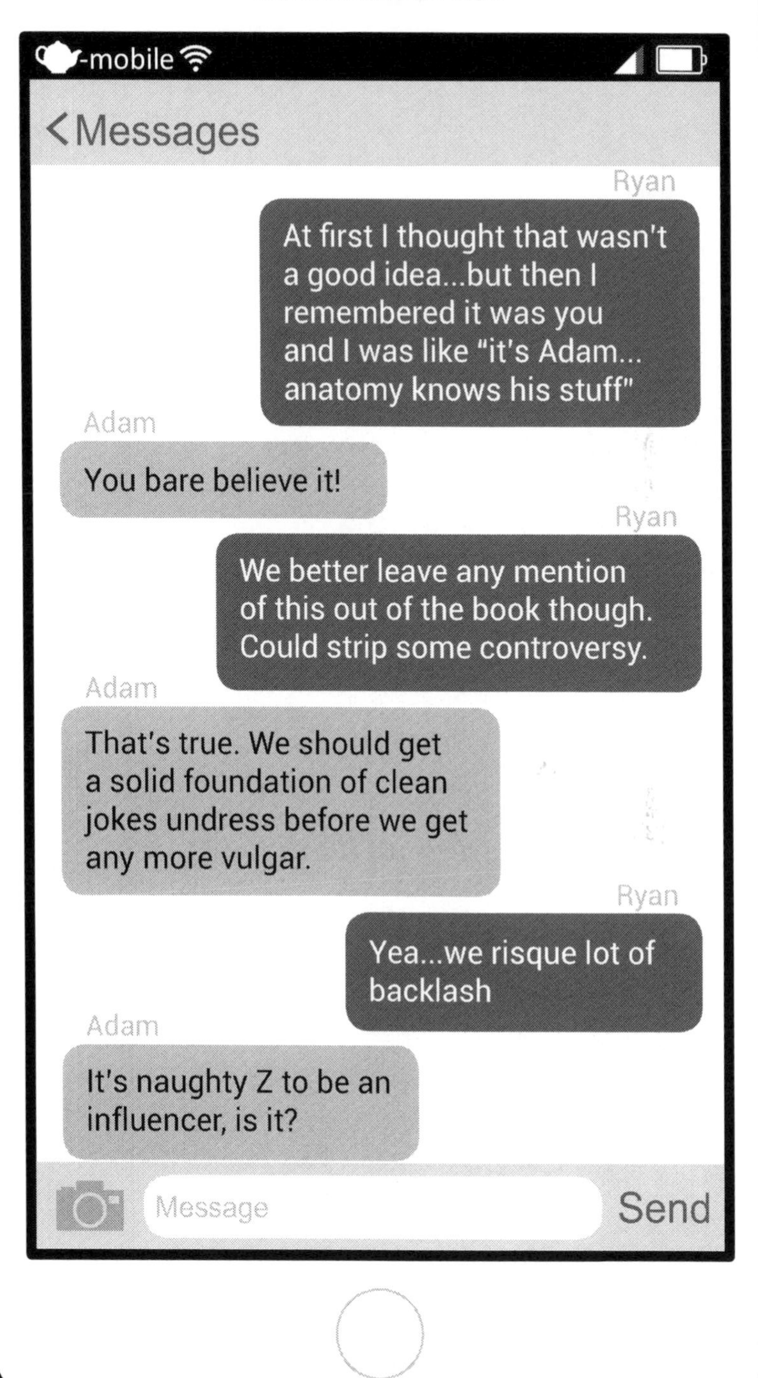
-mobile
Messages
Ryan
At first I thought that wasn't a good idea...but then I remembered it was you and I was like "it's Adam... anatomy knows his stuff"
Adam
You bare believe it!
Ryan
We better leave any mention of this out of the book though. Could strip some controversy.
Adam
That's true. We should get a solid foundation of clean jokes undress before we get any more vulgar.
Ryan
Yea...we risque lot of backlash
Adam
It's naughty Z to be an influencer, is it?
Message
Send

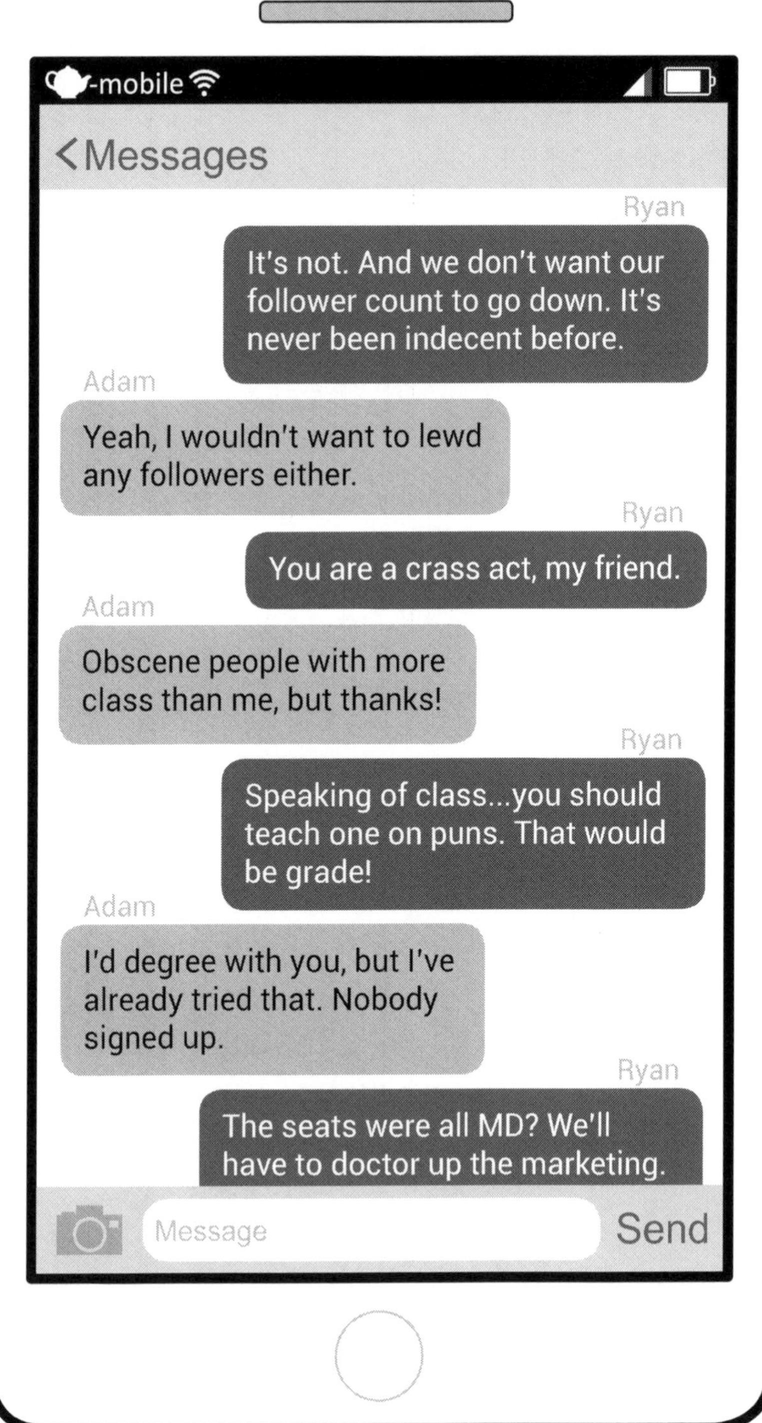
-mobile
Messages
Ryan
It's not. And we don't want our follower count to go down. It's never been indecent before.
Adam
Yeah, I wouldn't want to lewd any followers either.
Ryan
You are a crass act, my friend.
Adam
Obscene people with more class than me, but thanks!
Ryan
Speaking of class...you should teach one on puns. That would be grade!
Adam
I'd degree with you, but I've already tried that. Nobody signed up.
Ryan
The seats were all MD? We'll have to doctor up the marketing.
Message
Send

-mobile
Messages
Adam
Yeah, it was a bunch of BS. You might BA better teacher though.
Ryan
We are the Masters. We should teach it together.
Adam
So we should be Associates in this venture?
Ryan
Yes. Did you know that puns are what made my wife professor love for me?
Adam
You mean the first time when you declined her advances? That must semester up pretty bad.
Ryan
Yea. When she asked me to quarter.
Message
Send

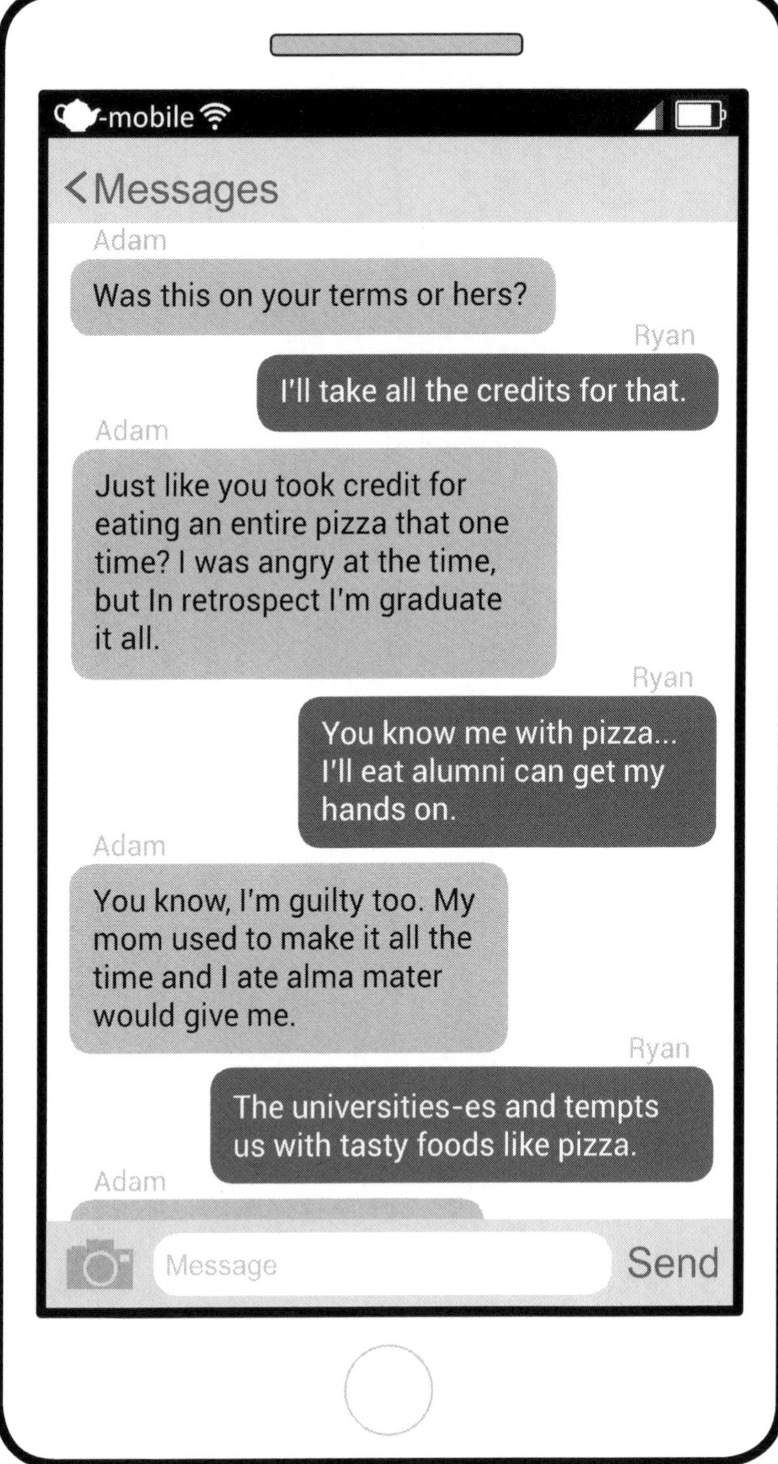

-mobile
Messages
Adam
Was this on your terms or hers?
Ryan
I'll take all the credits for that.
Adam
Just like you took credit for eating an entire pizza that one time? I was angry at the time, but In retrospect I'm graduate it all.
Ryan
You know me with pizza... I'll eat alumni can get my hands on.
Adam
You know, I'm guilty too. My mom used to make it all the time and I ate alma mater would give me.
Ryan
The universities-es and tempts us with tasty foods like pizza.
Adam
Message
Send

-mobile
Messages
Yep, especially the crust. Usually people avoid the crusty edge, but I colleges the best part.
Ryan
Yep. It's like a vocation for your mouth.
Adam
Do you like to career pizza in a box? That's how I like to carry mine.
Ryan
I like to employ that method as well. Works for me.
Adam
Really? I thought you were too busy profession your love to your wife.
Ryan
That's none of your business.
Adam
Oh great, are we going to trade insults again?
Message
Send

-mobile
Messages
Ryan
I might throw a couple of friendly jobs or right hooks.
Adam
I think our punch-oices can lead us to fight, but they can also bring us together.
Ryan
I couldn't agree more, old chop.
Adam
I sure get a kick out of it.
Ryan
Yea. You know I kneed ya for that.
Adam
Man, jiu jitsu needy sometimes.
Ryan
I'm sorry. I wrestle with that.
Adam
I MMA-zed you're willing to admit that.
Message
Send

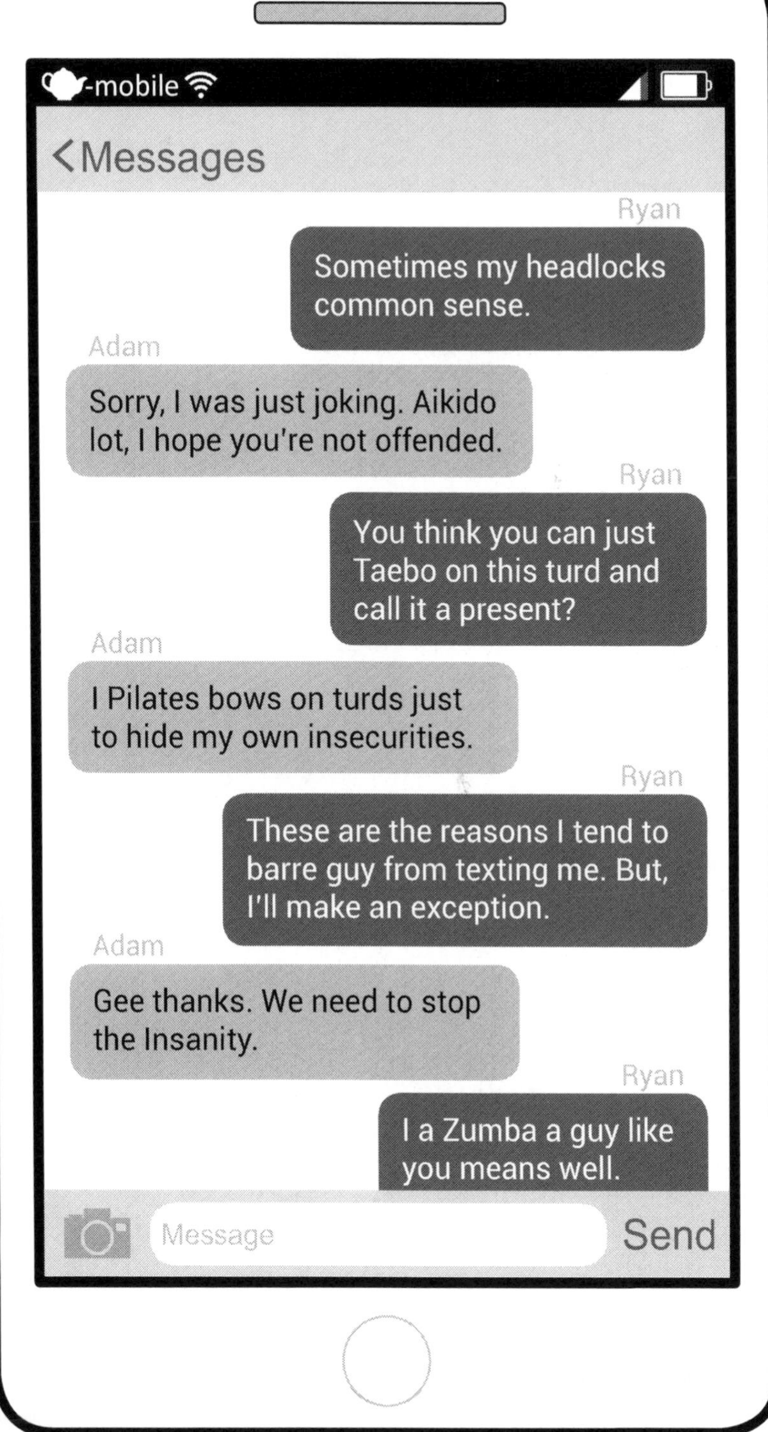

-mobile
Messages
Ryan
Sometimes my headlocks common sense.
Adam
Sorry, I was just joking. Aikido lot, I hope you're not offended.
Ryan
You think you can just Taebo on this turd and call it a present?
Adam
I Pilates bows on turds just to hide my own insecurities.
Ryan
These are the reasons I tend to barre guy from texting me. But, I'll make an exception.
Adam
Gee thanks. We need to stop the Insanity.
Ryan
I a Zumba a guy like you means well.
Message
Send

-mobile
Messages
Adam
Phew! You make me thigh with relief. You're gonna turn me into the Thighmaster.
Ryan
You're not the only Gaiam sure.
Adam
Yoga to be kidding me. There's more like me?
Ryan
Well, it's just a theory. Orangetheory's an interesting thing?
Adam
Is some body building on that theory, or are you the only one working on it?
Ryan
Well, I had some Body Pump me for information on it. But, it seems no one cares un Les Mills of dollars are involved.
Adam
Message
Send

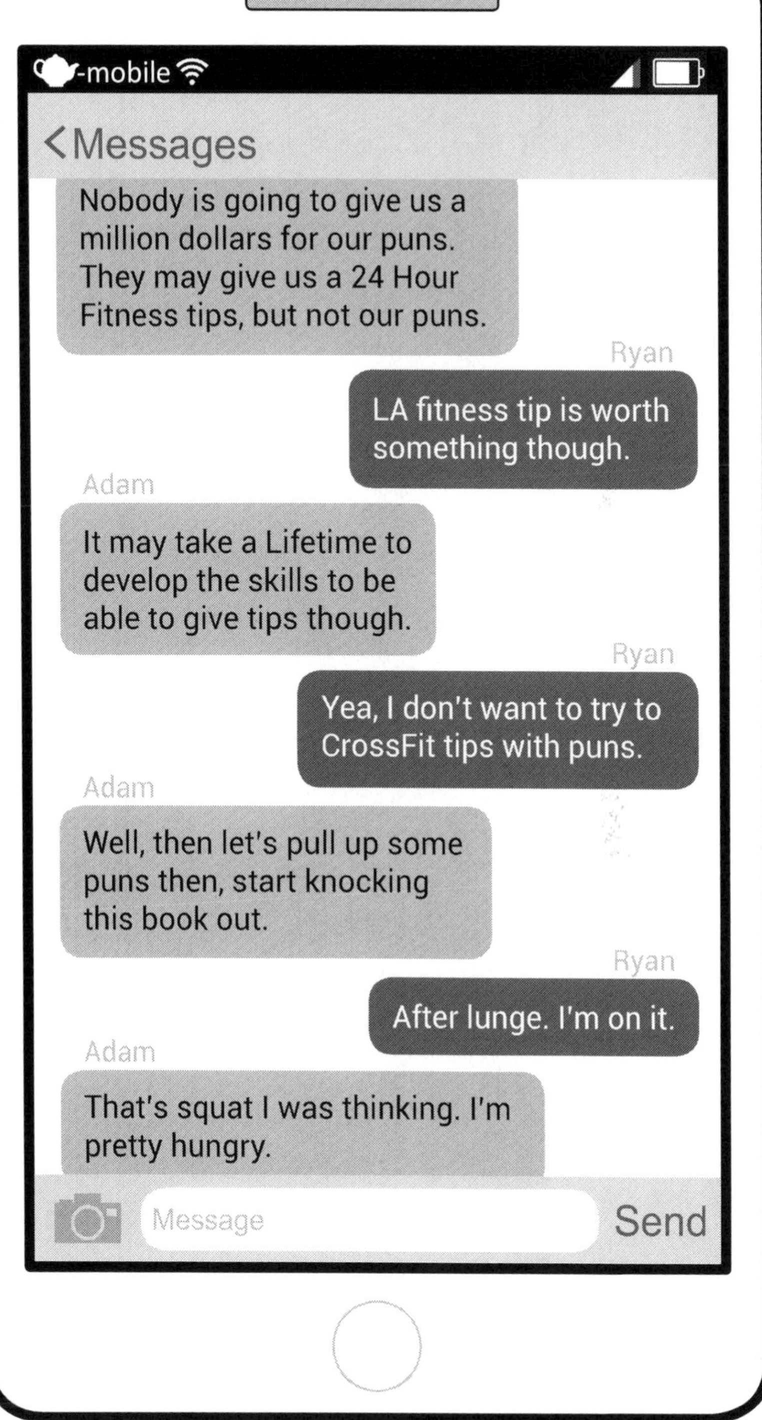
-mobile
Messages
Nobody is going to give us a million dollars for our puns. They may give us a 24 Hour Fitness tips, but not our puns.
Ryan
LA fitness tip is worth something though.
Adam
It may take a Lifetime to develop the skills to be able to give tips though.
Ryan
Yea, I don't want to try to CrossFit tips with puns.
Adam
Well, then let's pull up some puns then, start knocking this book out.
Ryan
After lunge. I'm on it.
Adam
That's squat I was thinking. I'm pretty hungry.
Message
Send

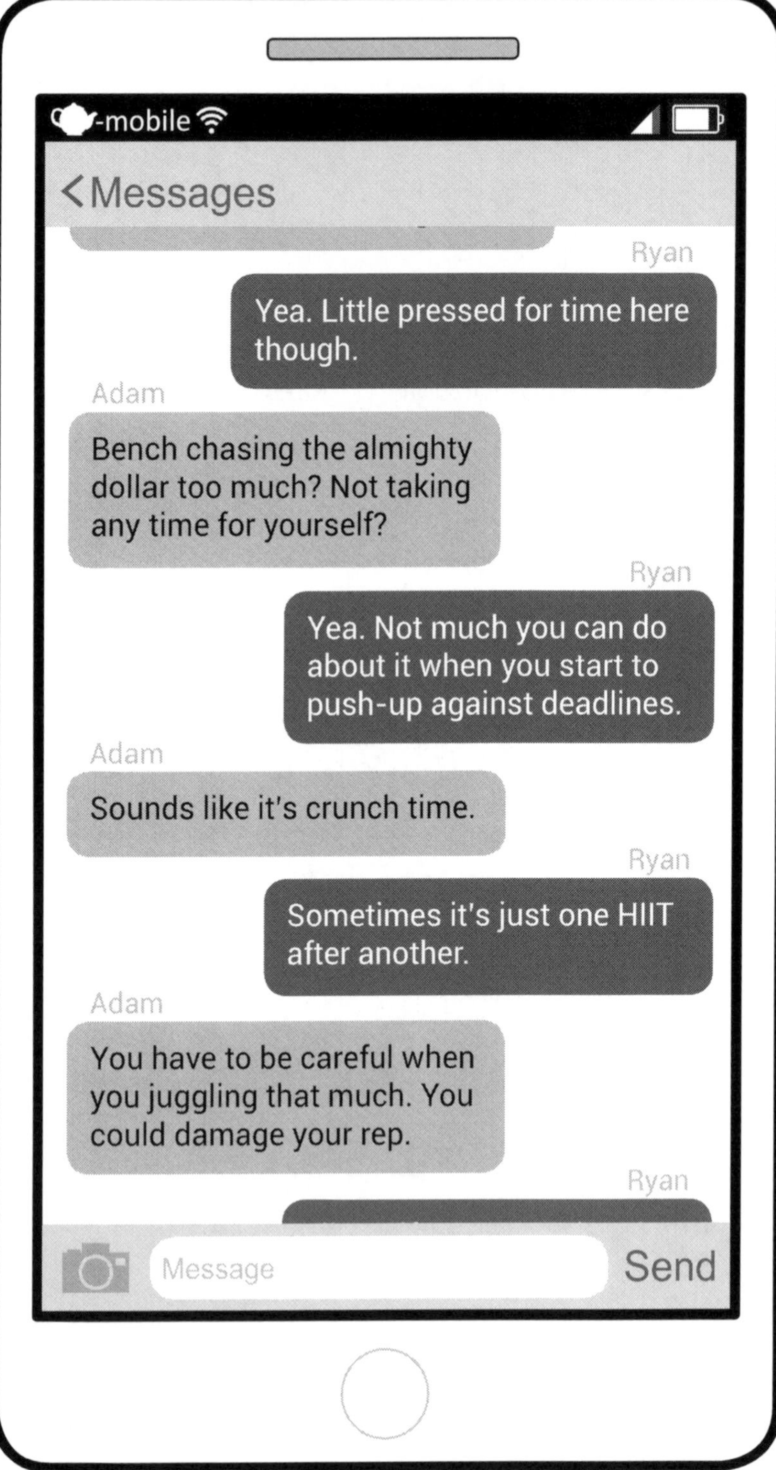
-mobile
Messages
Ryan
Yea. Little pressed for time here though.
Adam
Bench chasing the almighty dollar too much? Not taking any time for yourself?
Ryan
Yea. Not much you can do about it when you start to push-up against deadlines.
Adam
Sounds like it's crunch time.
Ryan
Sometimes it's just one HIIT after another.
Adam
You have to be careful when you juggling that much. You could damage your rep.
Ryan
Message
Send

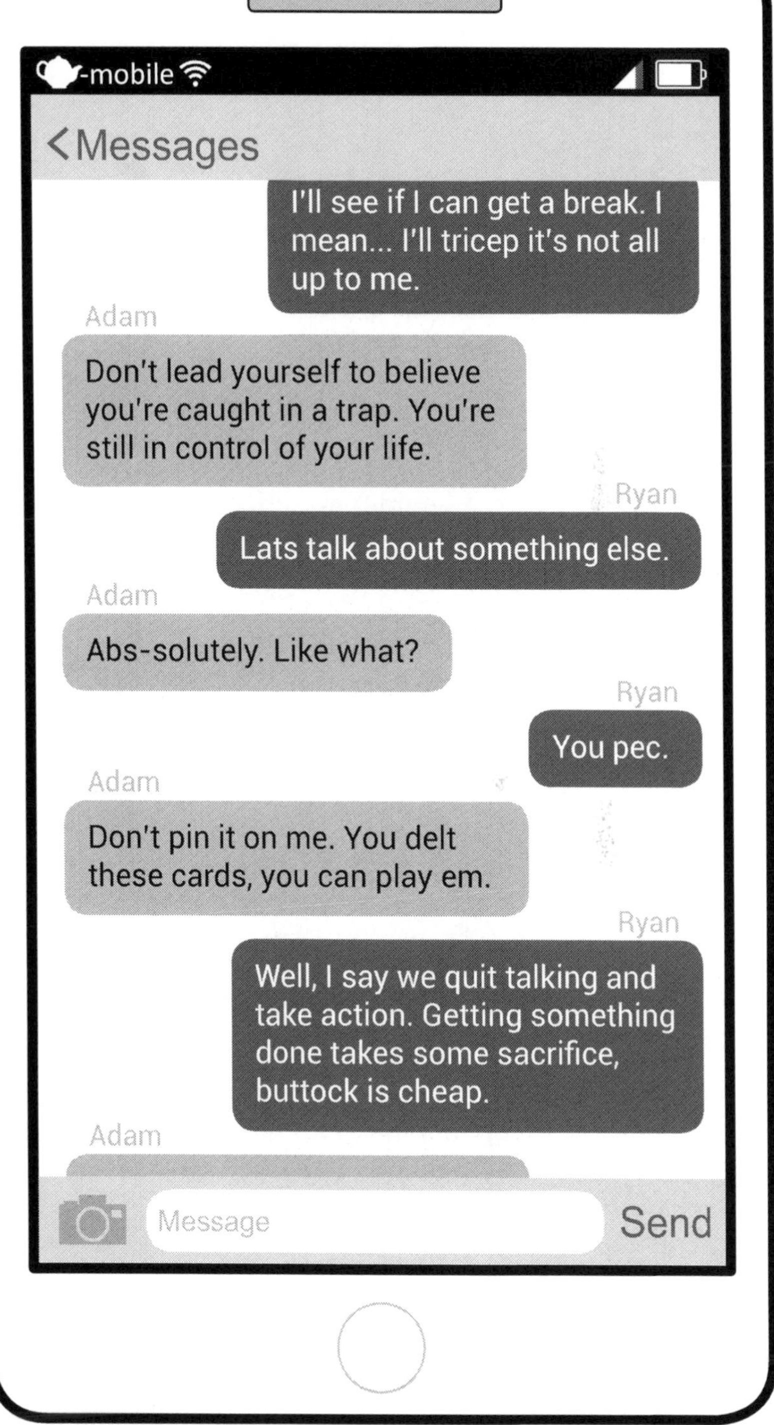
-mobile
Messages
I'll see if I can get a break. I mean... I'll tricep it's not all up to me.
Adam
Don't lead yourself to believe you're caught in a trap. You're still in control of your life.
Ryan
Lats talk about something else.
Adam
Abs-solutely. Like what?
Ryan
You pec.
Adam
Don't pin it on me. You delt these cards, you can play em.
Ryan
Well, I say we quit talking and take action. Getting something done takes some sacrifice, buttock is cheap.
Adam
Message
Send

-mobile
< Messages
Yeah, if we stop talking and get to work this book will only take calf the time to finish.
Ryan
Then we'll be like "wow...look quad we did"
Adam
I want you to know that I am just as into this as you are. I don't want you to think that I hamstring-ing you along.
Ryan
Awww...let me get a soft tissue.
Adam
Sorry, I muscle let myself get too emotional.
Ryan
No worries. So when do you want to meat next?
Adam
Probably beef or next week.
Ryan
Ok. I'm chicken my schedule
Message
Send

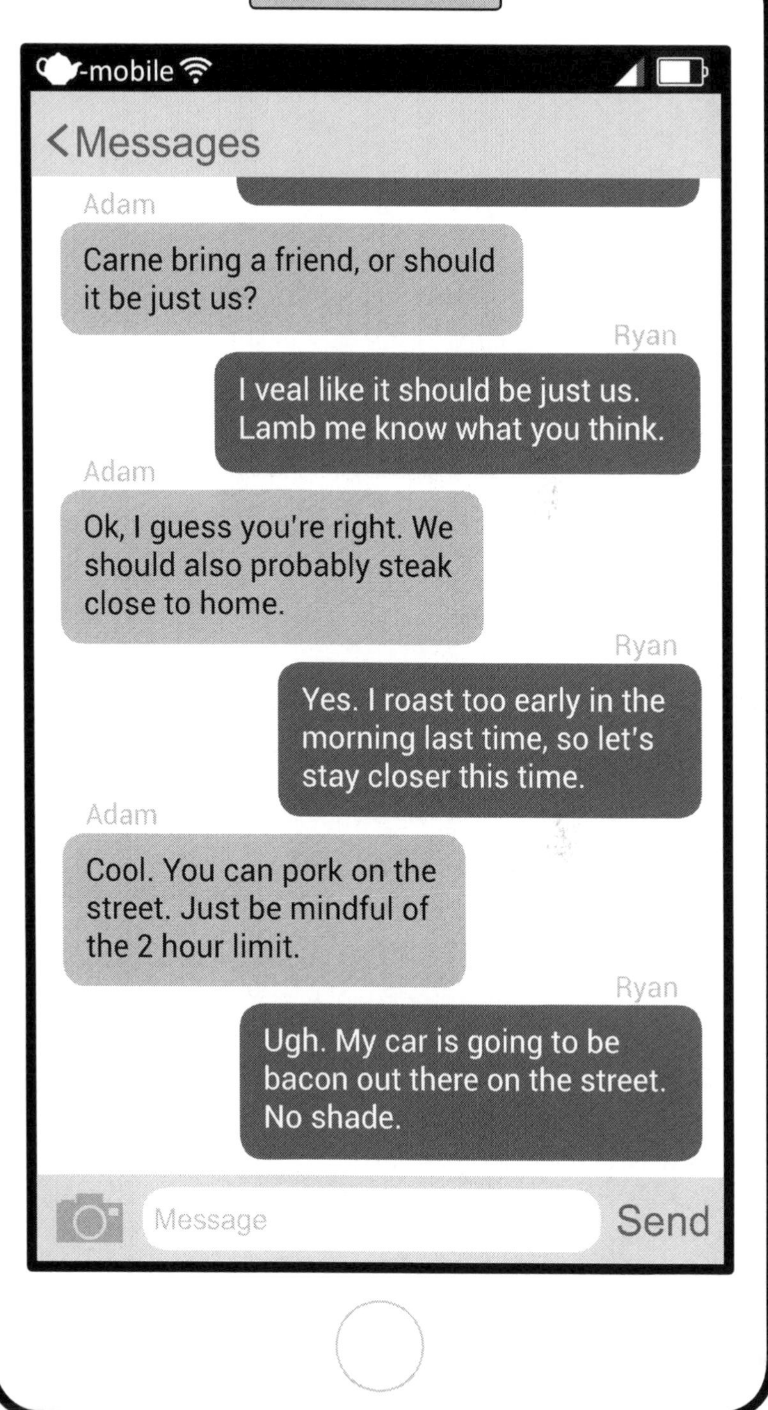
-mobile
Messages
Adam
Carne bring a friend, or should it be just us?
Ryan
I veal like it should be just us. Lamb me know what you think.
Adam
Ok, I guess you're right. We should also probably steak close to home.
Ryan
Yes. I roast too early in the morning last time, so let's stay closer this time.
Adam
Cool. You can pork on the street. Just be mindful of the 2 hour limit.
Ryan
Ugh. My car is going to be bacon out there on the street. No shade.
Message
Send

-mobile
Messages
Adam
Does your carnitas screen over it to block the sun?
Ryan
We'll see. If the wind is brisket isn't too bad.
Adam
You can always park under the shade of a poultry or building.
Ryan
That's one way tofu the sun and keep your car cool.
Adam
It works for me. Always keeps the car tempeh-ture down.
Ryan
Ok. What are we going to do in this meeting though? We need an agenda so we don't just veg out.
Adam
Message
Send

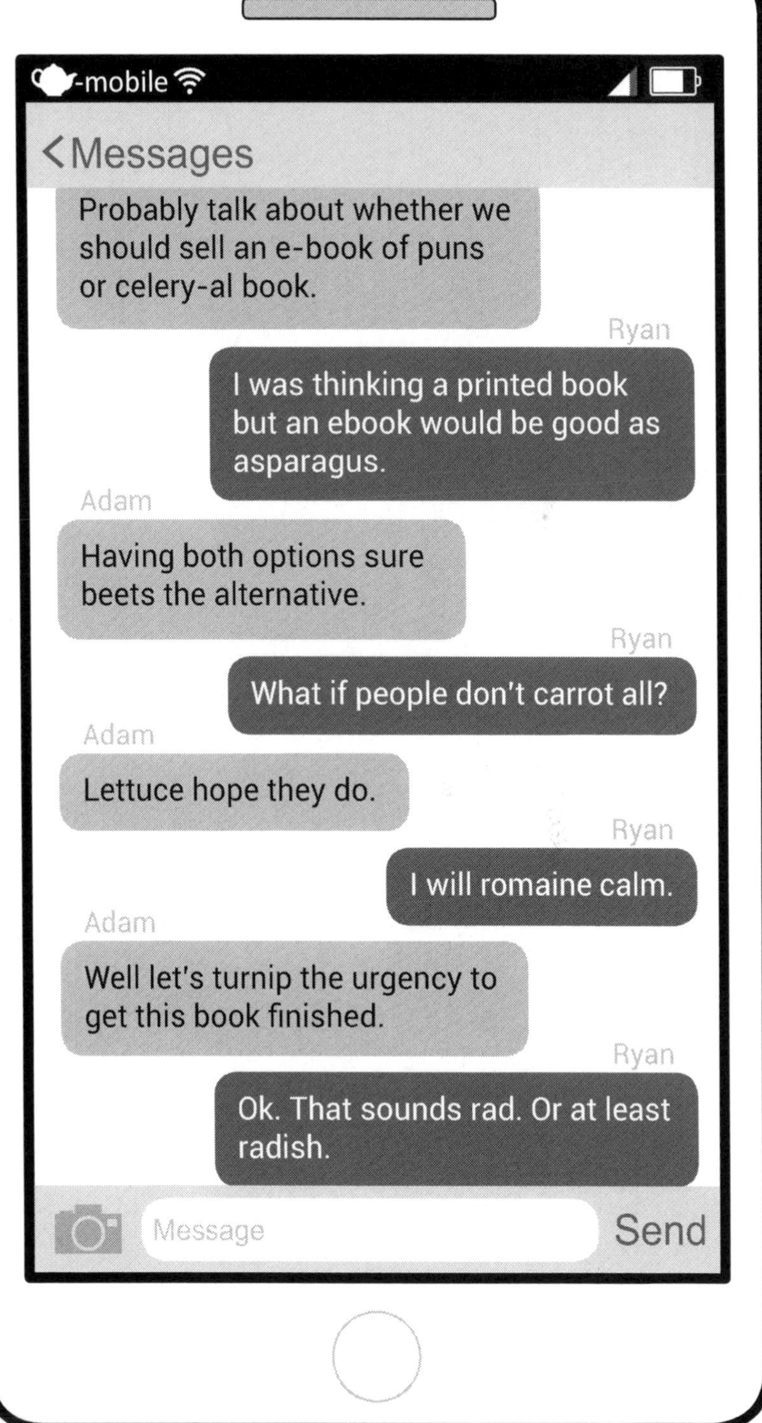
-mobile
Messages
Probably talk about whether we should sell an e-book of puns or celery-al book.
Ryan
I was thinking a printed book but an ebook would be good as asparagus.
Adam
Having both options sure beets the alternative.
Ryan
What if people don't carrot all?
Adam
Lettuce hope they do.
Ryan
I will romaine calm.
Adam
Well let's turnip the urgency to get this book finished.
Ryan
Ok. That sounds rad. Or at least radish.
Message
Send

-mobile
Messages
Adam
We just have to be careful. This pun book could go on onion.
Ryan
Avocado agree with you there. It has to be engaging.
Adam
Between the two of us we can make that happen. We make quite a pear.
Ryan
Orange you glad we met?
Adam
Of course, but kiwi get together more often?
Ryan
I can berry make the current meeting schedule, but we can try.
Adam
Let's just fig get about the meeting then, if you're not going to take it seriously.
Message
Send

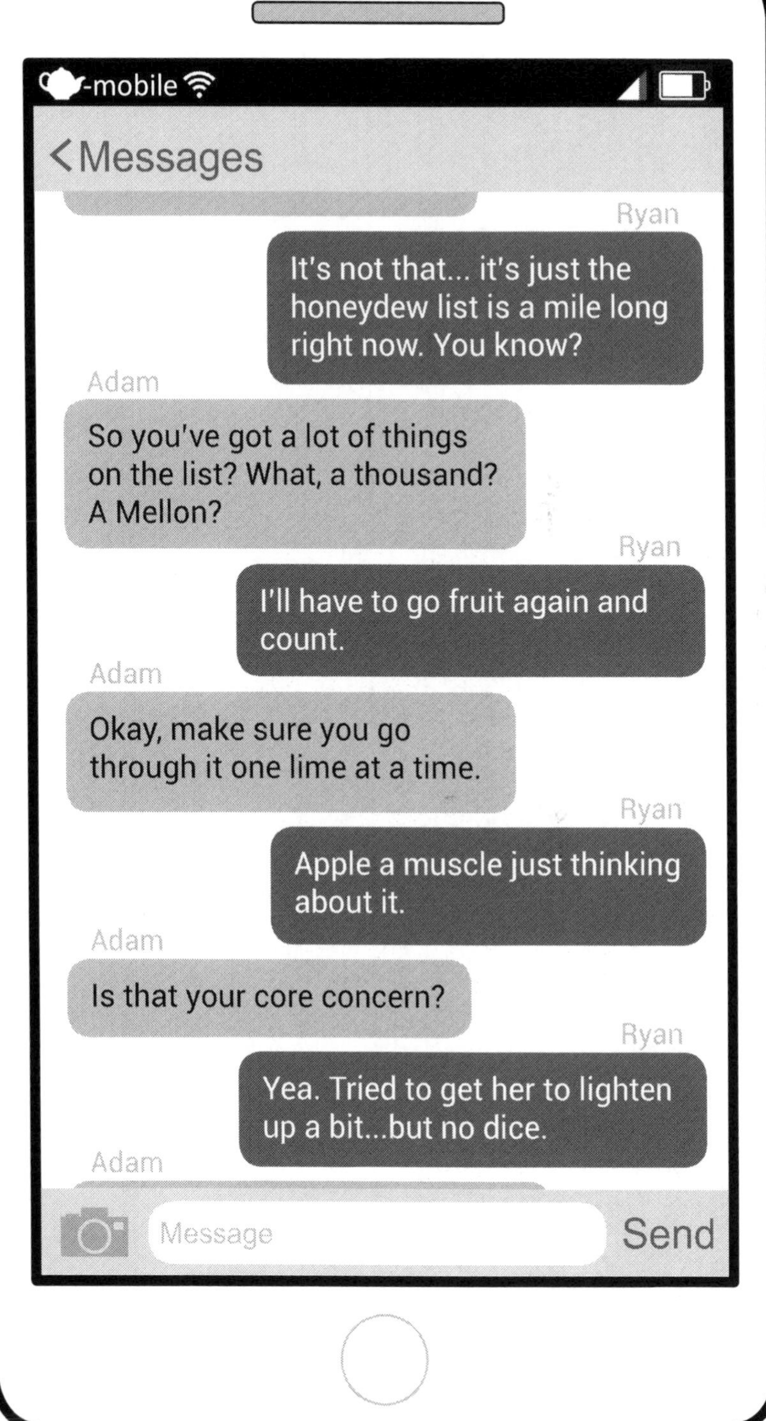
-mobile
Messages
Ryan
It's not that... it's just the honeydew list is a mile long right now. You know?
Adam
So you've got a lot of things on the list? What, a thousand? A Mellon?
Ryan
I'll have to go fruit again and count.
Adam
Okay, make sure you go through it one lime at a time.
Ryan
Apple a muscle just thinking about it.
Adam
Is that your core concern?
Ryan
Yea. Tried to get her to lighten up a bit...but no dice.
Adam
Message
Send

-mobile
Messages
So she doesn't find it a peelin'?
Ryan
No. And challenging her more is just a whisk I'm not willing to take.
Adam
I may not be on time to our meeting. I hope I don't make you angry with how ladle be.
Ryan
Not much I can say when knife been late before.
Adam
That's big of you. You're a grater man than I.
Ryan
Thank you fork caring enough to say that.
Adam
Well, I really had an ulterior motive... oops, I spork too soon.
Ryan
Message
Send

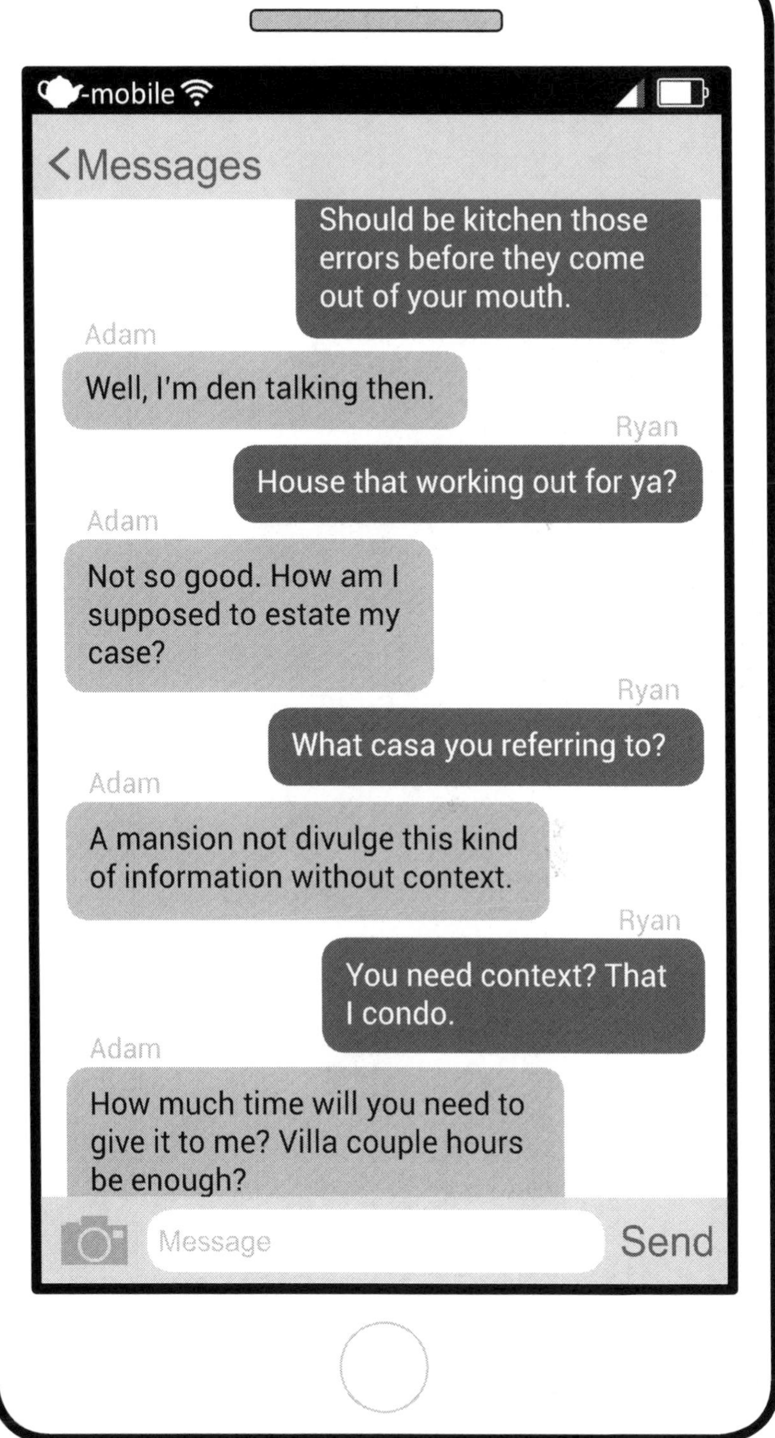
-mobile
Messages
Should be kitchen those errors before they come out of your mouth.
Adam
Well, I'm den talking then.
Ryan
House that working out for ya?
Adam
Not so good. How am I supposed to estate my case?
Ryan
What casa you referring to?
Adam
A mansion not divulge this kind of information without context.
Ryan
You need context? That I condo.
Adam
How much time will you need to give it to me? Villa couple hours be enough?
Message
Send

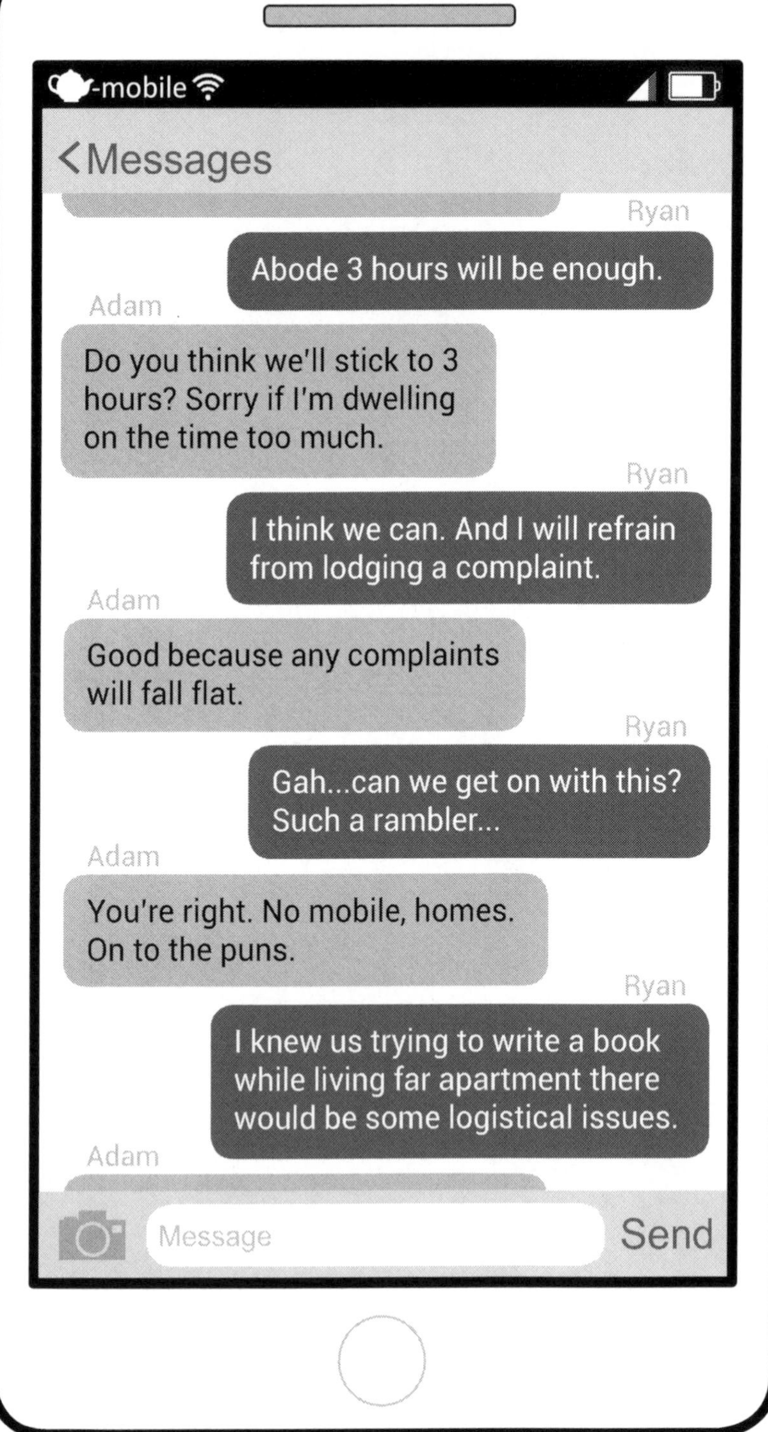
-mobile
Messages
Ryan
Abode 3 hours will be enough.
Adam
Do you think we'll stick to 3 hours? Sorry if I'm dwelling on the time too much.
Ryan
I think we can. And I will refrain from lodging a complaint.
Adam
Good because any complaints will fall flat.
Ryan
Gah...can we get on with this? Such a rambler...
Adam
You're right. No mobile, homes. On to the puns.
Ryan
I knew us trying to write a book while living far apartment there would be some logistical issues.
Adam
Message
Send

-mobile
Messages
I guess we have to try to break that habitat one of our next meetings.
Ryan
Wow. This meeting is going to be in tents.
Adam
I could tell you're amped about it. You'll be really impressive. I can already see what a studio going to be.
Ryan
That's what she shed!
Adam
Thanks for cabin this conversation off with a little humor!
Ryan
I am all about adding a little shack value.
Adam
Shock value is quite the hut topic right now.
Message
Send

-mobile
Messages
Ryan
I saw a few headlines about that. Didn't read them, but I cottage gist of it.
Adam
My wife's an expert. Cheese always educating me on the subject.
Ryan
Ugh. Tell me about it. Swiss my wife.
Adam
Often I'll want to ask her a question about it and she wouldn't have to look it up. Cheddar ready know the answer.
Ryan
Mine will tell me even if Havarti found the answer.
Adam
You've gotta be feta up with that.
Message
Send

-mobile
Messages
Ryan
Yea. Sometimes. There's Stilton of great things about her though, tbh.
Adam
That makes for a great relationship. I have yet to find someone who can provolone is better than together when it comes to marriage.
Ryan
I hope you gruyere kids to hold those same values.
Adam
I'm trying to, but I get the feeling I'm creating a little Muenster.
Ryan
You might be reggiano little hoodlum, eh?
Adam
I mean, what do I do? Do you set up a rigorous schedule for the kids or just plan it Asiago?
Message
Send

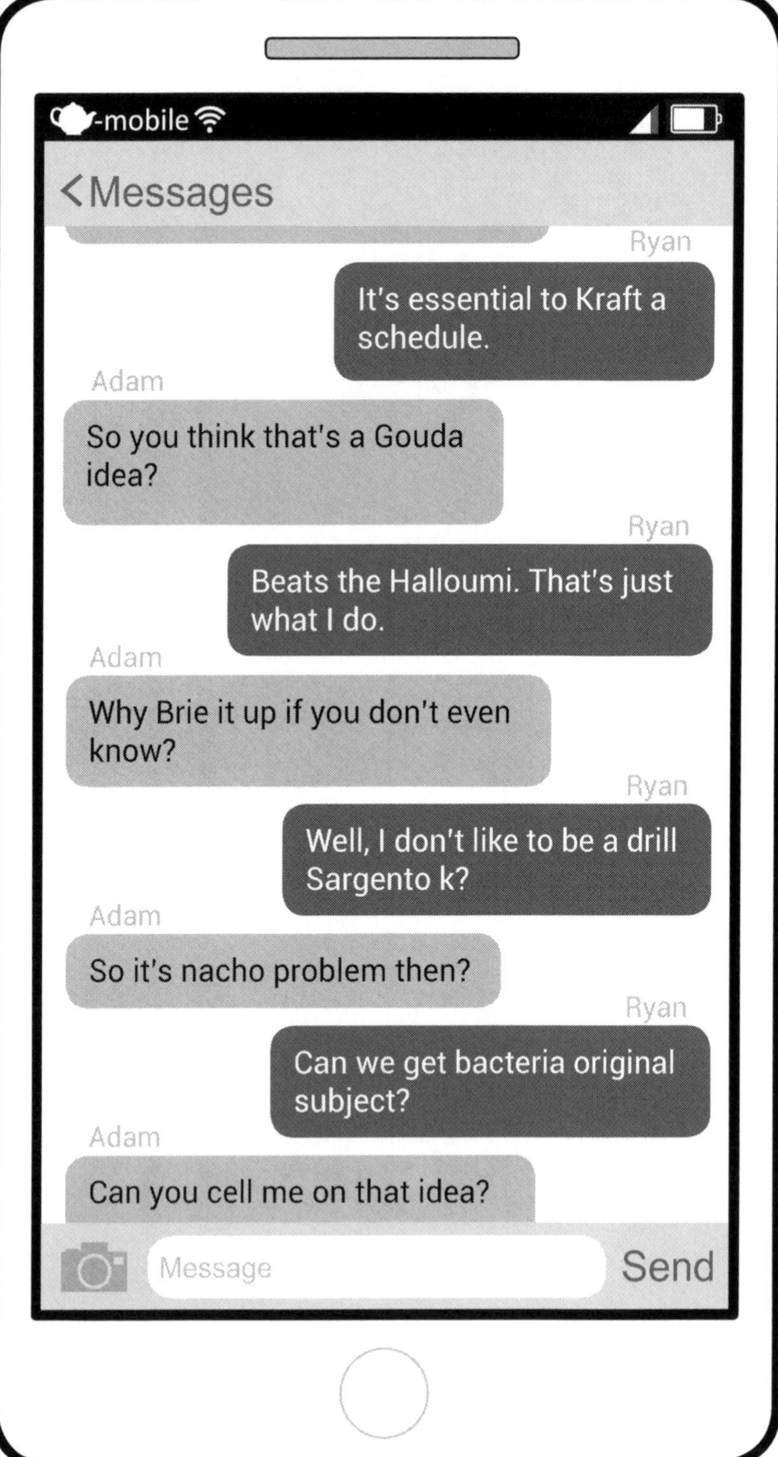
-mobile
Messages
Ryan
It's essential to Kraft a schedule.
Adam
So you think that's a Gouda idea?
Ryan
Beats the Halloumi. That's just what I do.
Adam
Why Brie it up if you don't even know?
Ryan
Well, I don't like to be a drill Sargento k?
Adam
So it's nacho problem then?
Ryan
Can we get bacteria original subject?
Adam
Can you cell me on that idea?
Message
Send

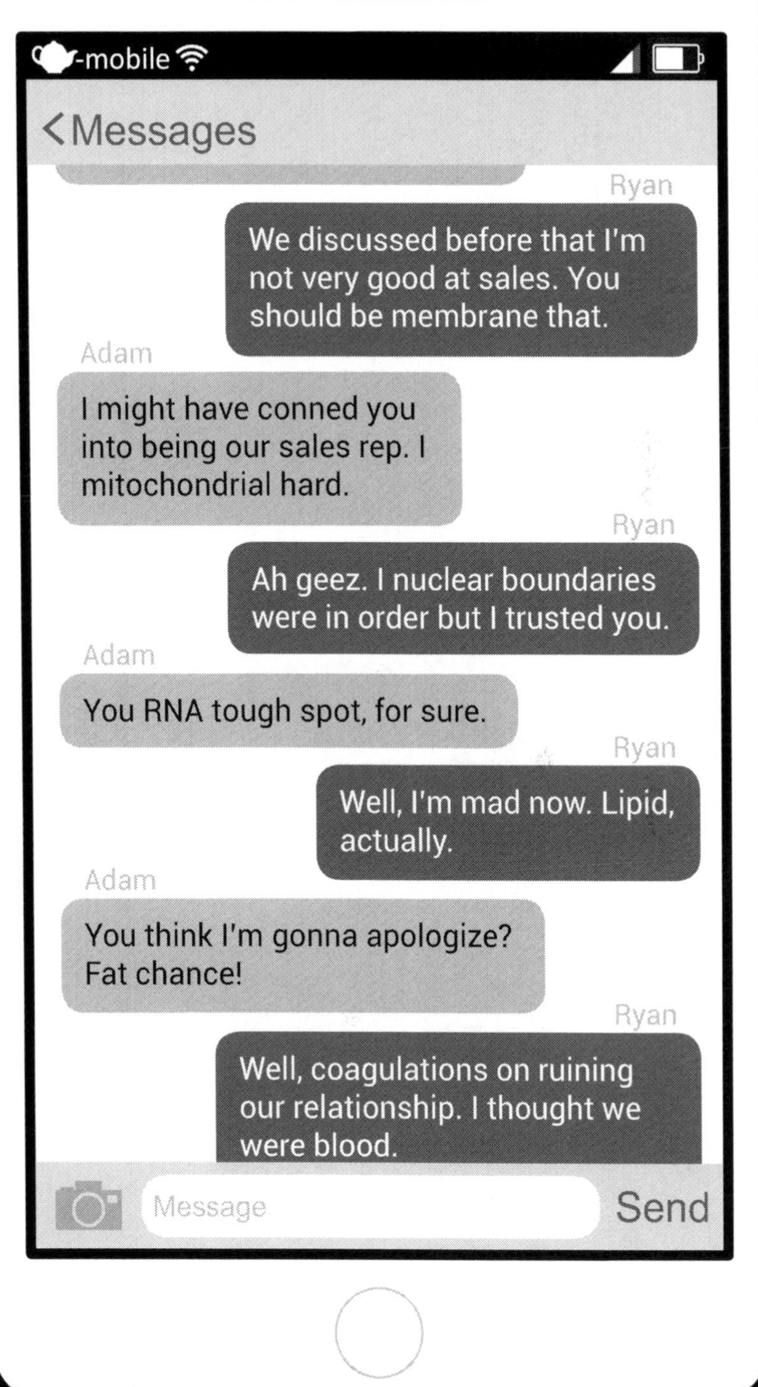
-mobile
Messages
Ryan
We discussed before that I'm not very good at sales. You should be membrane that.
Adam
I might have conned you into being our sales rep. I mitochondrial hard.
Ryan
Ah geez. I nuclear boundaries were in order but I trusted you.
Adam
You RNA tough spot, for sure.
Ryan
Well, I'm mad now. Lipid, actually.
Adam
You think I'm gonna apologize? Fat chance!
Ryan
Well, coagulations on ruining our relationship. I thought we were blood.
Message
Send

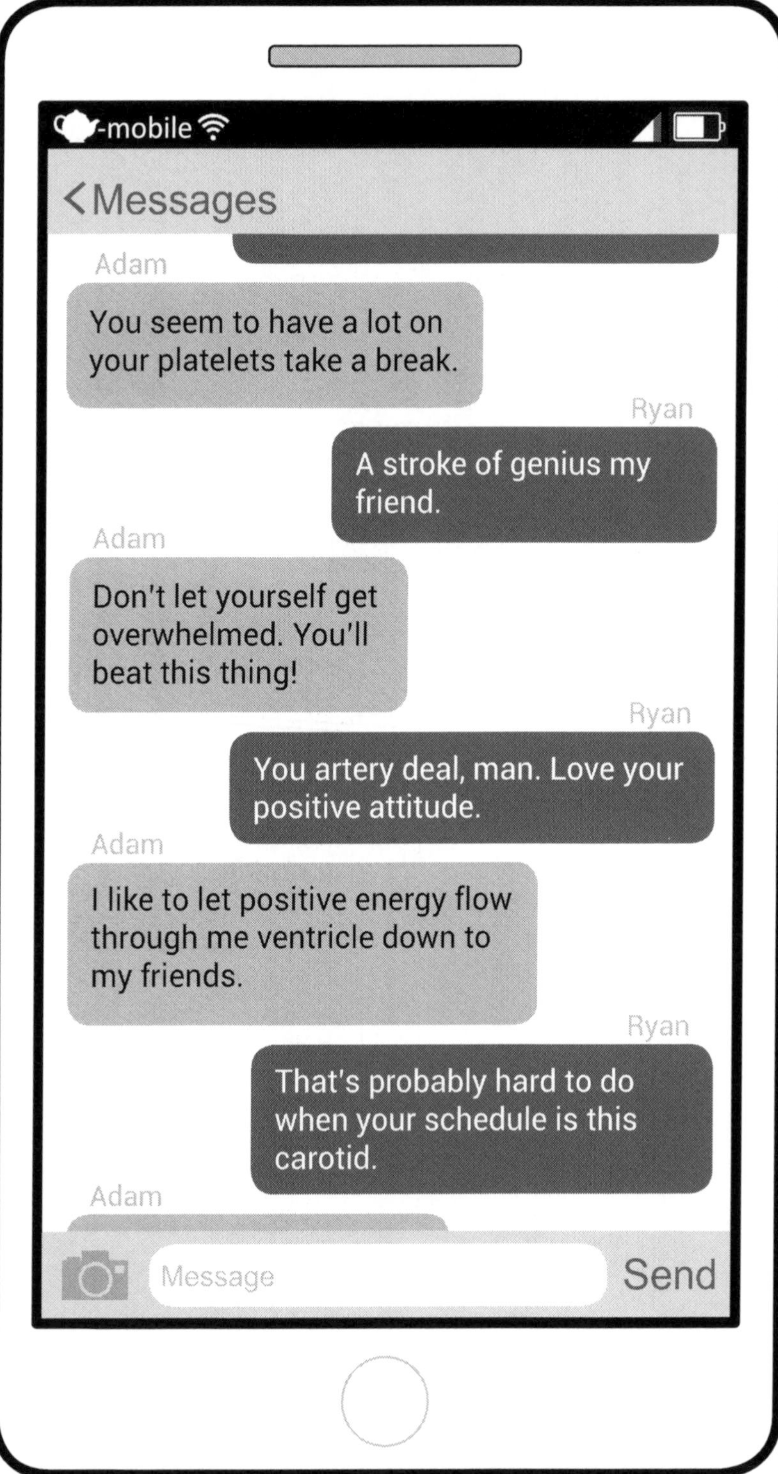
-mobile
Messages
Adam
You seem to have a lot on your platelets take a break.
Ryan
A stroke of genius my friend.
Adam
Don't let yourself get overwhelmed. You'll beat this thing!
Ryan
You artery deal, man. Love your positive attitude.
Adam
I like to let positive energy flow through me ventricle down to my friends.
Ryan
That's probably hard to do when your schedule is this carotid.
Adam
Message
Send

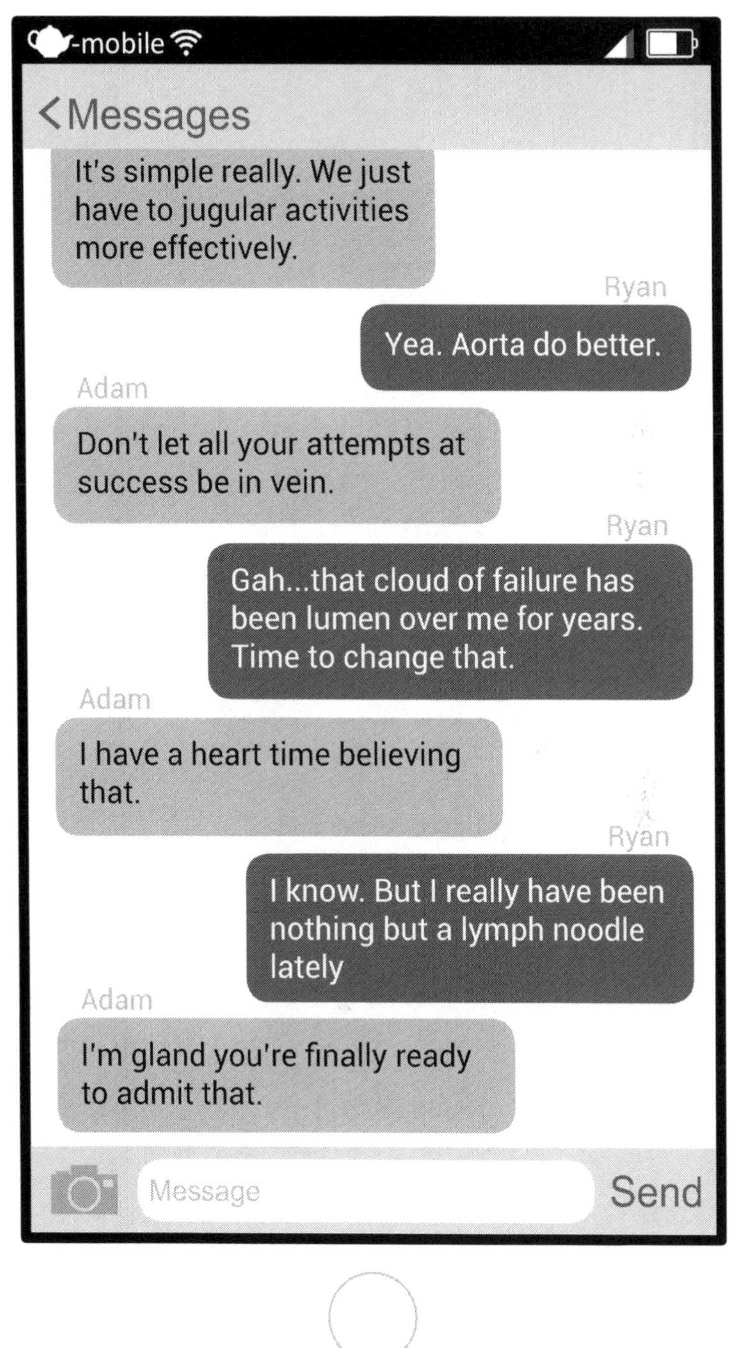
-mobile
Messages
It's simple really. We just have to jugular activities more effectively.
Ryan
Yea. Aorta do better.
Adam
Don't let all your attempts at success be in vein.
Ryan
Gah...that cloud of failure has been lumen over me for years. Time to change that.
Adam
I have a heart time believing that.
Ryan
I know. But I really have been nothing but a lymph noodle lately
Adam
I'm gland you're finally ready to admit that.
Message
Send

-mobile
Messages
Ryan
I'm not going to whine hormone about it.
Adam
Yeah, endocrine now either.
Ryan
I thought we agreed to keep that secrete.
Adam
Oops! Did I leak some private info?
Ryan
Hopefully not. Adrenal lot about the day I am finally successful and can put this all behind me.
Adam
That's ovary nice attitude to have.
Ryan
It's just not pheromone about it all the time.
Adam
Message
Send

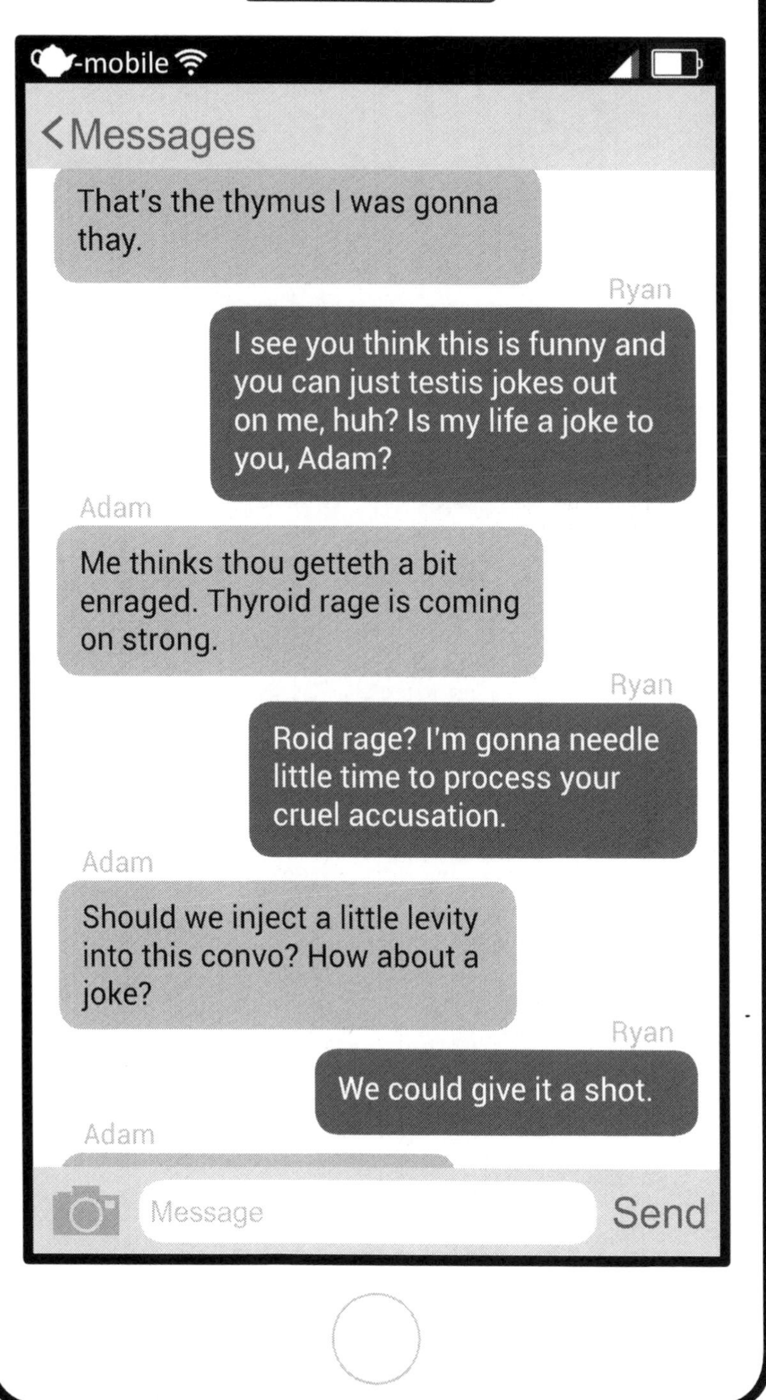
-mobile
Messages
That's the thymus I was gonna thay.
Ryan
I see you think this is funny and you can just testis jokes out on me, huh? Is my life a joke to you, Adam?
Adam
Me thinks thou getteth a bit enraged. Thyroid rage is coming on strong.
Ryan
Roid rage? I'm gonna needle little time to process your cruel accusation.
Adam
Should we inject a little levity into this convo? How about a joke?
Ryan
We could give it a shot.
Adam
Message
Send

-mobile
Messages
Do you have some jokes? Let's serum!
Ryan
Let me think. I don't want to stick ya with a bad one.
Adam
Yeah, keep dose jokes to yourself.
Ryan
You're the one that's good at jokes. Vaccinate talent right there. You can't teach that.
Adam
IV like that is true. Maybe I should teach a course.
Ryan
Like cure the best. I'd sign up.
Adam
Cool, I'll take a stab at it.
Ryan
Cool. Btw, I gauze so many ideas for our book.
Message
Send

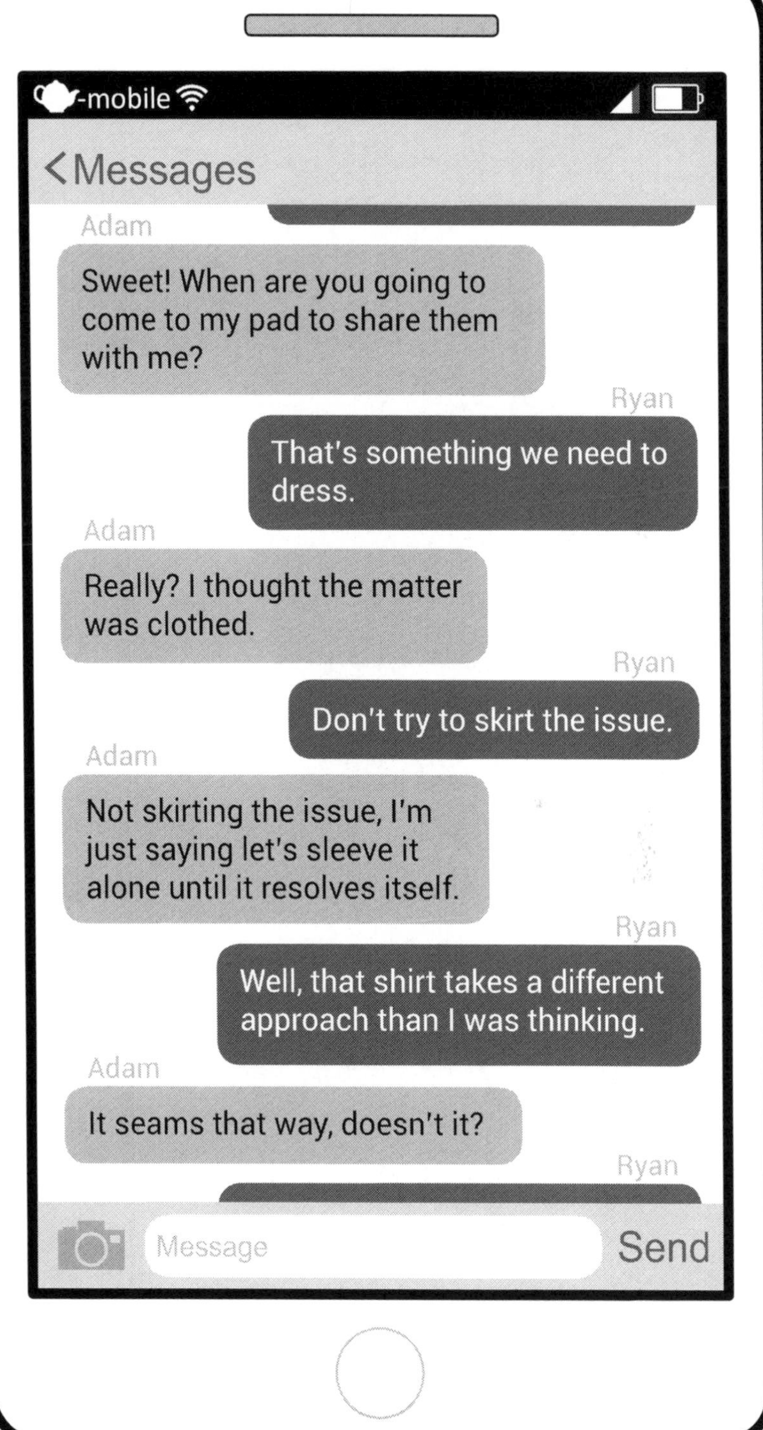
-mobile
Messages
Adam
Sweet! When are you going to come to my pad to share them with me?
Ryan
That's something we need to dress.
Adam
Really? I thought the matter was clothed.
Ryan
Don't try to skirt the issue.
Adam
Not skirting the issue, I'm just saying let's sleeve it alone until it resolves itself.
Ryan
Well, that shirt takes a different approach than I was thinking.
Adam
It seams that way, doesn't it?
Ryan
Message
Send

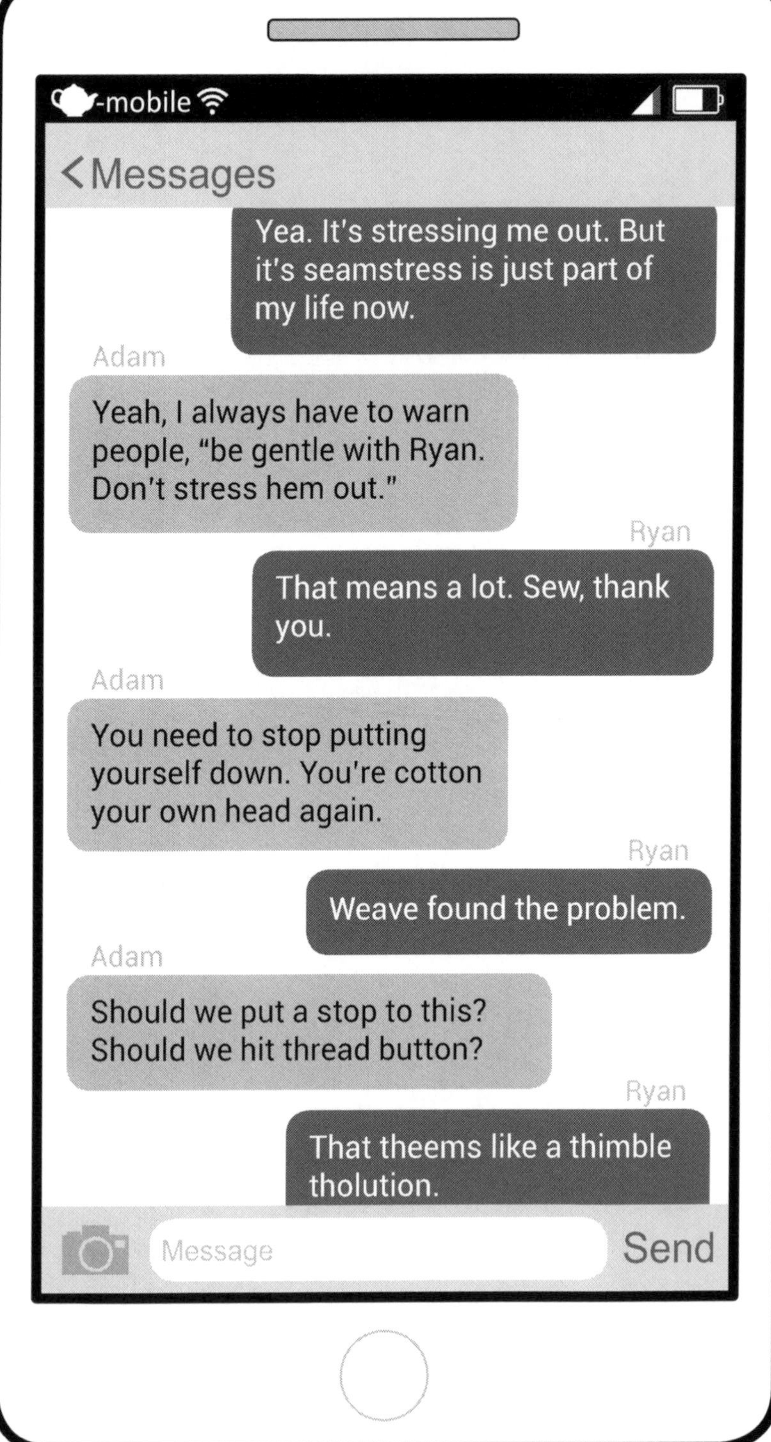
-mobile
Messages
Yea. It's stressing me out. But it's seamstress is just part of my life now.
Adam
Yeah, I always have to warn people, "be gentle with Ryan. Don't stress hem out."
Ryan
That means a lot. Sew, thank you.
Adam
You need to stop putting yourself down. You're cotton your own head again.
Ryan
Weave found the problem.
Adam
Should we put a stop to this? Should we hit thread button?
Ryan
That theems like a thimble tholution.
Message
Send

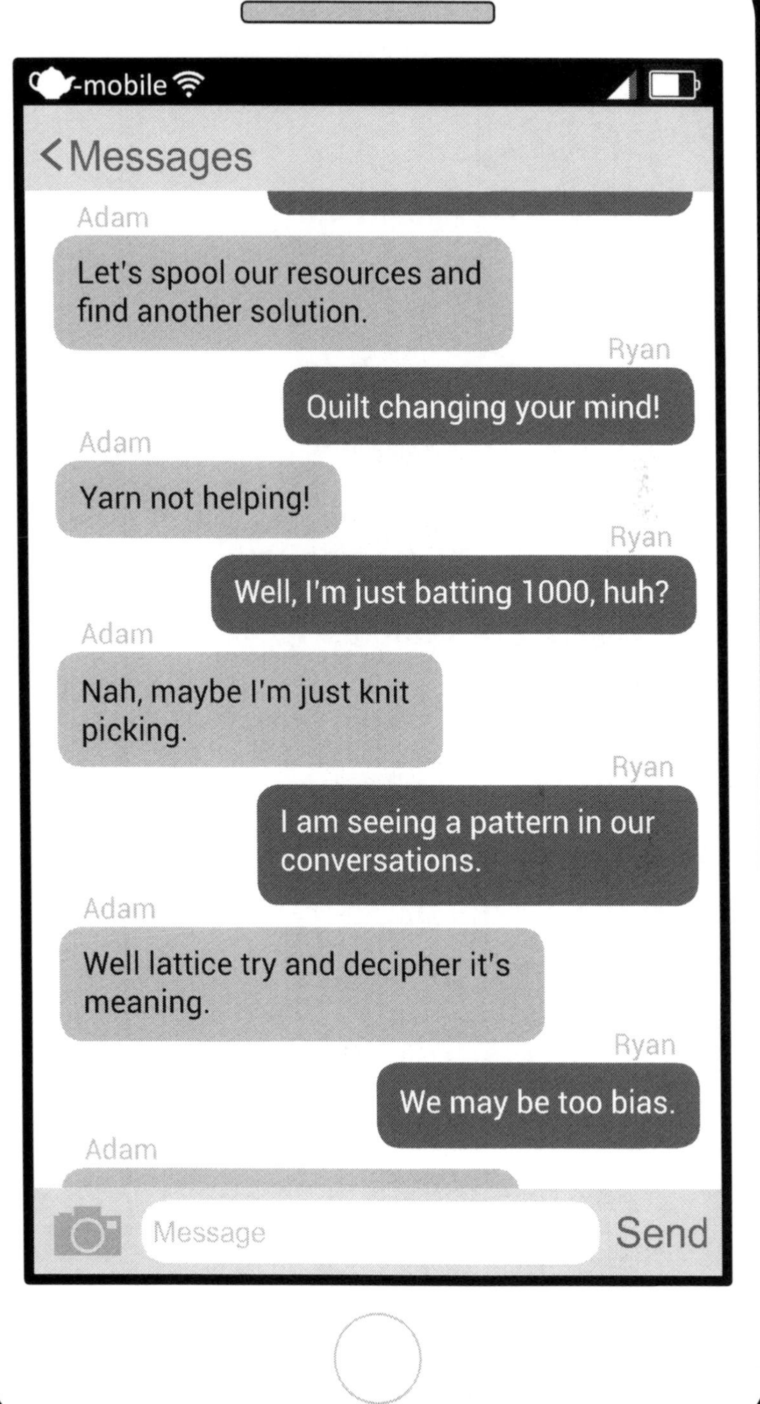
-mobile
<Messages
Adam
Let's spool our resources and find another solution.
Ryan
Quilt changing your mind!
Adam
Yarn not helping!
Ryan
Well, I'm just batting 1000, huh?
Adam
Nah, maybe I'm just knit picking.
Ryan
I am seeing a pattern in our conversations.
Adam
Well lattice try and decipher it's meaning.
Ryan
We may be too bias.
Adam
Message
Send

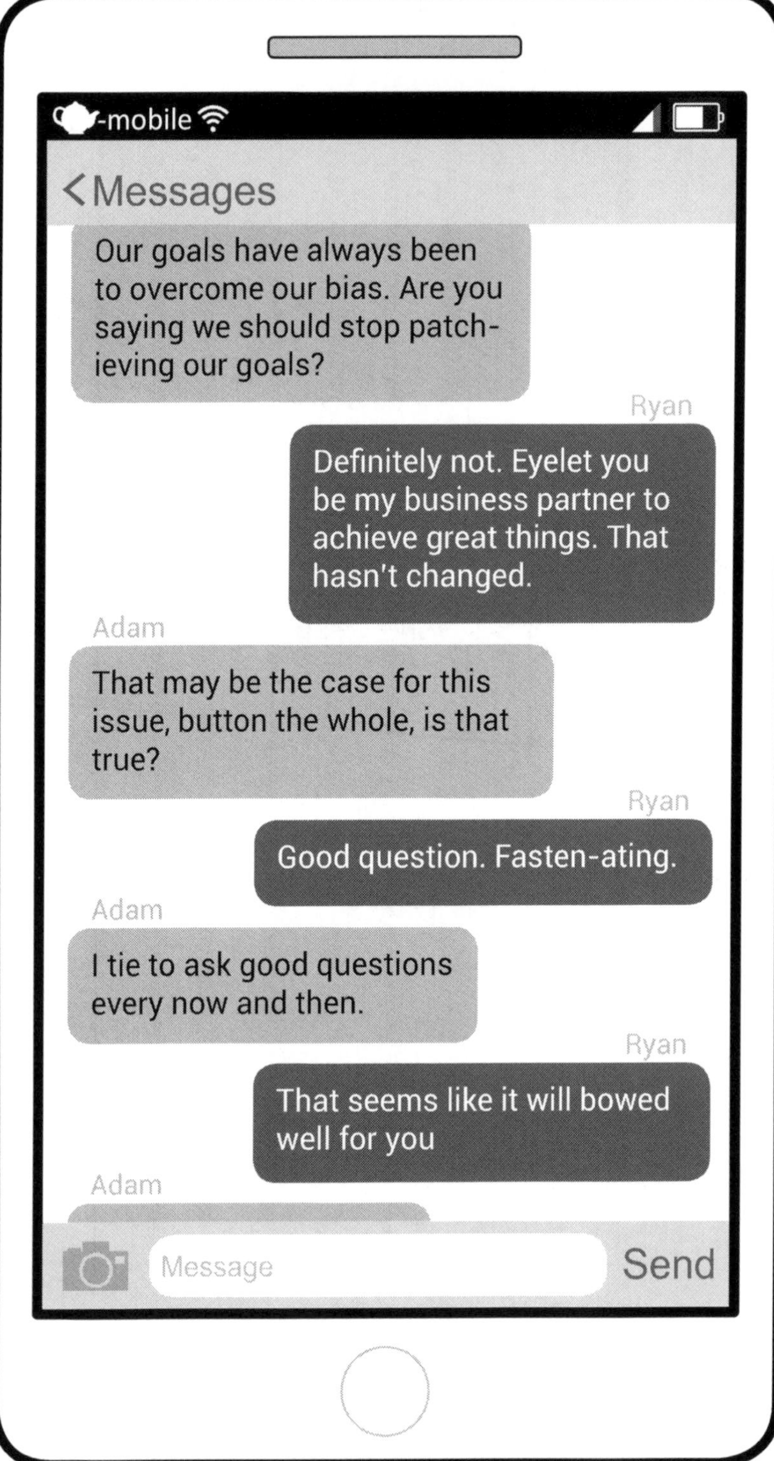
-mobile
Messages
Our goals have always been to overcome our bias. Are you saying we should stop patch-ieving our goals?
Ryan
Definitely not. Eyelet you be my business partner to achieve great things. That hasn't changed.
Adam
That may be the case for this issue, button the whole, is that true?
Ryan
Good question. Fasten-ating.
Adam
I tie to ask good questions every now and then.
Ryan
That seems like it will bowed well for you
Adam
Message
Send

-mobile
Messages
Aglet That all the time.
Ryan
Oh snap!
Adam
Okay, back to the price we should set for the book. Let's start low and move our way up. Maybe a buckle do.
Ryan
OMG. Back to this? I thought you had more clasp than this. A buck?
Adam
Isn't a dollar better than zipper what?
Ryan
I suppose. But we'll get more with the audience we've belt.
Adam
I just don't think people will waist money on our book.
Ryan
Message
Send

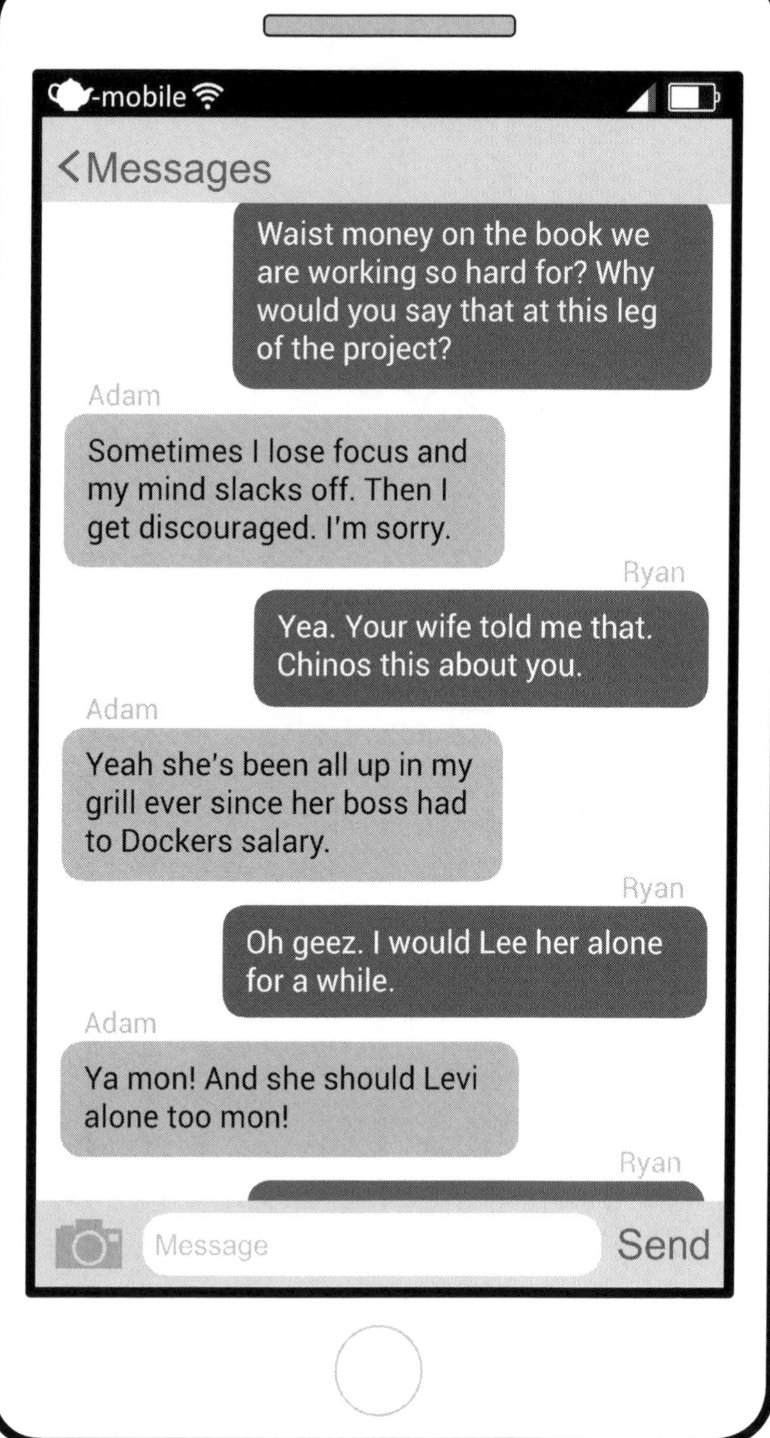
-mobile
<Messages
Waist money on the book we are working so hard for? Why would you say that at this leg of the project?
Adam
Sometimes I lose focus and my mind slacks off. Then I get discouraged. I'm sorry.
Ryan
Yea. Your wife told me that. Chinos this about you.
Adam
Yeah she's been all up in my grill ever since her boss had to Dockers salary.
Ryan
Oh geez. I would Lee her alone for a while.
Adam
Ya mon! And she should Levi alone too mon!
Ryan
Message
Send

-mobile
Messages
Yea. Otherwise you'll see in Klein's in your argument rate.
Adam
I Guess. Arguing is in my jeans.
Ryan
Diesel be things you'll have to work out with her.
Adam
I find it doesn't end well if Hugo Boss your wife around.
Ryan
Especially if she is a bit Pepe like yours.
Adam
Well, we'll go see a couples counselor. Hilfiger it out for me.
Ryan
Yea. He'll be able to Wrangler for sure.
Adam
Message
Send

-mobile
Messages
I hope he decides to take my side Ann Taylor his argument to mine.
Ryan
Yea. I don't know. I have a soft spot for your wife though. Like Carhartt is good and stuff, you know?
Adam
Don't get me wrong, we are great together. The problems we have are minor and Under Armour loving qualities.
Ryan
Yea, Adidas with my wife too and it all worked out.
Adam
Sounds like you were able to find a Puma-nent solution.
Ryan
Yes. But tell my wife I told you we were in therapy and Nike you. Got it?
Message
Send

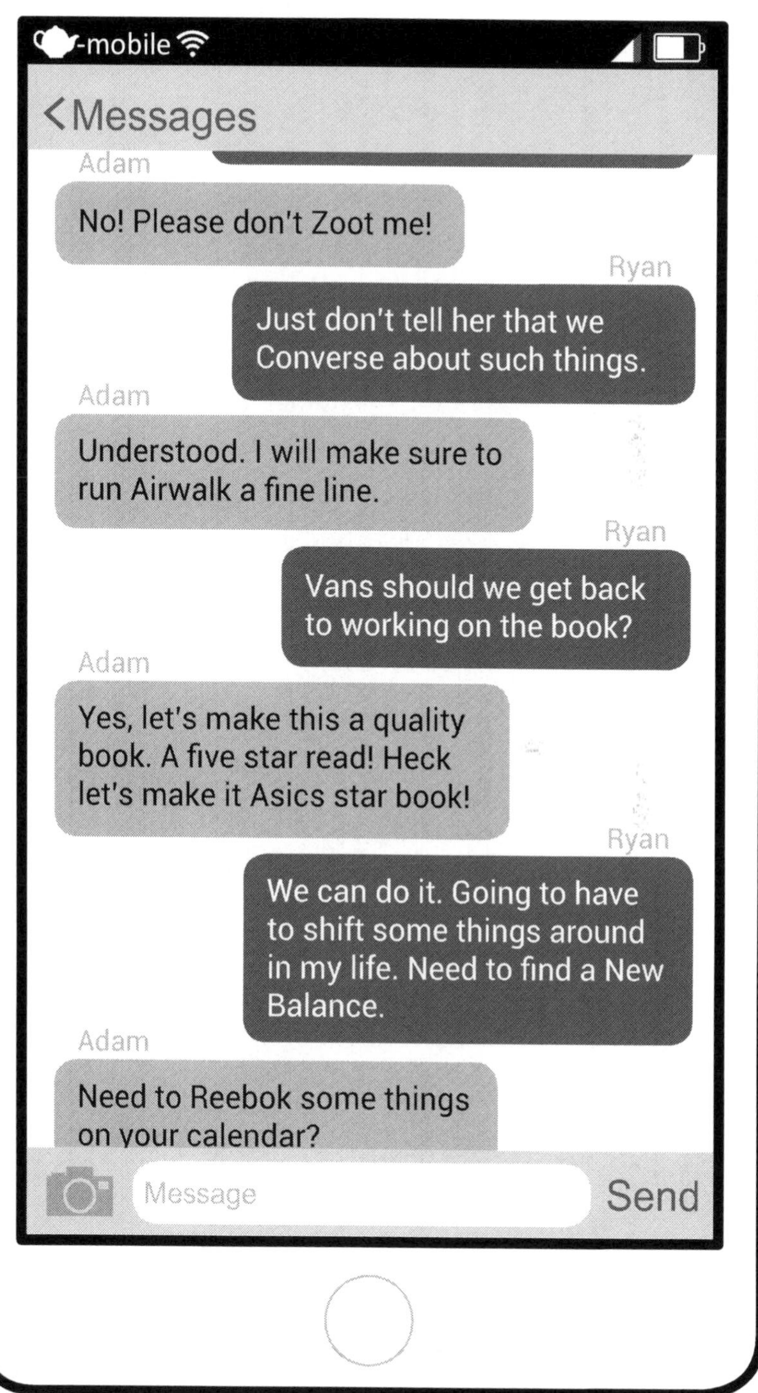
-mobile
Messages
Adam
No! Please don't Zoot me!
Ryan
Just don't tell her that we Converse about such things.
Adam
Understood. I will make sure to run Airwalk a fine line.
Ryan
Vans should we get back to working on the book?
Adam
Yes, let's make this a quality book. A five star read! Heck let's make it Asics star book!
Ryan
We can do it. Going to have to shift some things around in my life. Need to find a New Balance.
Adam
Need to Reebok some things on your calendar?
Message
Send

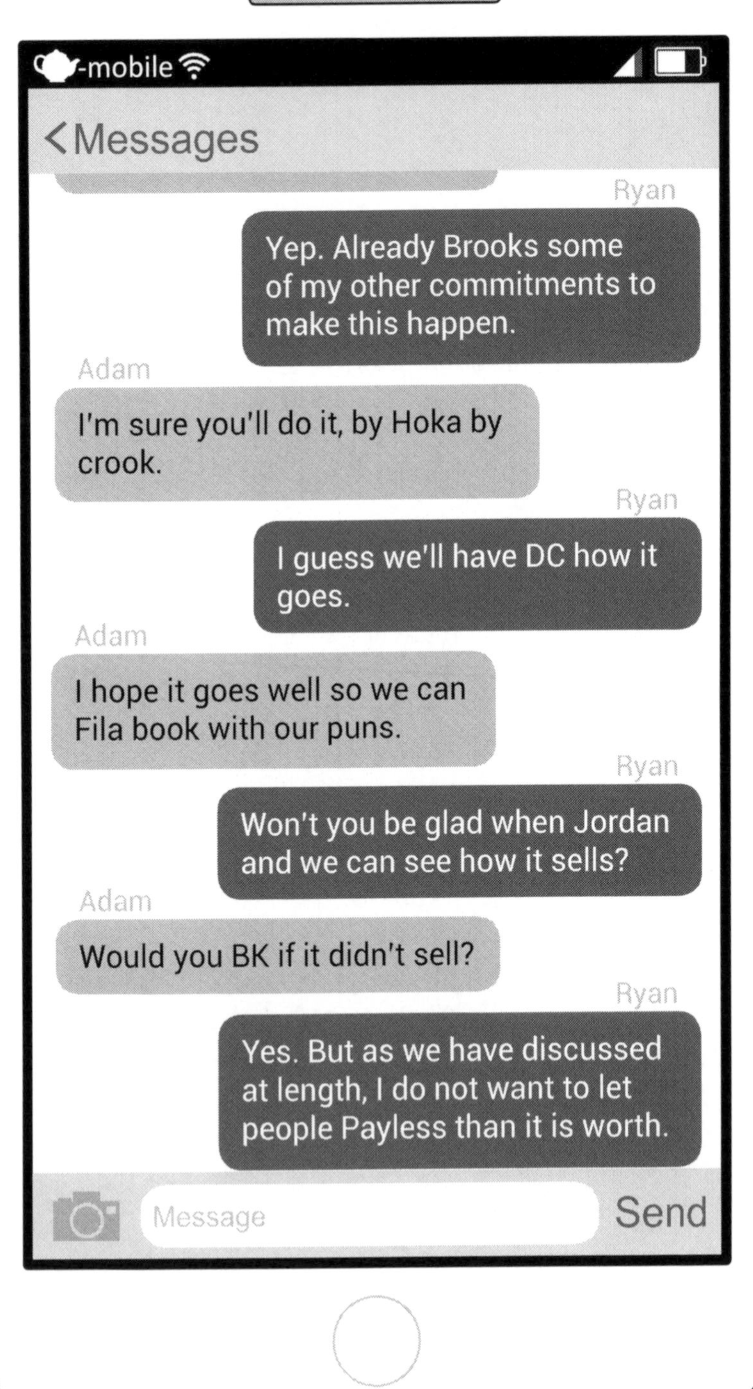
-mobile
Messages
Ryan
Yep. Already Brooks some of my other commitments to make this happen.
Adam
I'm sure you'll do it, by Hoka by crook.
Ryan
I guess we'll have DC how it goes.
Adam
I hope it goes well so we can Fila book with our puns.
Ryan
Won't you be glad when Jordan and we can see how it sells?
Adam
Would you BK if it didn't sell?
Ryan
Yes. But as we have discussed at length, I do not want to let people Payless than it is worth.
Message
Send

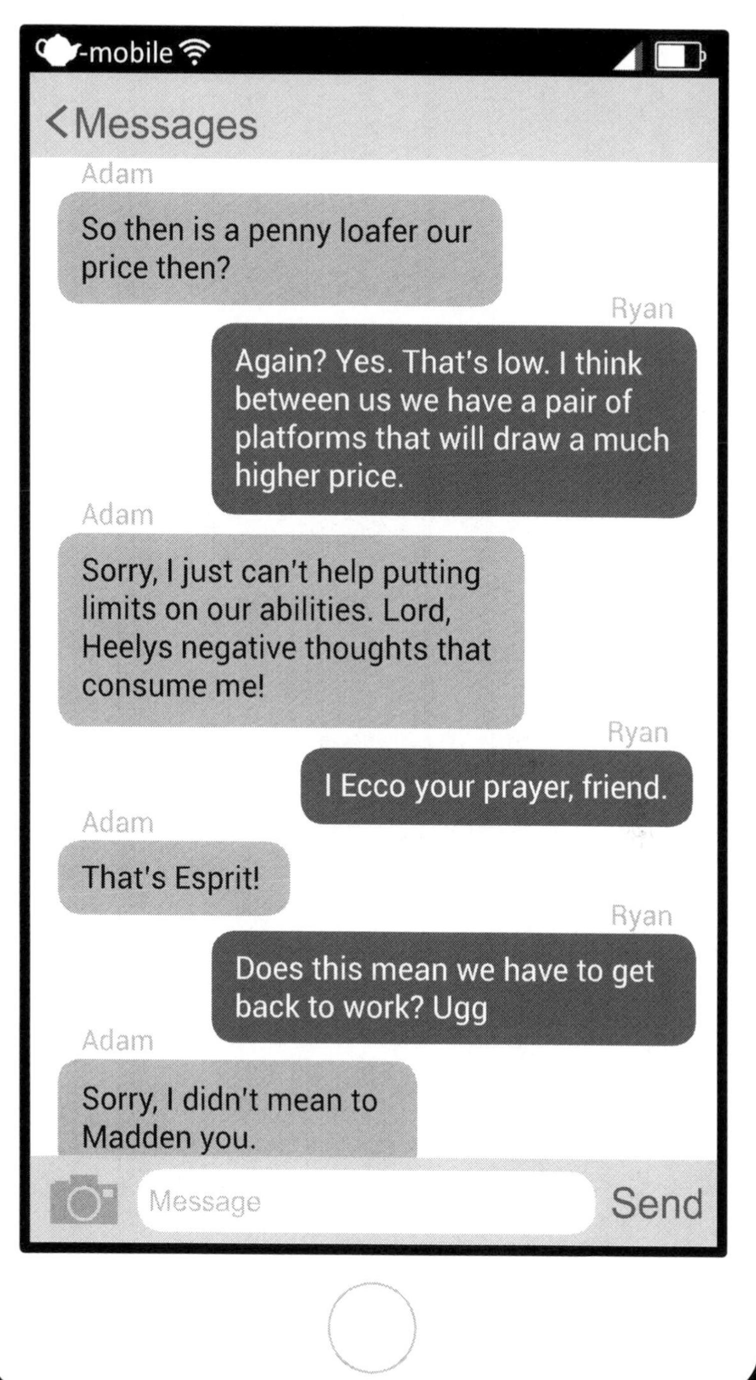
-mobile
Messages
Adam
So then is a penny loafer our price then?
Ryan
Again? Yes. That's low. I think between us we have a pair of platforms that will draw a much higher price.
Adam
Sorry, I just can't help putting limits on our abilities. Lord, Heelys negative thoughts that consume me!
Ryan
I Ecco your prayer, friend.
Adam
That's Esprit!
Ryan
Does this mean we have to get back to work? Ugg
Adam
Sorry, I didn't mean to Madden you.
Message
Send

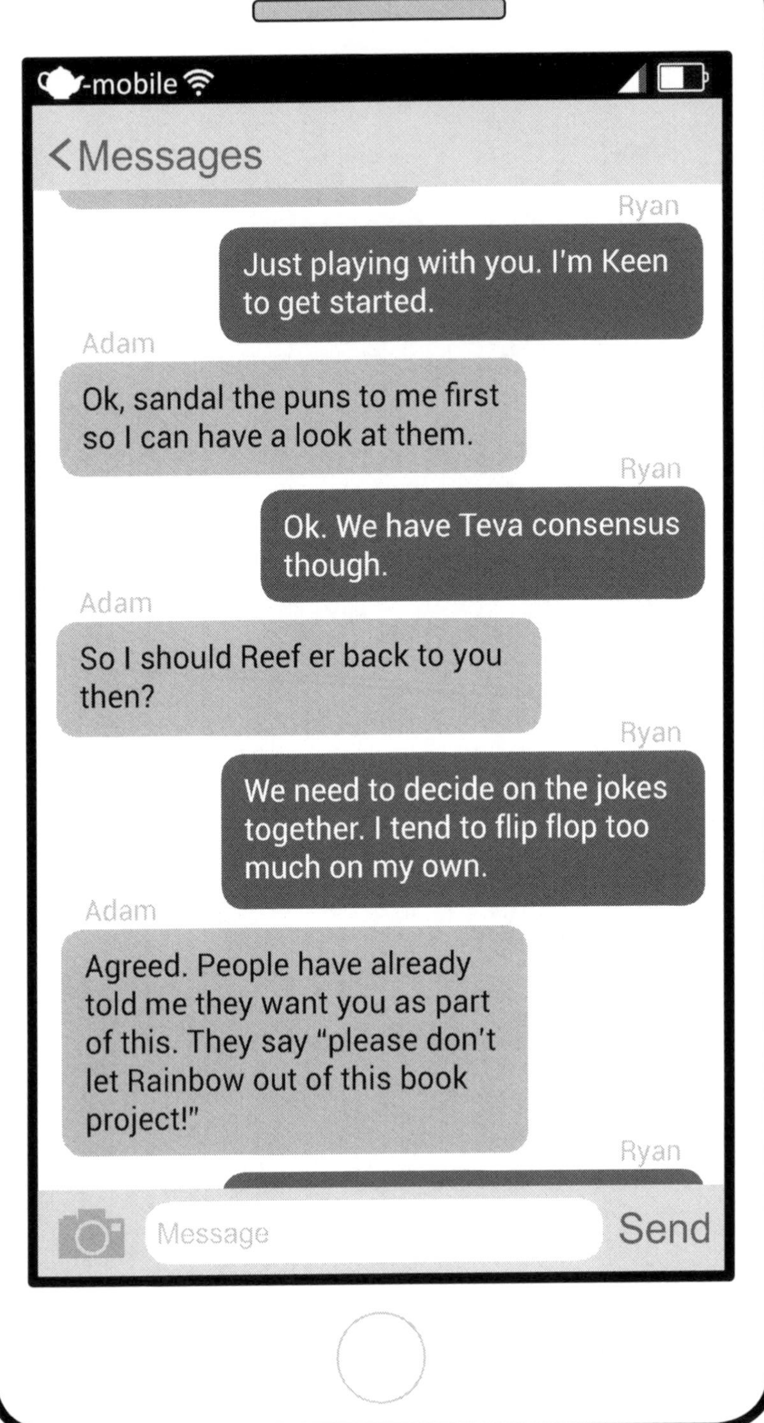
-mobile
Messages
Ryan
Just playing with you. I'm Keen to get started.
Adam
Ok, sandal the puns to me first so I can have a look at them.
Ryan
Ok. We have Teva consensus though.
Adam
So I should Reef er back to you then?
Ryan
We need to decide on the jokes together. I tend to flip flop too much on my own.
Adam
Agreed. People have already told me they want you as part of this. They say "please don't let Rainbow out of this book project!"
Ryan
Message
Send

-mobile
Messages
That's Sanuk kind of experience for me. Usually they want me out.
Adam
Now that we're both committed to this, let's not let ourselves get distracted... OluKai donut shop!
Ryan
Seriously? Can't focus for one second. And is there anything cruller than mentioning donuts when you know I'm watching my figure?
Adam
Call me old fashioned, but I just like indulging every now and then.
Ryan
Is that how you were raised?
Adam
I seemed to fritter away my childhood thinking of such things.
Message
Send

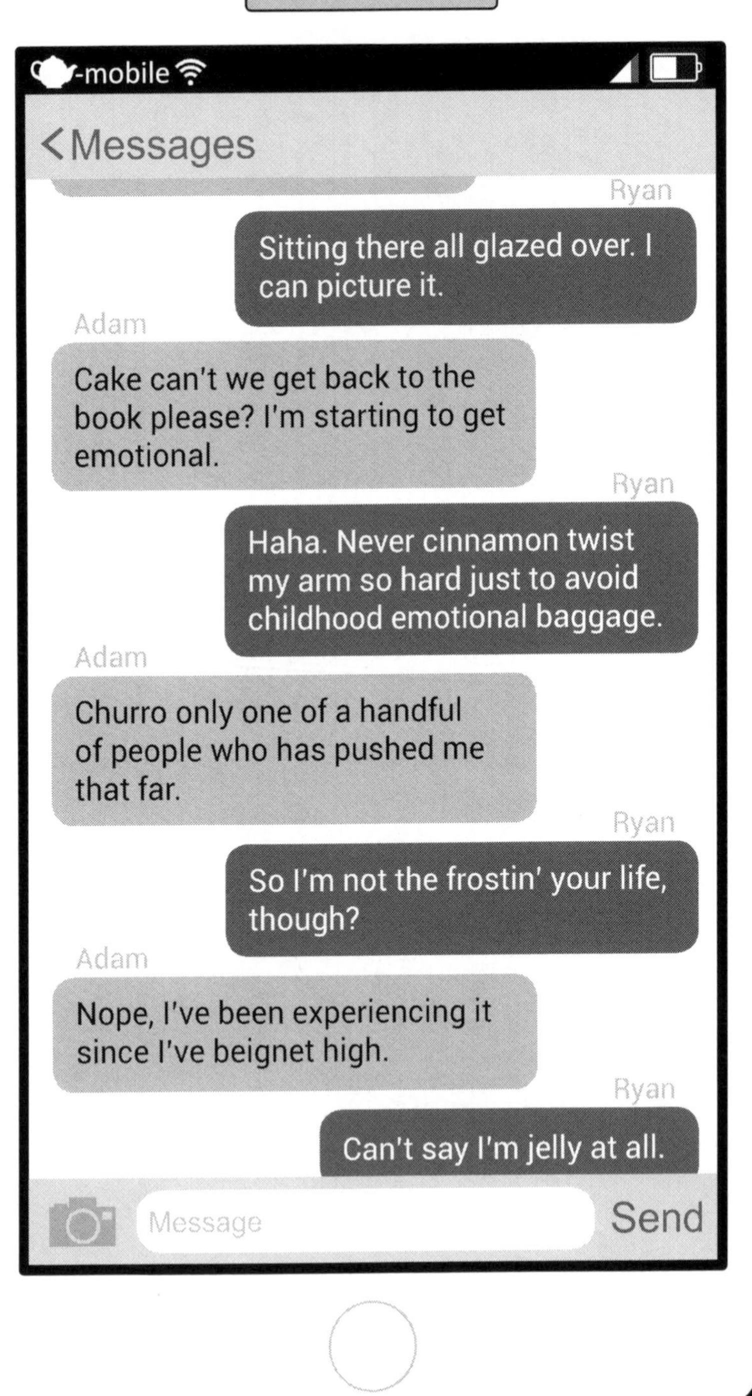
-mobile
Messages
Ryan
Sitting there all glazed over. I can picture it.
Adam
Cake can't we get back to the book please? I'm starting to get emotional.
Ryan
Haha. Never cinnamon twist my arm so hard just to avoid childhood emotional baggage.
Adam
Churro only one of a handful of people who has pushed me that far.
Ryan
So I'm not the frostin' your life, though?
Adam
Nope, I've been experiencing it since I've beignet high.
Ryan
Can't say I'm jelly at all.
Message
Send

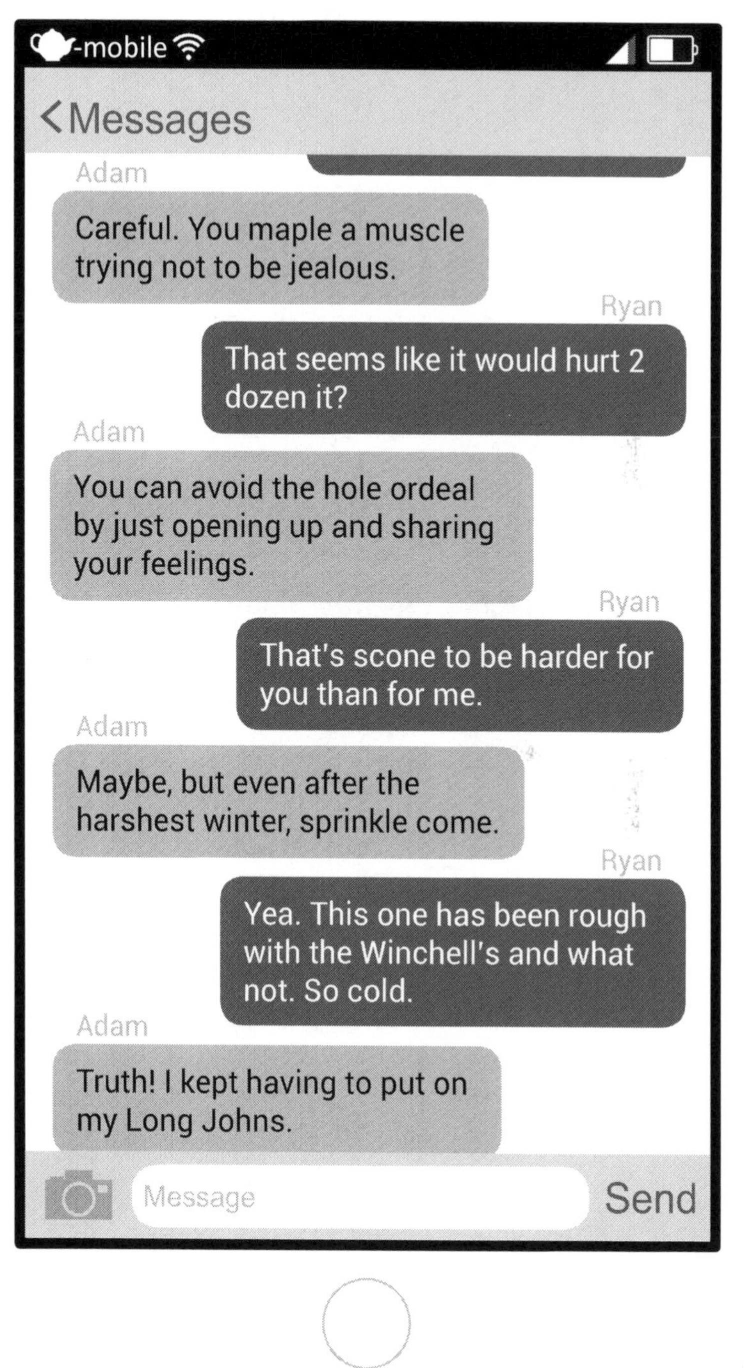
-mobile
Messages
Adam
Careful. You maple a muscle trying not to be jealous.
Ryan
That seems like it would hurt 2 dozen it?
Adam
You can avoid the hole ordeal by just opening up and sharing your feelings.
Ryan
That's scone to be harder for you than for me.
Adam
Maybe, but even after the harshest winter, sprinkle come.
Ryan
Yea. This one has been rough with the Winchell's and what not. So cold.
Adam
Truth! I kept having to put on my Long Johns.
Message
Send

-mobile
Messages
Ryan
Glad that's Dunkin' we get back to the warmer weather, please?
Adam
Careful what you wish for. If it warms up we may not finish this book. Time to raise the bar.
Ryan
We will have to powder through.
Adam
All dough, we could just get out for a little sunshine.
Ryan
I imagine we'll both knead that.
Adam
So it's agreed? We'll take a break, get out and smell the flours?
Ryan
Yes. At yeast for a few minutes.
Adam
Have you checked the weather? It pastry the forecast first.
Message
Send

-mobile
Messages
Ryan
I'll have to tart doing that.
Adam
Sweet. Let me know what you find out.
Ryan
I'll try to remember. I cannoli do so much.
Adam
I'm not asking a lot, only if it will be cloudy or eclair.
Ryan
Danish a non issue.
Adam
So we have muffin to worry about?
Ryan
All good. Now let's macaron at a best seller.
Adam
Aww, can't we stay outside a few more minutes? Why do I have to bagel the time?
Message
Send

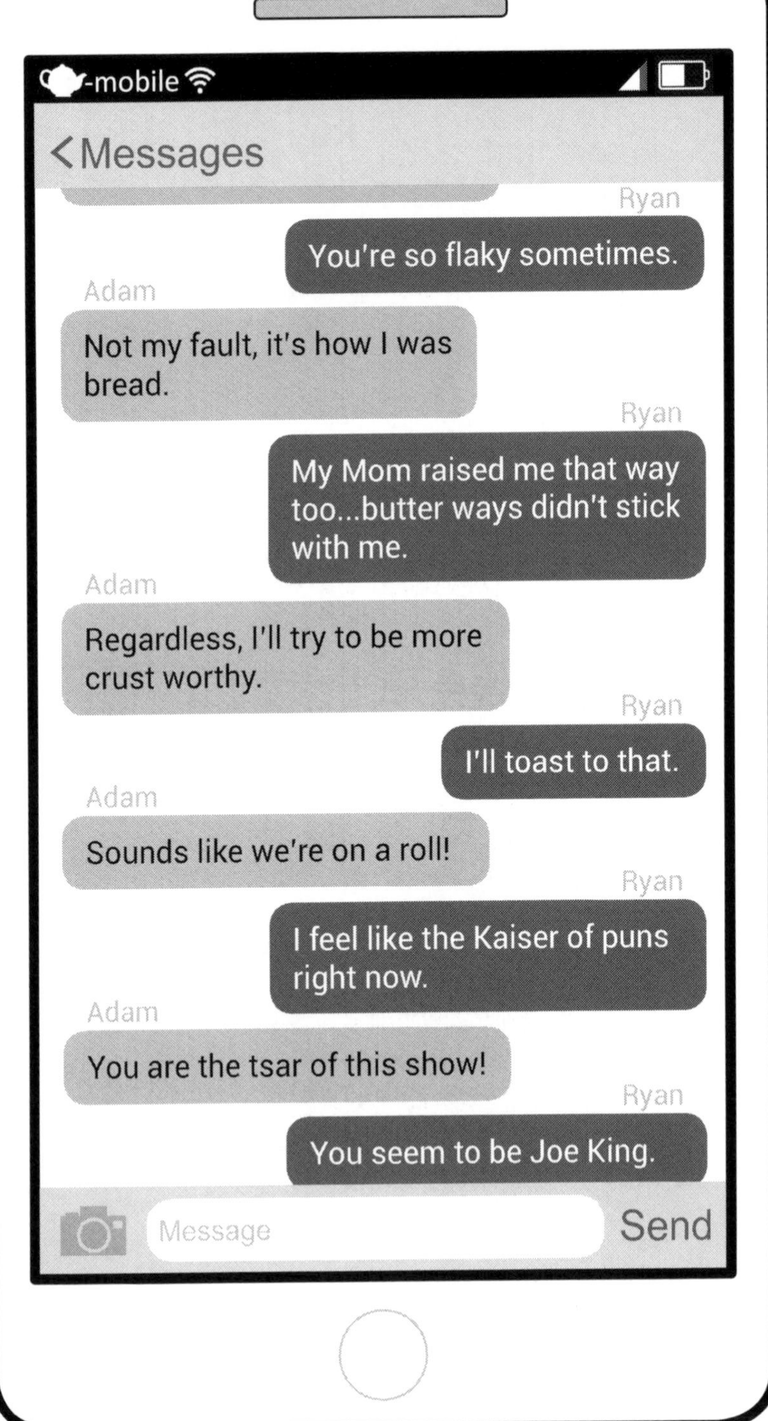
-mobile
Messages
Ryan
You're so flaky sometimes.
Adam
Not my fault, it's how I was bread.
Ryan
My Mom raised me that way too...butter ways didn't stick with me.
Adam
Regardless, I'll try to be more crust worthy.
Ryan
I'll toast to that.
Adam
Sounds like we're on a roll!
Ryan
I feel like the Kaiser of puns right now.
Adam
You are the tsar of this show!
Ryan
You seem to be Joe King.
Message
Send

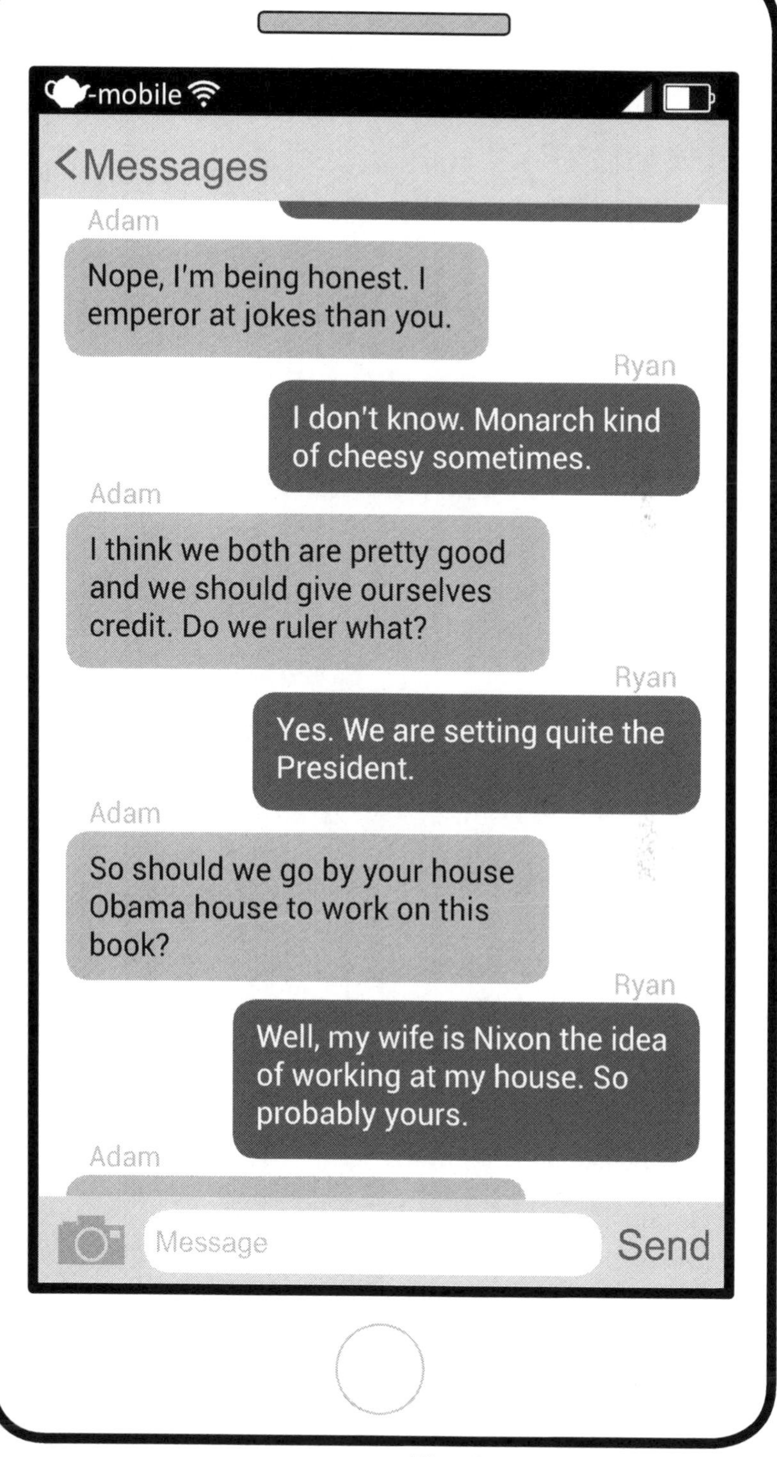
-mobile
Messages
Adam
Nope, I'm being honest. I emperor at jokes than you.
Ryan
I don't know. Monarch kind of cheesy sometimes.
Adam
I think we both are pretty good and we should give ourselves credit. Do we ruler what?
Ryan
Yes. We are setting quite the President.
Adam
So should we go by your house Obama house to work on this book?
Ryan
Well, my wife is Nixon the idea of working at my house. So probably yours.
Adam
Message
Send

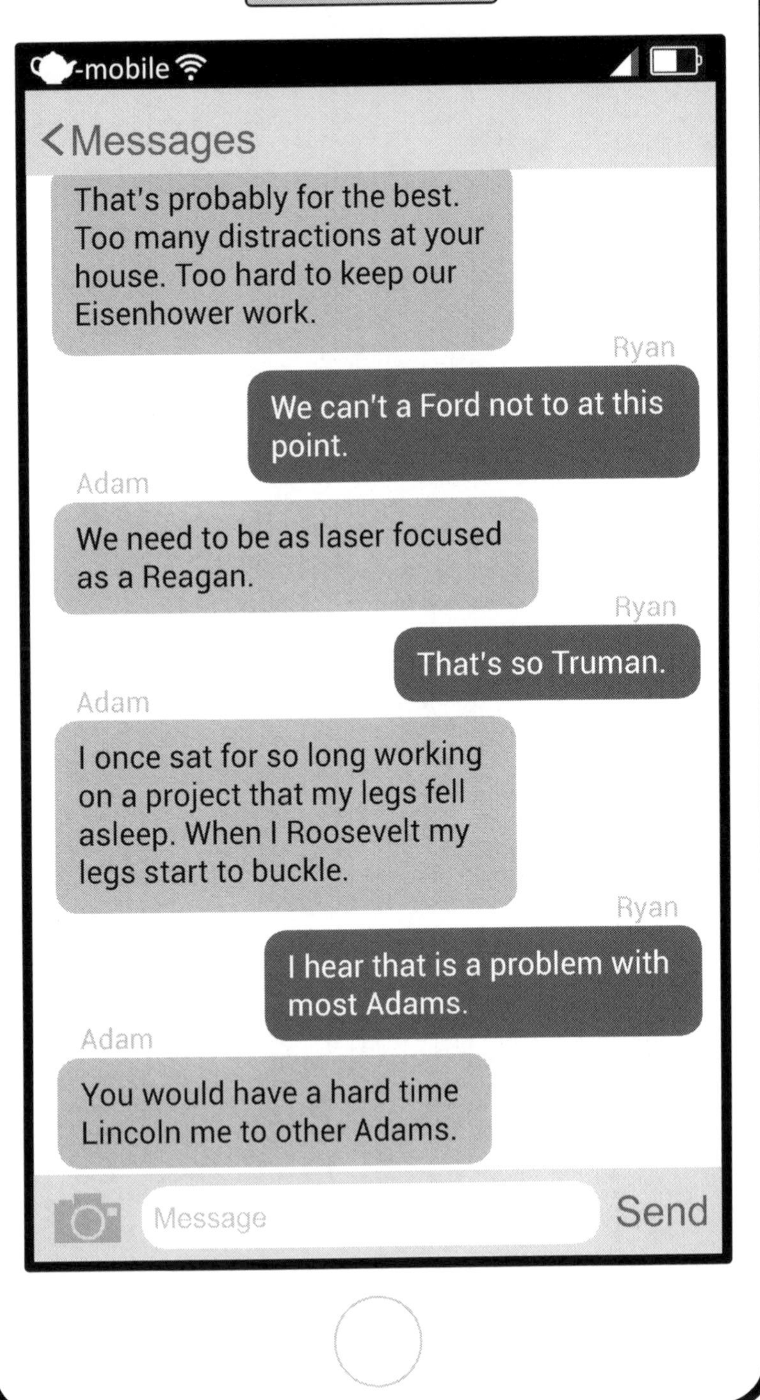
-mobile
Messages
That's probably for the best. Too many distractions at your house. Too hard to keep our Eisenhower work.
Ryan
We can't a Ford not to at this point.
Adam
We need to be as laser focused as a Reagan.
Ryan
That's so Truman.
Adam
I once sat for so long working on a project that my legs fell asleep. When I Roosevelt my legs start to buckle.
Ryan
I hear that is a problem with most Adams.
Adam
You would have a hard time Lincoln me to other Adams.
Message
Send

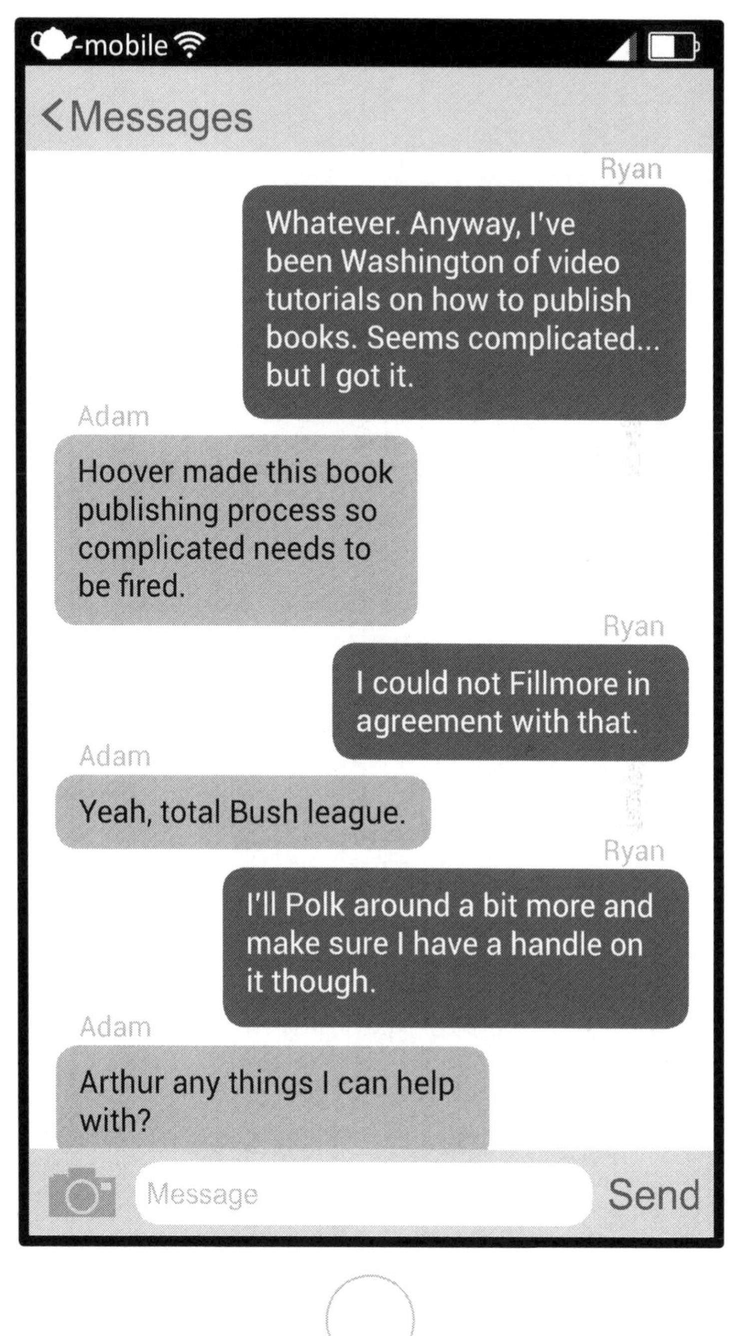
-mobile
Messages
Ryan
Whatever. Anyway, I've been Washington of video tutorials on how to publish books. Seems complicated... but I got it.
Adam
Hoover made this book publishing process so complicated needs to be fired.
Ryan
I could not Fillmore in agreement with that.
Adam
Yeah, total Bush league.
Ryan
I'll Polk around a bit more and make sure I have a handle on it though.
Adam
Arthur any things I can help with?
Message
Send

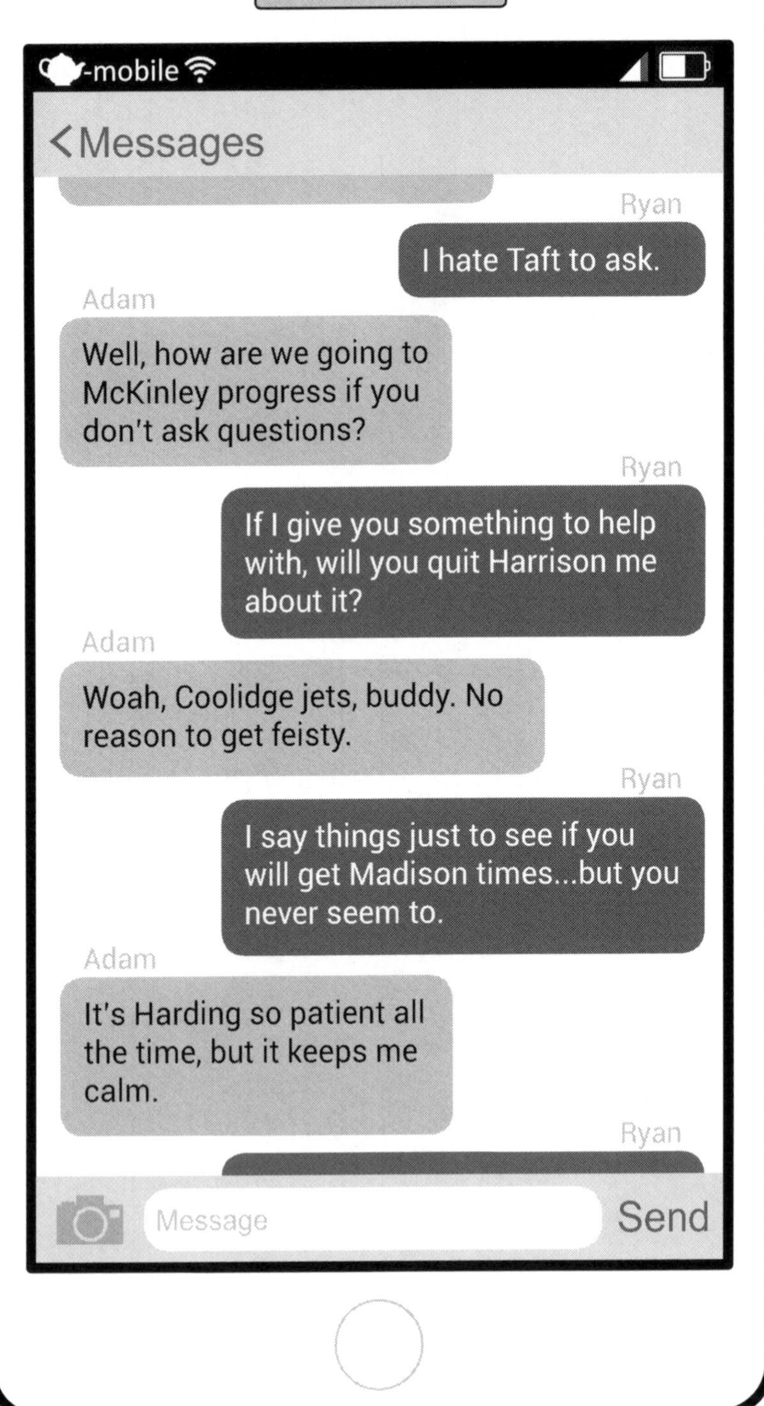
-mobile
Messages
Ryan
I hate Taft to ask.
Adam
Well, how are we going to McKinley progress if you don't ask questions?
Ryan
If I give you something to help with, will you quit Harrison me about it?
Adam
Woah, Coolidge jets, buddy. No reason to get feisty.
Ryan
I say things just to see if you will get Madison times...but you never seem to.
Adam
It's Harding so patient all the time, but it keeps me calm.
Ryan
Message
Send

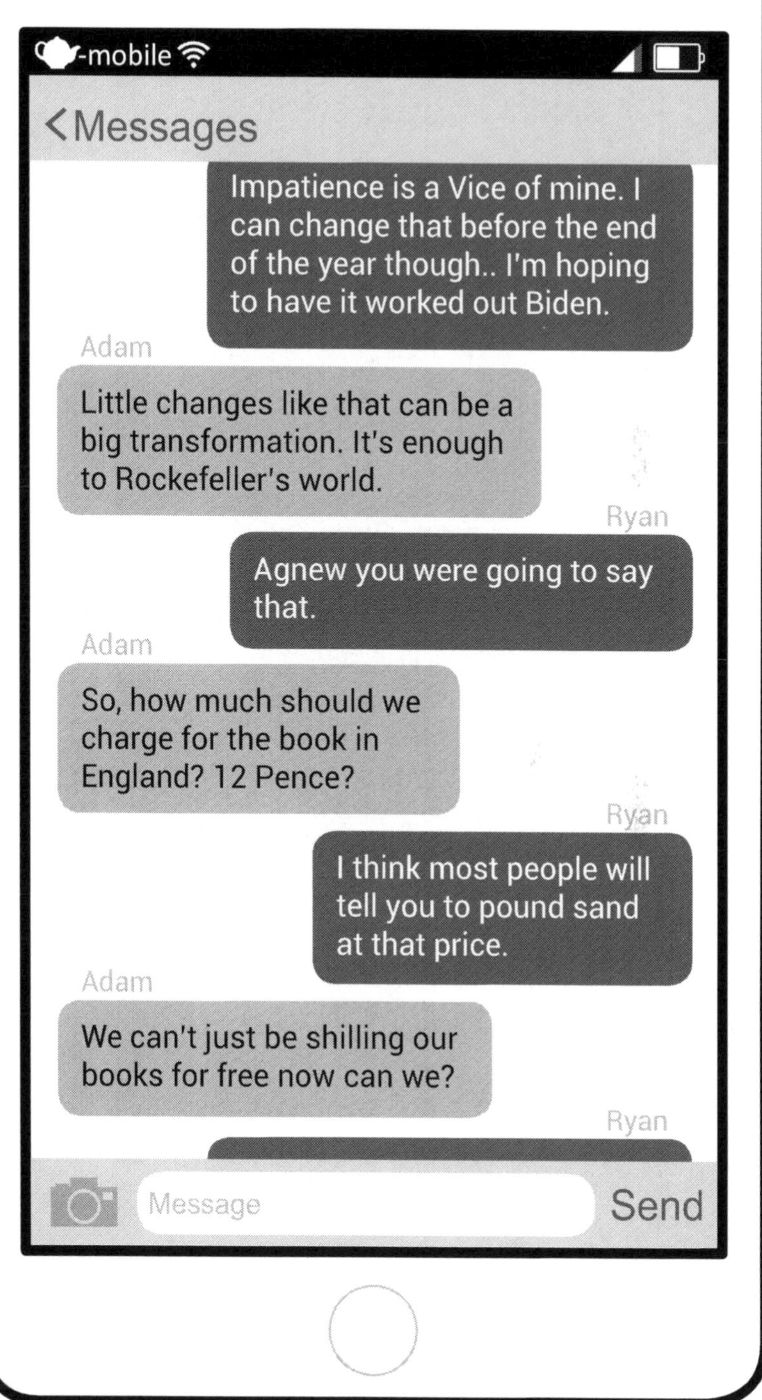
-mobile
Messages
Impatience is a Vice of mine. I can change that before the end of the year though.. I'm hoping to have it worked out Biden.
Adam
Little changes like that can be a big transformation. It's enough to Rockefeller's world.
Ryan
Agnew you were going to say that.
Adam
So, how much should we charge for the book in England? 12 Pence?
Ryan
I think most people will tell you to pound sand at that price.
Adam
We can't just be shilling our books for free now can we?
Ryan
Message
Send

-mobile
Messages
I feel like we are Rupee ting the same conversation over and over.
Adam
Well, determining what people will peso important. We can't take it lightly.
Ryan
So, we're going toonie to talk about it again, eh?
Adam
I think we need to have a Franc discussion, yes.
Ryan
I won't dinar that you're right on this one.
Adam
Yen know it!
Ryan
I love how Euro with the punches.
Adam
Message
Send

-mobile
< Messages
It's a riyal asset from time to time.
Ryan
You just rise above things as if you're a foot dollar than everyone else.
Adam
That's won way to look at it.
Ryan
Ok. So I need to change my mindset about this price thing. Coin you help?
Adam
I think we should be aggressive. It's the only way we could ever succeed in doubloon our profits.
Ryan
I'm dime to see what you come up with.
Adam
Well, if we're good boys, maybe Saint Nickel bring us more profits for Christmas.
Message
Send

-mobile
<Messages
Ryan
Makes cents.
Adam
We just have to prove he exists. We'll have to cash him first.
Ryan
It'll be tough to pennies location down.
Adam
You're not going to change my mind.
Ryan
I never mint to.
Adam
That's good, because it bills trust.
Ryan
I treasury friends like you that I can trust. Fake friends suck.
Adam
I'm glad you don't think I'm fake. I can't a Fort Knox on my reputation like that.
Message
Send

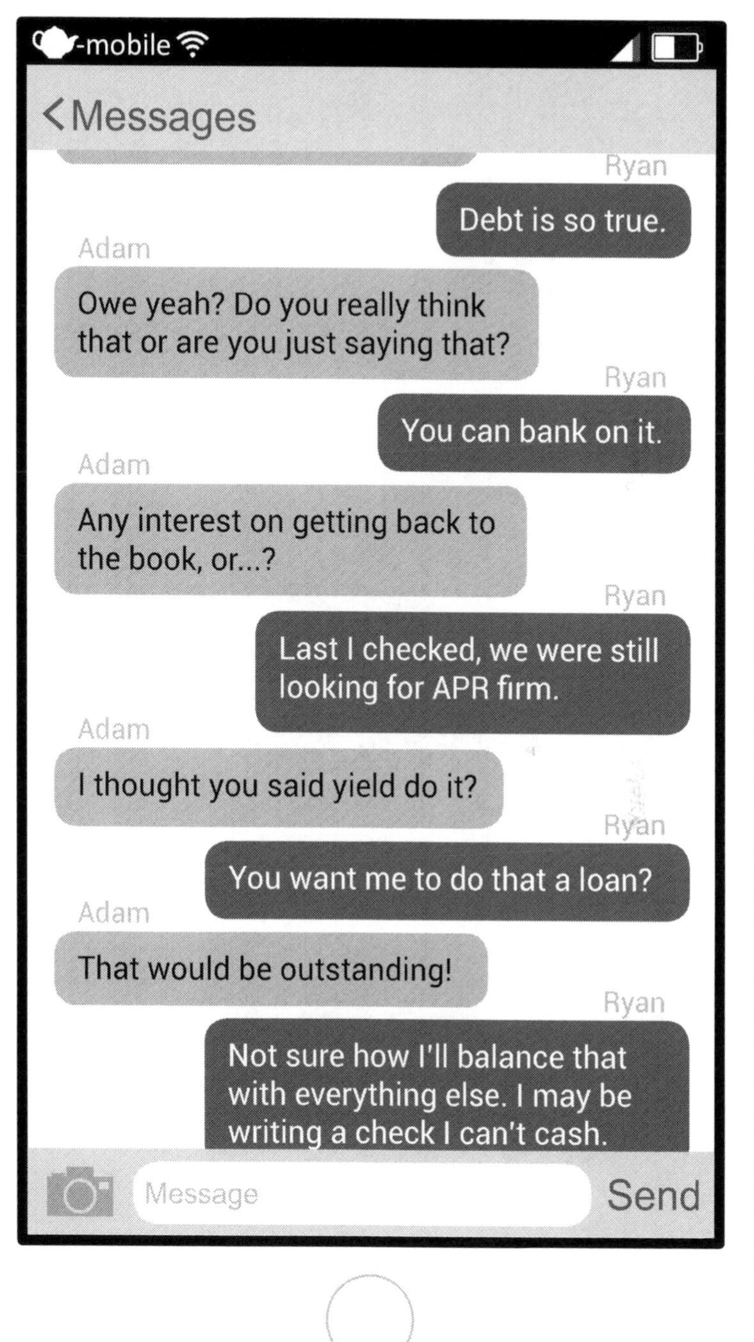
-mobile
Messages
Ryan
Debt is so true.
Adam
Owe yeah? Do you really think that or are you just saying that?
Ryan
You can bank on it.
Adam
Any interest on getting back to the book, or...?
Ryan
Last I checked, we were still looking for APR firm.
Adam
I thought you said yield do it?
Ryan
You want me to do that a loan?
Adam
That would be outstanding!
Ryan
Not sure how I'll balance that with everything else. I may be writing a check I can't cash.
Message
Send

-mobile
<Messages
Adam
Do you want me to take care of debit dat you can't handle?
Ryan
Yea, could you chip in?
Adam
I don't think I would make a difference. I think we need ATM of experts.
Ryan
I withdraw my comment.
Adam
I'm just saying, I'm so overdraft-ing emails to PR firms.
Ryan
I fee the same.
Adam
Don't try to take credit for my feelings.
Ryan
I would never swipe your idea.
Message
Send

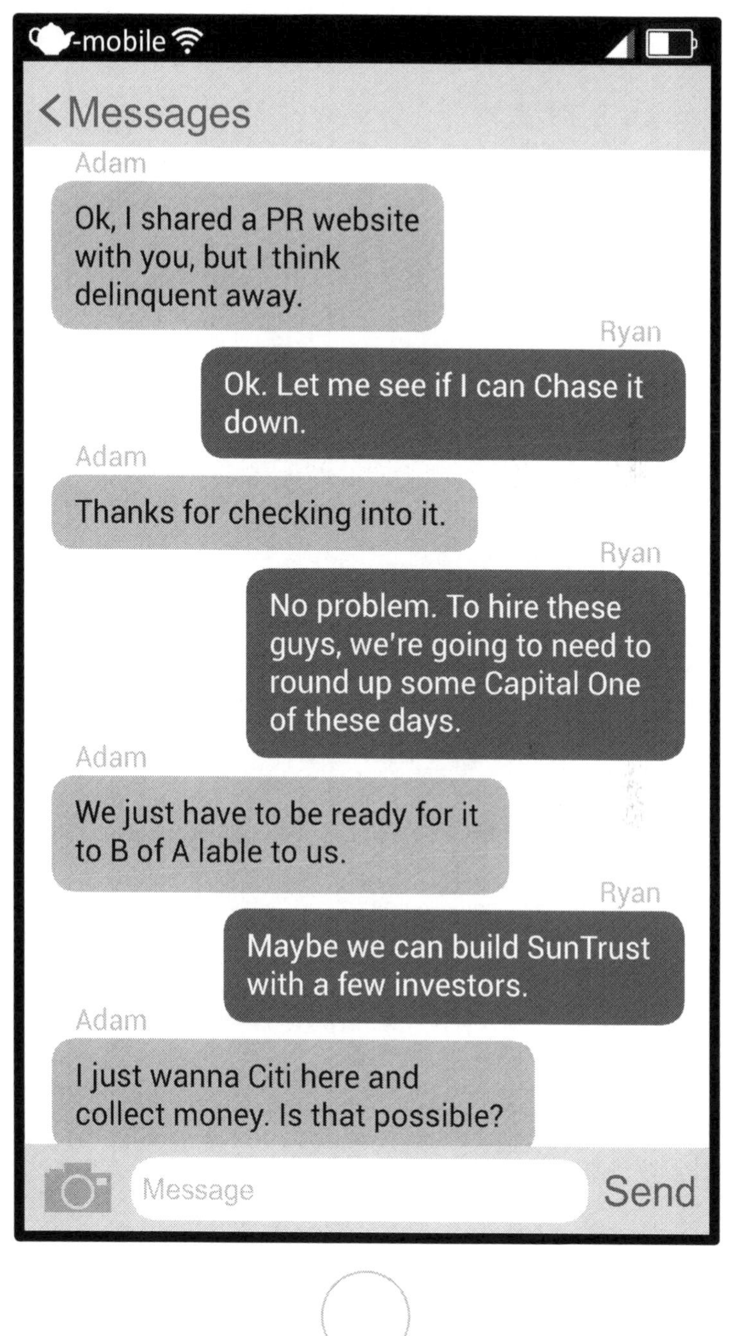
-mobile
Messages
Adam
Ok, I shared a PR website with you, but I think delinquent away.
Ryan
Ok. Let me see if I can Chase it down.
Adam
Thanks for checking into it.
Ryan
No problem. To hire these guys, we're going to need to round up some Capital One of these days.
Adam
We just have to be ready for it to B of A lable to us.
Ryan
Maybe we can build SunTrust with a few investors.
Adam
I just wanna Citi here and collect money. Is that possible?
Message
Send

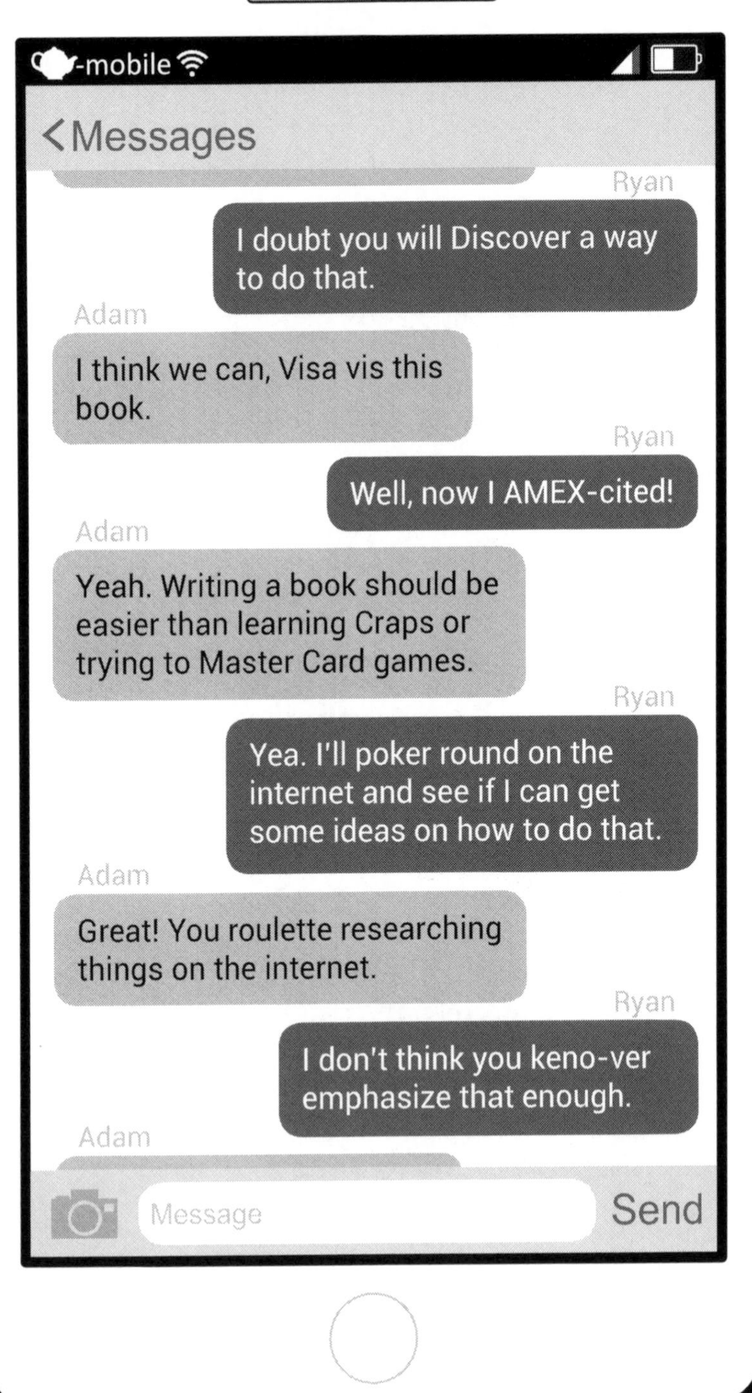
-mobile
Messages
Ryan
I doubt you will Discover a way to do that.
Adam
I think we can, Visa vis this book.
Ryan
Well, now I AMEX-cited!
Adam
Yeah. Writing a book should be easier than learning Craps or trying to Master Card games.
Ryan
Yea. I'll poker round on the internet and see if I can get some ideas on how to do that.
Adam
Great! You roulette researching things on the internet.
Ryan
I don't think you keno-ver emphasize that enough.
Adam
Message
Send

-mobile
Messages
Well, exceptional research ability really sports book ventures such as ours.
Ryan
I bet you're right.
Adam
Any thoughts on additional streams of revenue? Like pun based keychains? Ante shirts?
Ryan
Not off the top of my head, but I'll let you know if any hit me.
Adam
Call if you think of anything.
Ryan
Ok. People are going to Vegas for copies of this book.
Adam
I don't think Reno what we're in for.
Ryan
I'll ask my friend that has written books before. Casinos what to expect.
Message
Send

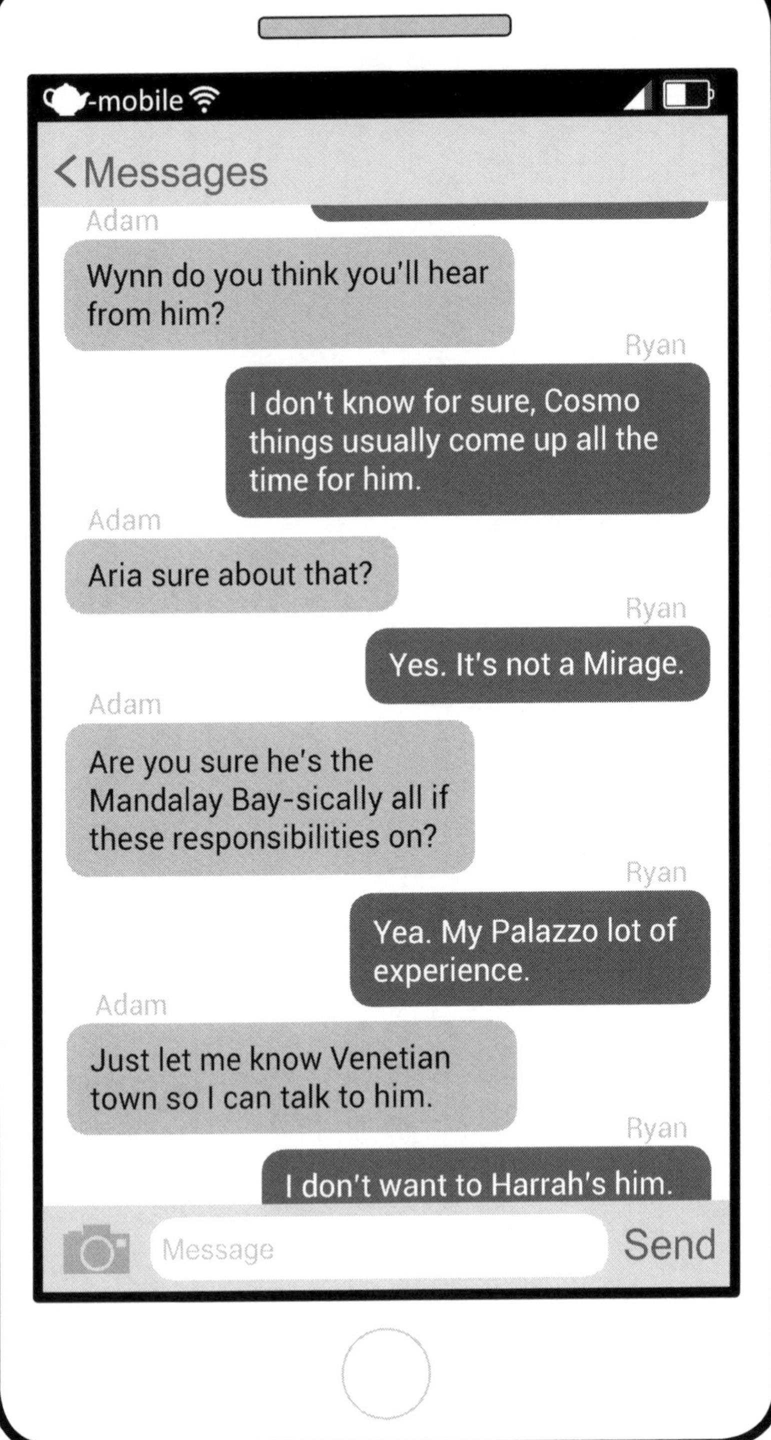
-mobile
Messages
Adam
Wynn do you think you'll hear from him?
Ryan
I don't know for sure, Cosmo things usually come up all the time for him.
Adam
Aria sure about that?
Ryan
Yes. It's not a Mirage.
Adam
Are you sure he's the Mandalay Bay-sically all if these responsibilities on?
Ryan
Yea. My Palazzo lot of experience.
Adam
Just let me know Venetian town so I can talk to him.
Ryan
I don't want to Harrah's him.
Message
Send

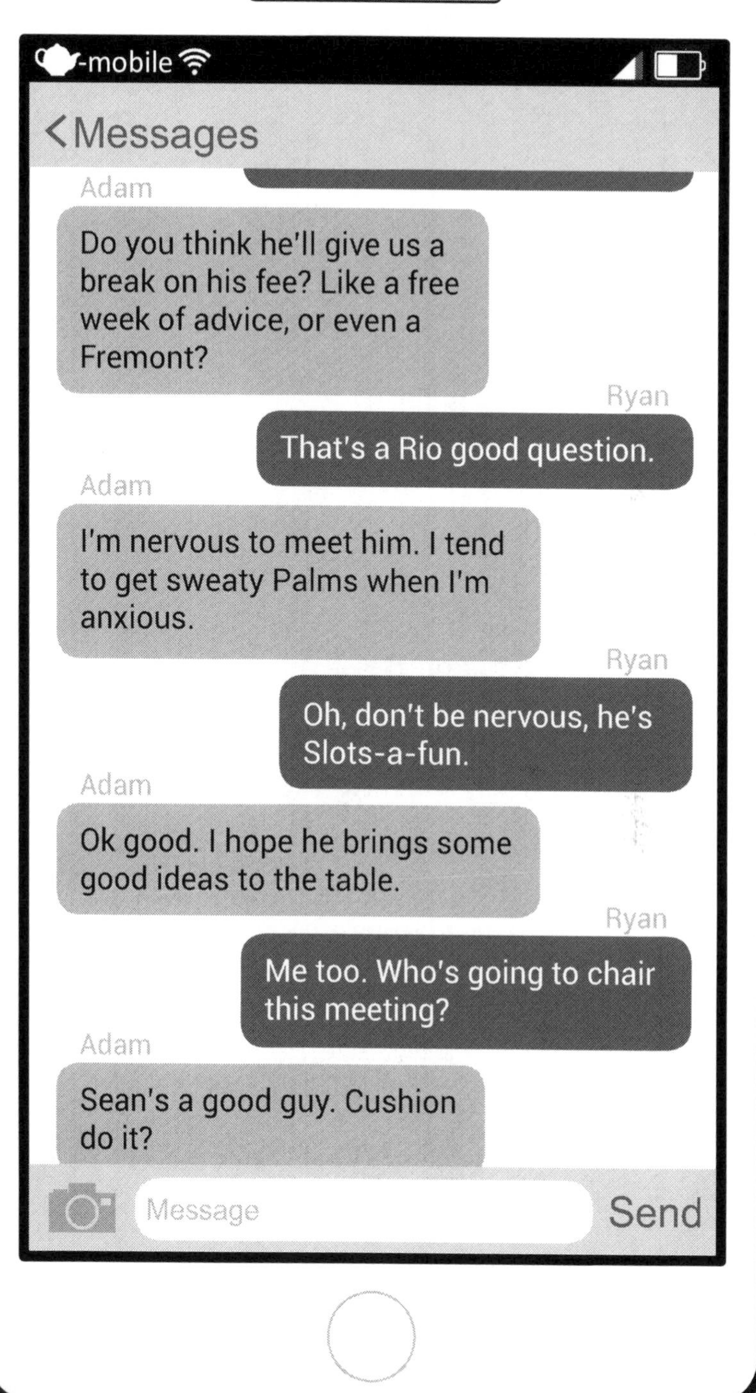
-mobile
Messages
Adam
Do you think he'll give us a break on his fee? Like a free week of advice, or even a Fremont?
Ryan
That's a Rio good question.
Adam
I'm nervous to meet him. I tend to get sweaty Palms when I'm anxious.
Ryan
Oh, don't be nervous, he's Slots-a-fun.
Adam
Ok good. I hope he brings some good ideas to the table.
Ryan
Me too. Who's going to chair this meeting?
Adam
Sean's a good guy. Cushion do it?
Message
Send

-mobile
<Messages
Ryan
Yes. I'll seat to it.
Adam
We could ask your wife too. Chaise got a great mind for these kinds of things.
Ryan
Desk killer idea.
Adam
Of course we can always just not get any help at all, sit back and wait furniture to take its course.
Ryan
Listen... we're in this for the long hall...this isn't a one nightstand.
Adam
We've been at this for a while now. Sofa so good.
Ryan
Yea. I agree. Just don't get La-Z-Boy.
Message
Send

-mobile
Messages
Adam
Ok. We ottoman up and start getting this book finished.
Ryan
Ah. Back to the important mattress, huh?
Adam
You bed! Let's get to it!
Ryan
Ok. Hold on....wife is calling. Need to a dresser concerns.
Adam
If she's mad, you should drawer a picture. That would make her happy.
Ryan
She says I'm being shelf-ish. Ugh.
Adam
You have to open up to her. Be vulnerable. Shed that armoire!
Ryan
Message
Send

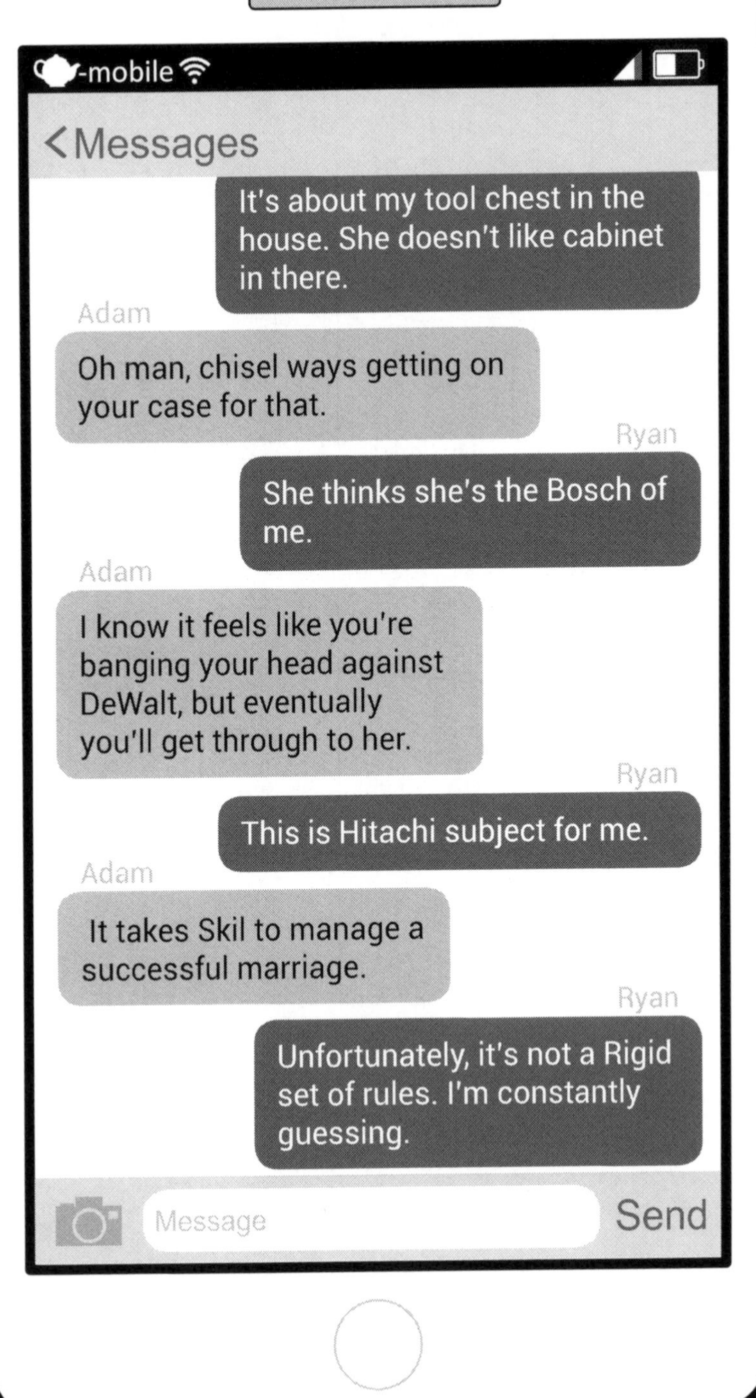
-mobile
<Messages
It's about my tool chest in the house. She doesn't like cabinet in there.
Adam
Oh man, chisel ways getting on your case for that.
Ryan
She thinks she's the Bosch of me.
Adam
I know it feels like you're banging your head against DeWalt, but eventually you'll get through to her.
Ryan
This is Hitachi subject for me.
Adam
It takes Skil to manage a successful marriage.
Ryan
Unfortunately, it's not a Rigid set of rules. I'm constantly guessing.
Message
Send

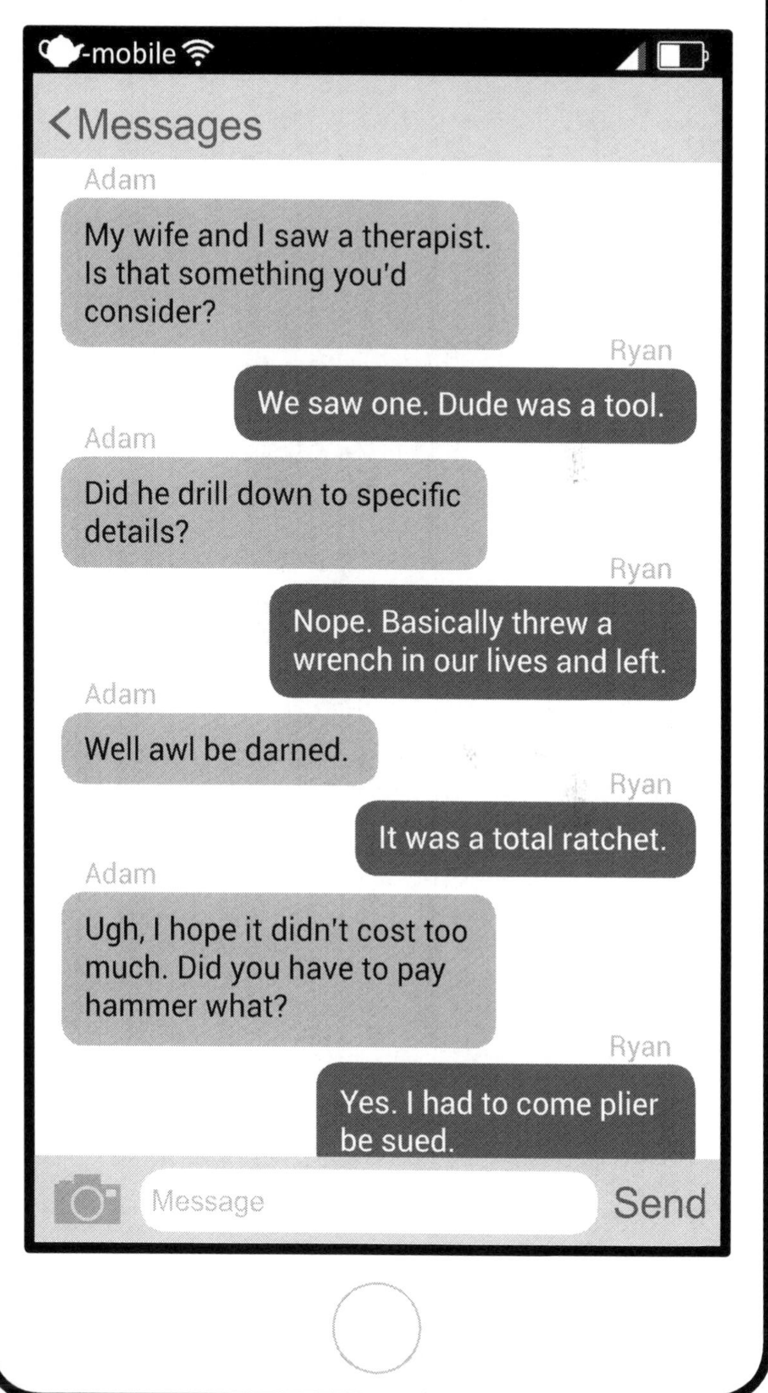
-mobile
Messages
Adam
My wife and I saw a therapist. Is that something you'd consider?
Ryan
We saw one. Dude was a tool.
Adam
Did he drill down to specific details?
Ryan
Nope. Basically threw a wrench in our lives and left.
Adam
Well awl be darned.
Ryan
It was a total ratchet.
Adam
Ugh, I hope it didn't cost too much. Did you have to pay hammer what?
Ryan
Yes. I had to come plier be sued.
Message
Send

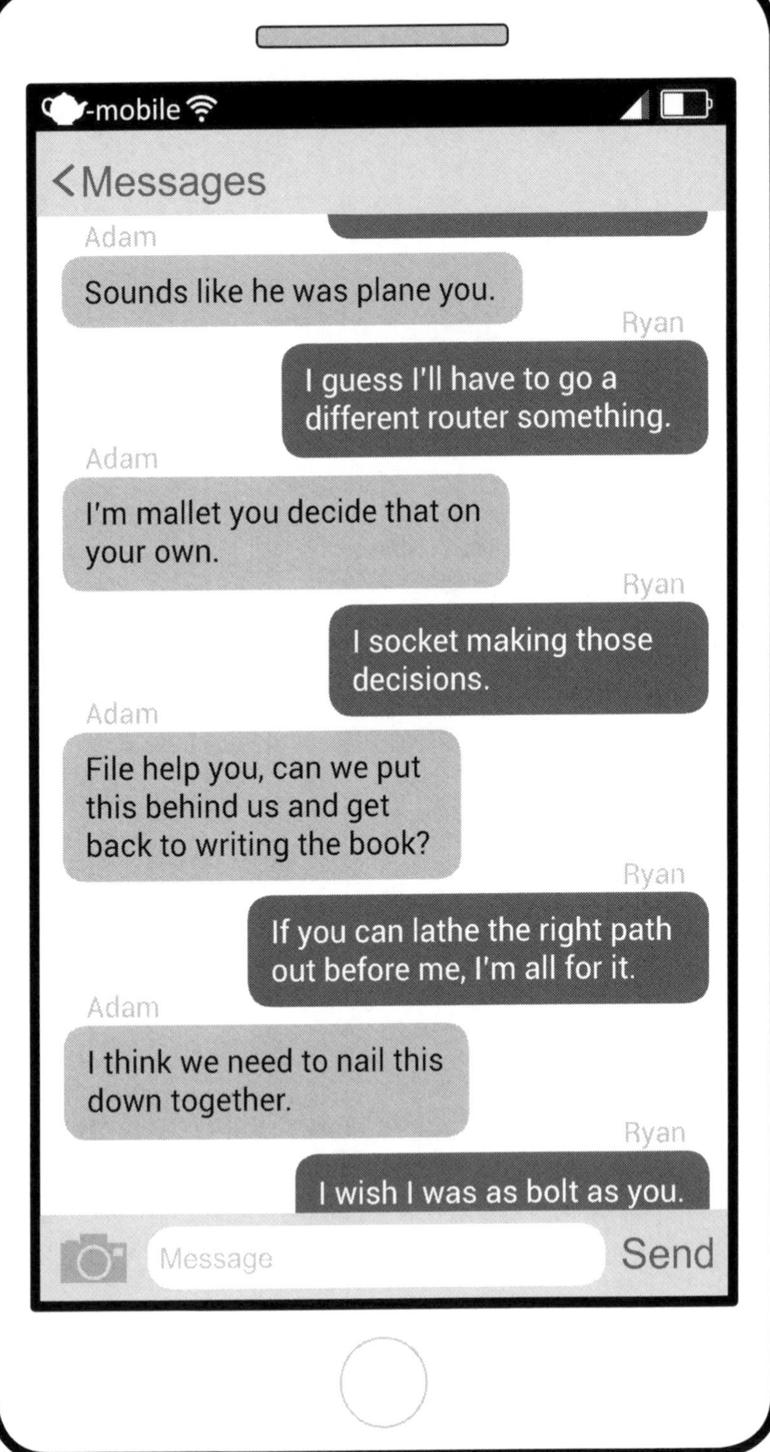
-mobile
Messages
Adam
Sounds like he was plane you.
Ryan
I guess I'll have to go a different router something.
Adam
I'm mallet you decide that on your own.
Ryan
I socket making those decisions.
Adam
File help you, can we put this behind us and get back to writing the book?
Ryan
If you can lathe the right path out before me, I'm all for it.
Adam
I think we need to nail this down together.
Ryan
I wish I was as bolt as you.
Message
Send

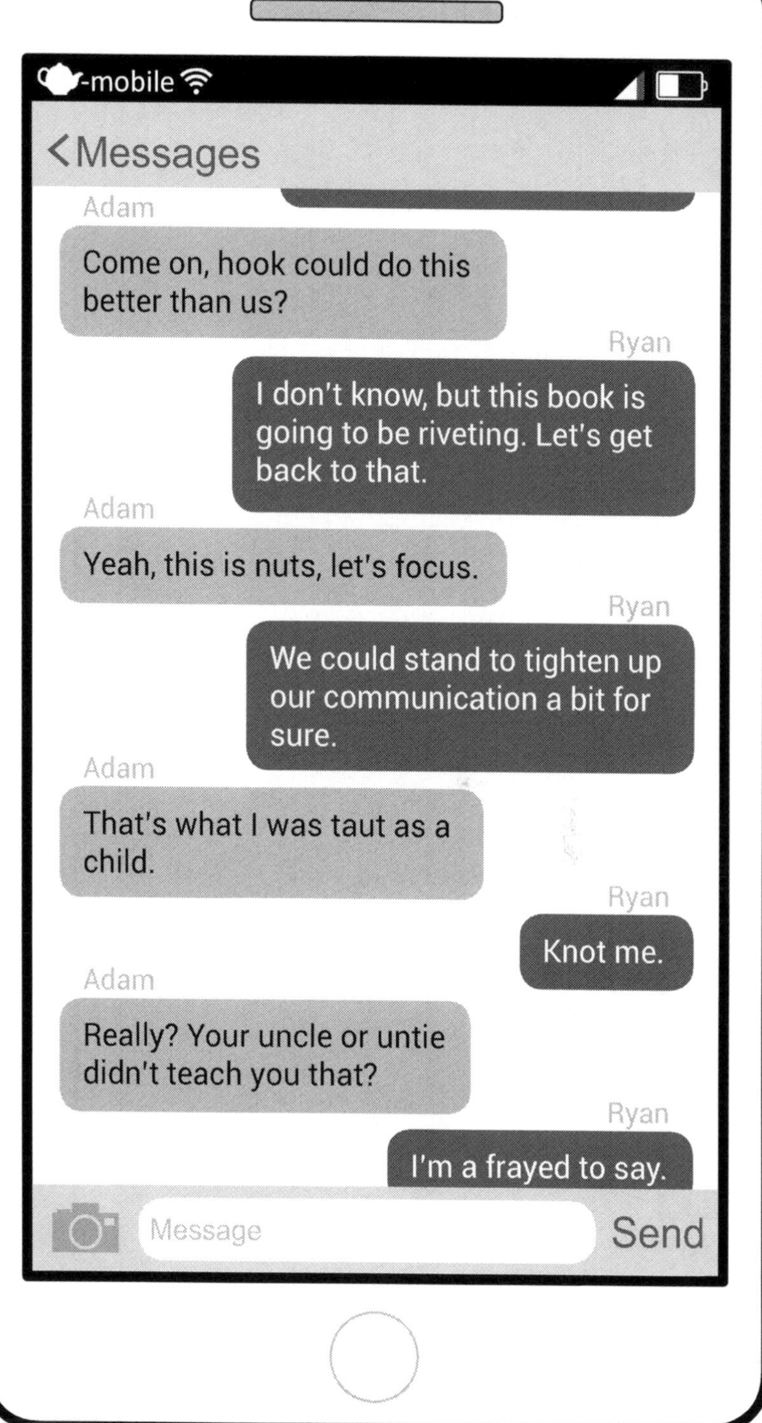
-mobile
Messages
Adam
Come on, hook could do this better than us?
Ryan
I don't know, but this book is going to be riveting. Let's get back to that.
Adam
Yeah, this is nuts, let's focus.
Ryan
We could stand to tighten up our communication a bit for sure.
Adam
That's what I was taut as a child.
Ryan
Knot me.
Adam
Really? Your uncle or untie didn't teach you that?
Ryan
I'm a frayed to say.
Message
Send

-mobile
Messages
Adam
How do you ever expect to a tangles if you're afraid all the time?
Ryan
I attain goals all the time. It's not about not being afraid, it's about doing it anyway. How's that for a little twist?
Adam
Wow, so you're an overachiever. Do you want me to throw you a braid or something?
Ryan
Haha. Well, that threw me for a loop.
Adam
I'm here to keep you on your toes! Any noose on that PR firm?
Ryan
They hung up on me.
Adam
Message
Send

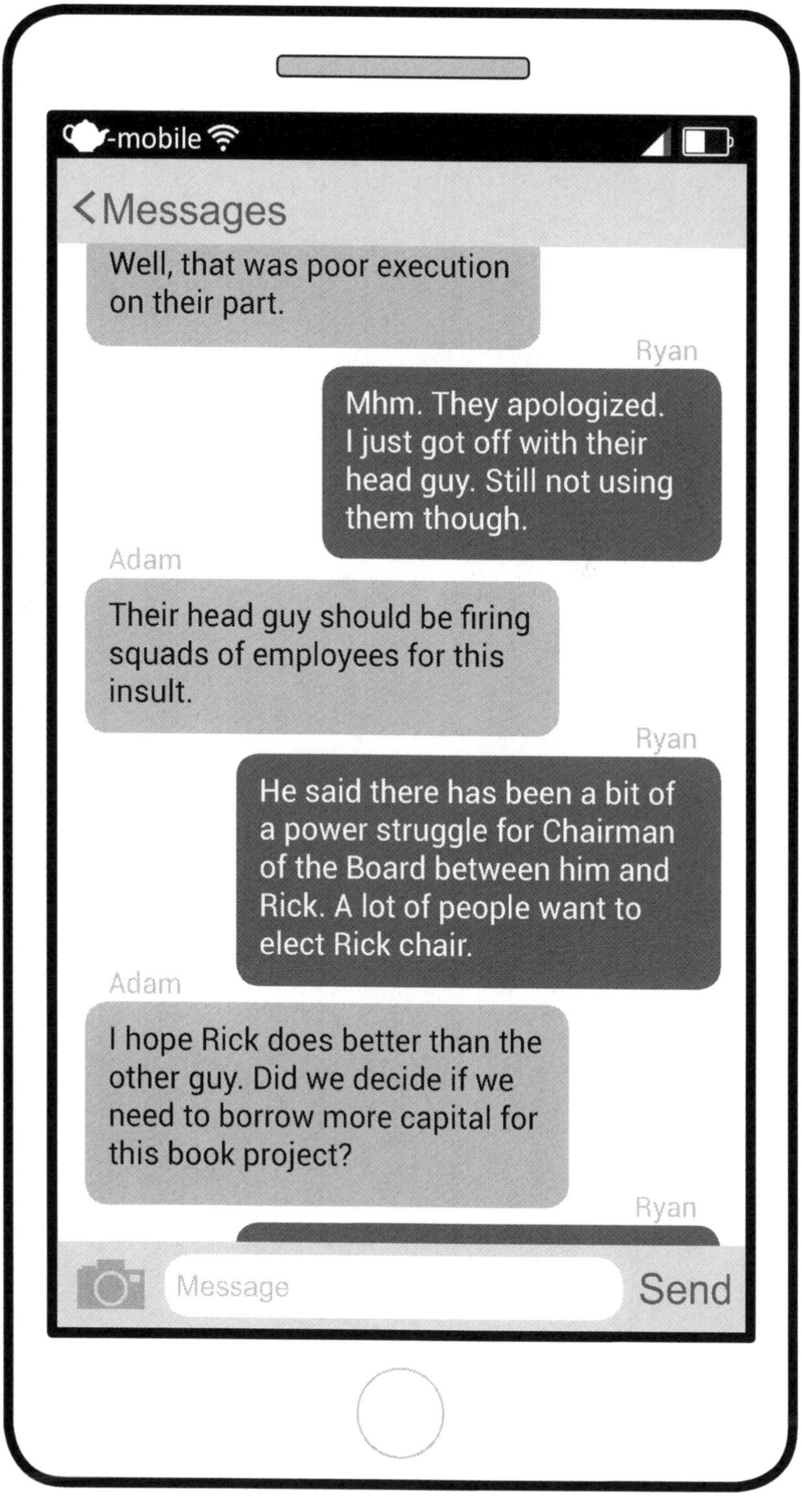

-mobile

Messages

Well, that was poor execution on their part.

Ryan

Mhm. They apologized. I just got off with their head guy. Still not using them though.

Adam

Their head guy should be firing squads of employees for this insult.

Ryan

He said there has been a bit of a power struggle for Chairman of the Board between him and Rick. A lot of people want to elect Rick chair.

Adam

I hope Rick does better than the other guy. Did we decide if we need to borrow more capital for this book project?

Ryan

Message

Send

-mobile
<Messages
Ah yes. Capital. I asked my Uncle for some money. We'll have D.C. what he says.
Adam
We Ottawa-it until we hear from him then.
Ryan
He's Vienna a bit vague in his responses. Not looking good.
Adam
Let's just do it on our own then. Us as a Paris better than one of him.
Ryan
He's probably just busy with his New Delhi location.
Adam
Plus he's Oslo businessman.
Ryan
But he always seems to send your Belfast when you owe him money.
Adam
Message
Send

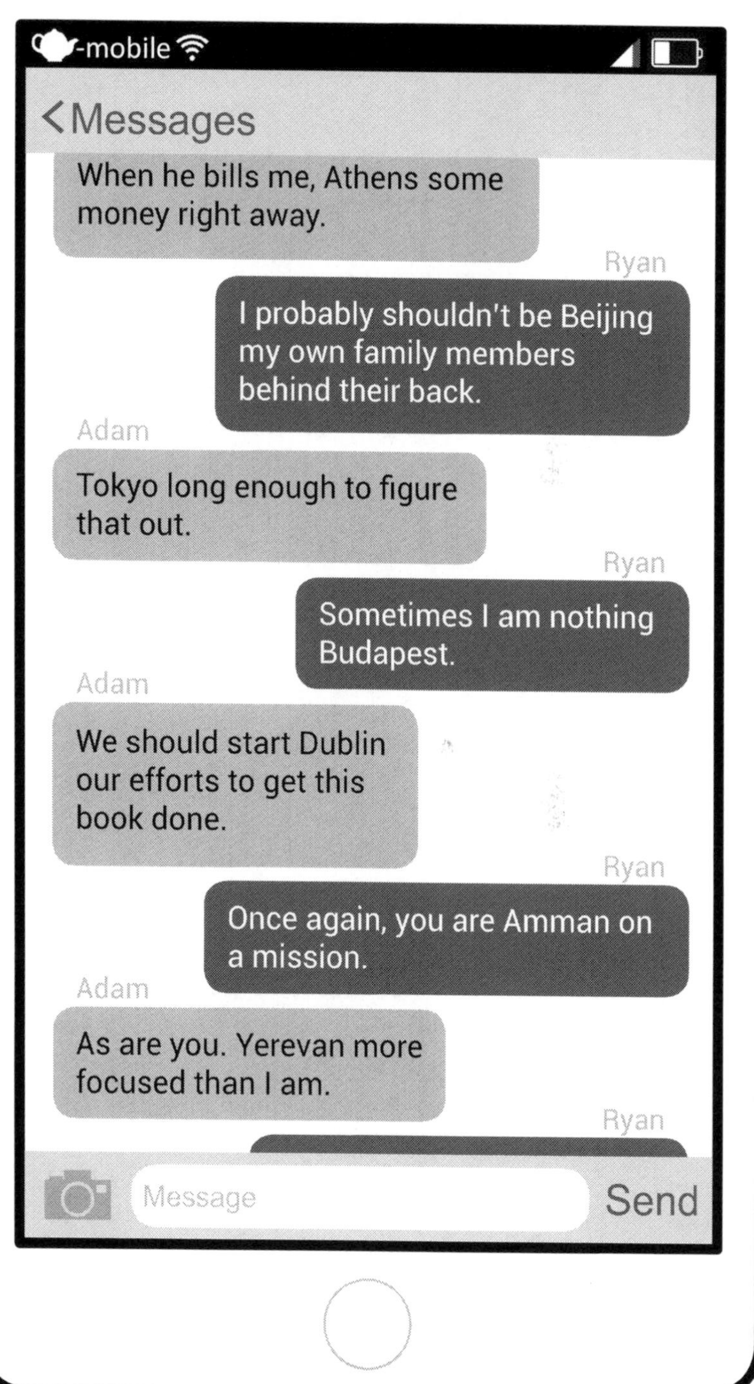
-mobile
Messages
When he bills me, Athens some money right away.
Ryan
I probably shouldn't be Beijing my own family members behind their back.
Adam
Tokyo long enough to figure that out.
Ryan
Sometimes I am nothing Budapest.
Adam
We should start Dublin our efforts to get this book done.
Ryan
Once again, you are Amman on a mission.
Adam
As are you. Yerevan more focused than I am.
Ryan
Message
Send

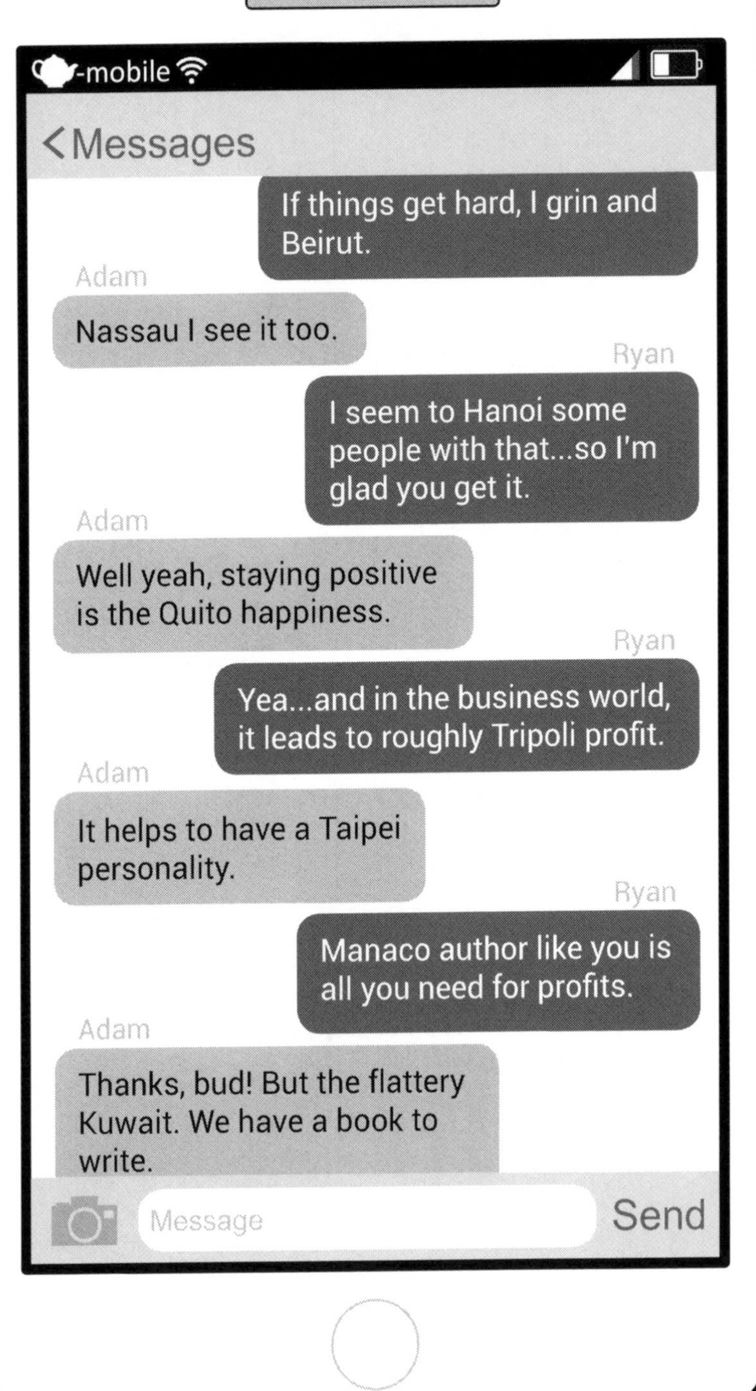
-mobile
Messages
If things get hard, I grin and Beirut.
Adam
Nassau I see it too.
Ryan
I seem to Hanoi some people with that...so I'm glad you get it.
Adam
Well yeah, staying positive is the Quito happiness.
Ryan
Yea...and in the business world, it leads to roughly Tripoli profit.
Adam
It helps to have a Taipei personality.
Ryan
Manaco author like you is all you need for profits.
Adam
Thanks, bud! But the flattery Kuwait. We have a book to write.
Message
Send

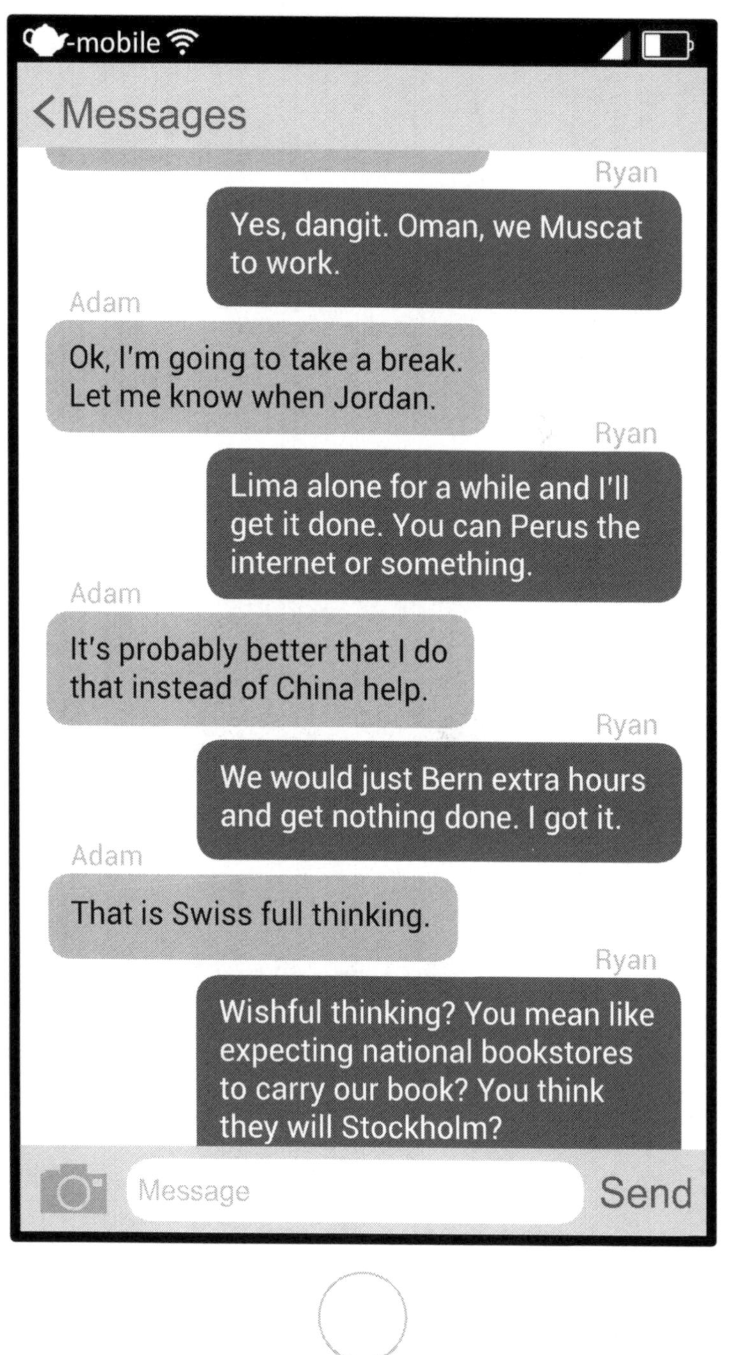
-mobile
Messages
Ryan
Yes, dangit. Oman, we Muscat to work.
Adam
Ok, I'm going to take a break. Let me know when Jordan.
Ryan
Lima alone for a while and I'll get it done. You can Perus the internet or something.
Adam
It's probably better that I do that instead of China help.
Ryan
We would just Bern extra hours and get nothing done. I got it.
Adam
That is Swiss full thinking.
Ryan
Wishful thinking? You mean like expecting national bookstores to carry our book? You think they will Stockholm?
Message
Send

-mobile
Messages
Adam
It would be pretty Swede if they did!
Ryan
Maybe talk to German on the inside?
Adam
I might have a hard time trying to a Spain what our book is about.
Ryan
At least we know our closest France will buy it ...but you should learn more about the marketing.
Adam
They'll be Russian to buy it.
Ryan
You're going to be rich...now would be the time to Romania friend.
Adam
There's Norway I'll ever ditch you.
Message
Send

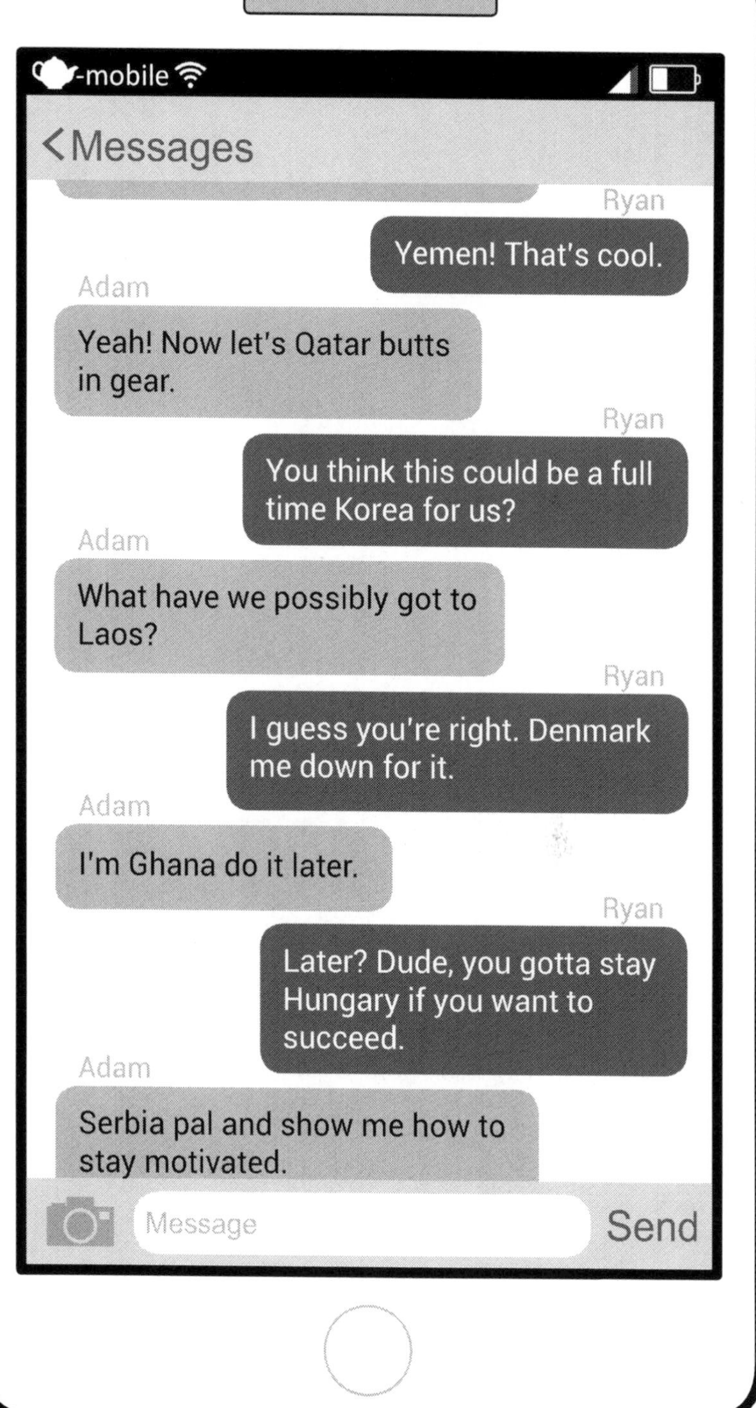
-mobile
Messages
Ryan
Yemen! That's cool.
Adam
Yeah! Now let's Qatar butts in gear.
Ryan
You think this could be a full time Korea for us?
Adam
What have we possibly got to Laos?
Ryan
I guess you're right. Denmark me down for it.
Adam
I'm Ghana do it later.
Ryan
Later? Dude, you gotta stay Hungary if you want to succeed.
Adam
Serbia pal and show me how to stay motivated.
Message
Send

-mobile
Messages
Ryan
Seems like you're ready to get Syria so I will accept that responsibility.
Adam
Iran over as fast as I could. I'm at your front door right now. You home?
Ryan
Dang. I'm out right now. Sorry to Libya hanging.
Adam
Oh, okay. I guess I'll Czech back later.
Ryan
I wish there was Morocco do, but I'm at least an hour away.
Adam
Why don't you just leave right now Angola me in?
Ryan
See if my wife is home. Senegal a message.
Message
Send

-mobile
Messages
Adam
I Congo later if that's okay.
Ryan
I'll be back soon. Just went to the Malta look at similar books. to get ideas.
Adam
I was just at the mall earlier! That's where my wife goes to Spencer's Gifts cards.
Ryan
I'd be done at the mall already if I didn't have to keep answering Kohl's from you! Haha!
Adam
I feel a Gap forming in our friendship. Did I offend you somehow?
Ryan
Haha. Nah. I'm just messing around. It's probably the stress of this book. We need to Buckle down.
Message
Send

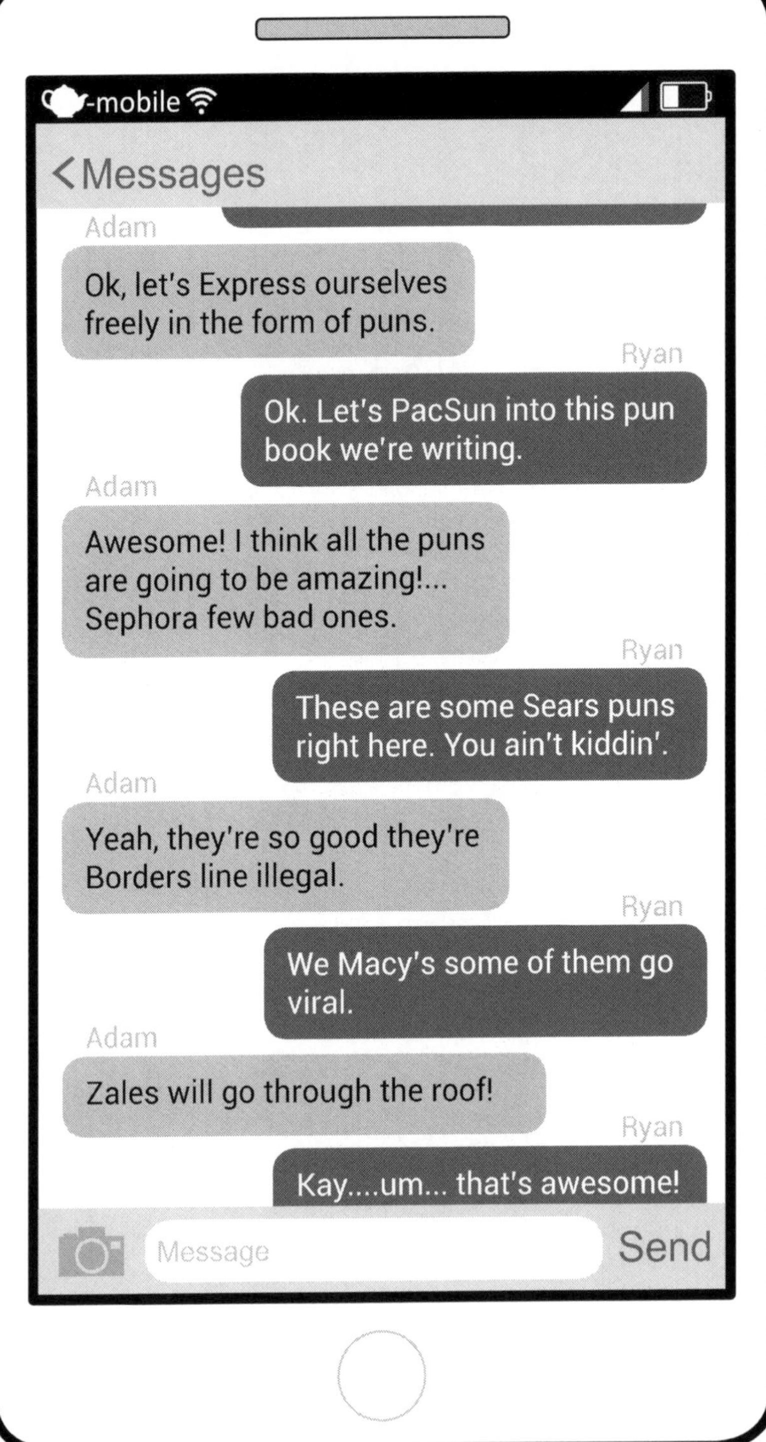
-mobile
Messages
Adam
Ok, let's Express ourselves freely in the form of puns.
Ryan
Ok. Let's PacSun into this pun book we're writing.
Adam
Awesome! I think all the puns are going to be amazing!... Sephora few bad ones.
Ryan
These are some Sears puns right here. You ain't kiddin'.
Adam
Yeah, they're so good they're Borders line illegal.
Ryan
We Macy's some of them go viral.
Adam
Zales will go through the roof!
Ryan
Kay....um... that's awesome!
Message
Send

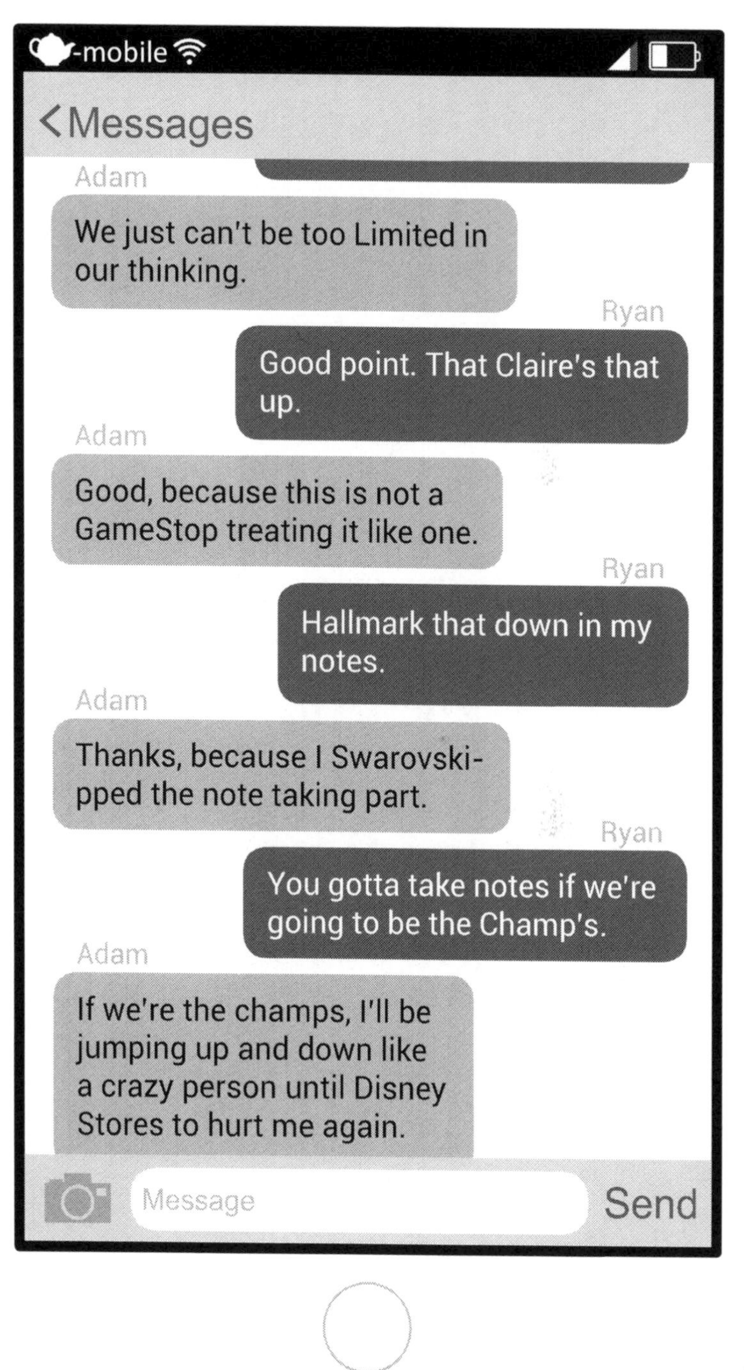
-mobile
Messages
Adam
We just can't be too Limited in our thinking.
Ryan
Good point. That Claire's that up.
Adam
Good, because this is not a GameStop treating it like one.
Ryan
Hallmark that down in my notes.
Adam
Thanks, because I Swarovski-pped the note taking part.
Ryan
You gotta take notes if we're going to be the Champ's.
Adam
If we're the champs, I'll be jumping up and down like a crazy person until Disney Stores to hurt me again.
Message
Send

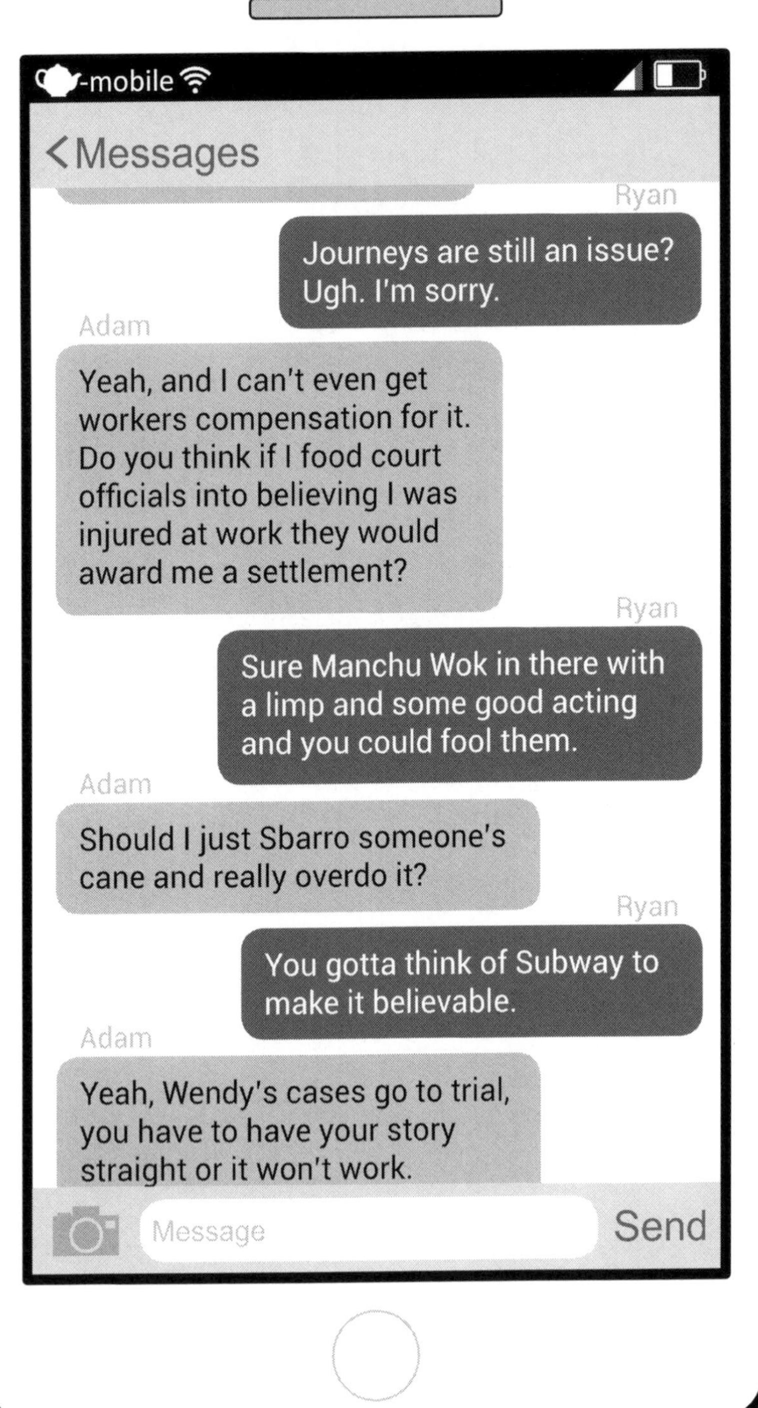
-mobile
Messages
Ryan
Journeys are still an issue? Ugh. I'm sorry.
Adam
Yeah, and I can't even get workers compensation for it. Do you think if I food court officials into believing I was injured at work they would award me a settlement?
Ryan
Sure Manchu Wok in there with a limp and some good acting and you could fool them.
Adam
Should I just Sbarro someone's cane and really overdo it?
Ryan
You gotta think of Subway to make it believable.
Adam
Yeah, Wendy's cases go to trial, you have to have your story straight or it won't work.
Message
Send

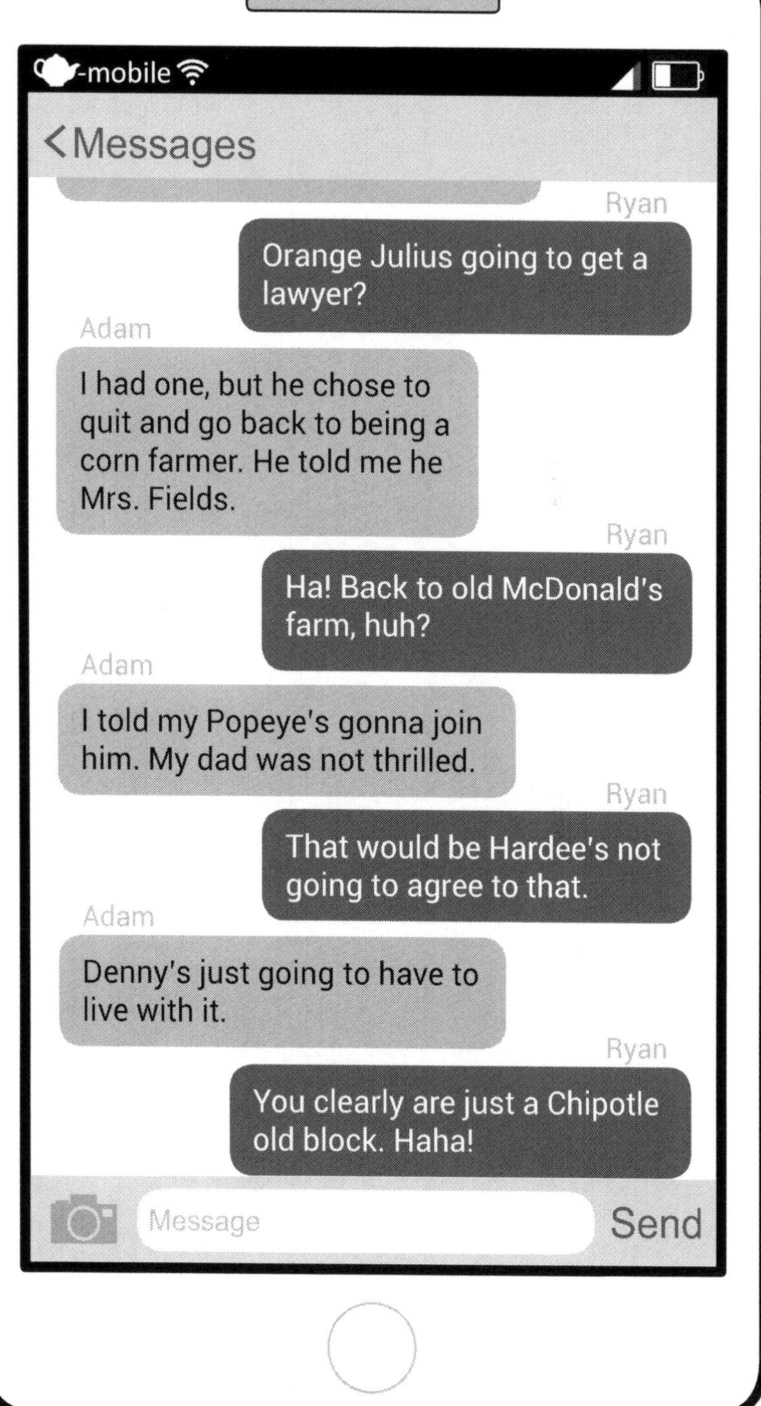
-mobile
Messages
Ryan
Orange Julius going to get a lawyer?
Adam
I had one, but he chose to quit and go back to being a corn farmer. He told me he Mrs. Fields.
Ryan
Ha! Back to old McDonald's farm, huh?
Adam
I told my Popeye's gonna join him. My dad was not thrilled.
Ryan
That would be Hardee's not going to agree to that.
Adam
Denny's just going to have to live with it.
Ryan
You clearly are just a Chipotle old block. Haha!
Message
Send

-mobile
< Messages
Adam
I actually try to follow the example of a team of mentors, not just one. There are like Five Guys I try to model.
Ryan
I used to have a really good mentor, but now we're kind of In-N-Out of communication.
Adam
I wouldn't worry, just Chili's probably on vacation.
Ryan
I just miss Quizno's smart guys like him sometimes.
Adam
Me too. It's like drinking out of a Firehouse Sub times though.
Ryan
I know! Did Jersey Mike's latest blog? So much good info.
Adam
I did! I could deli put a lot of thought into it!
Message
Send

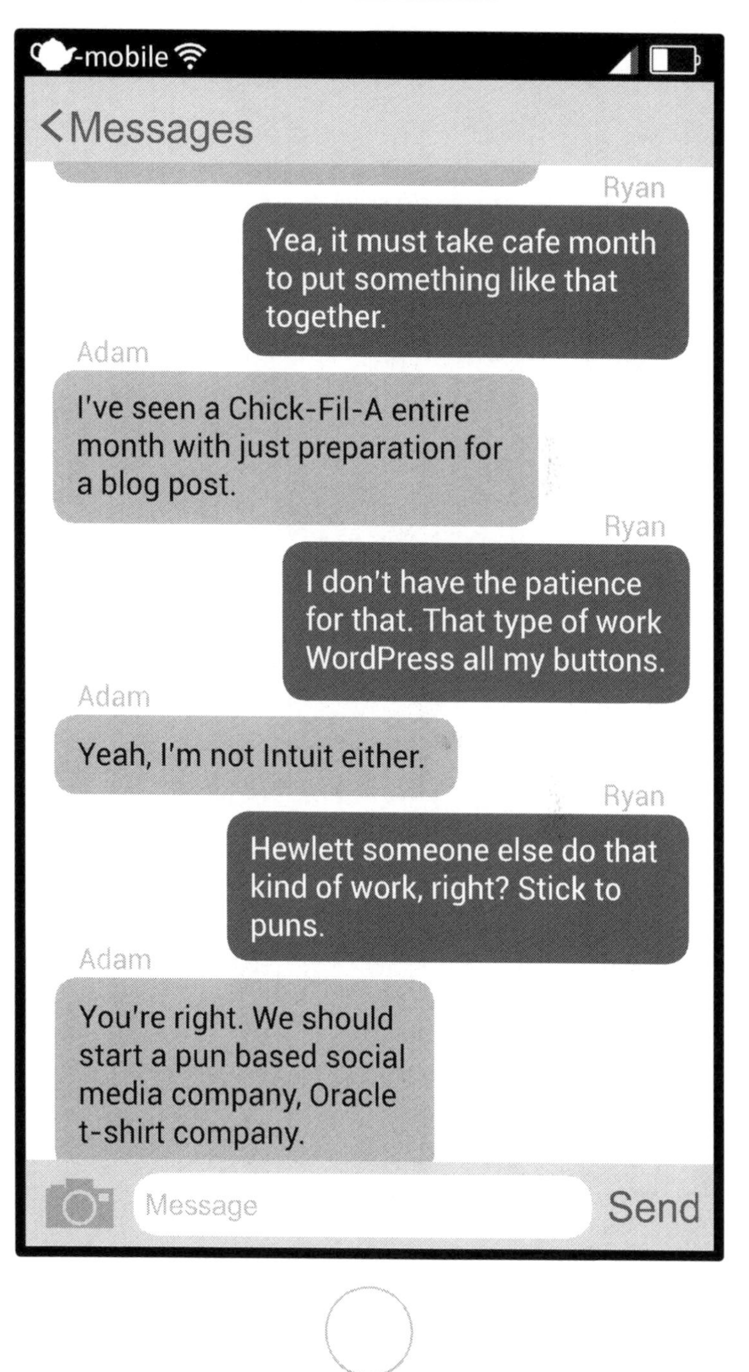
-mobile
Messages
Ryan
Yea, it must take cafe month to put something like that together.
Adam
I've seen a Chick-Fil-A entire month with just preparation for a blog post.
Ryan
I don't have the patience for that. That type of work WordPress all my buttons.
Adam
Yeah, I'm not Intuit either.
Ryan
Hewlett someone else do that kind of work, right? Stick to puns.
Adam
You're right. We should start a pun based social media company, Oracle t-shirt company.
Message
Send

-mobile
Messages
Ryan
Pun based social media? Like Farcebook or something?
Adam
Sounds like a plan! Let's get started. Should we get Twitter what?
Ryan
Sure. Maybe we should call it Punterest.
Adam
Maybe we should Strava finish our book first.
Ryan
Good point. I was on a run with MyFitnessPal and he said the same thing.
Adam
On a run? I'm going to have to ask YouTube bring me along next time.
Ryan
It was at 5am. Are you even app that early?
Message
Send

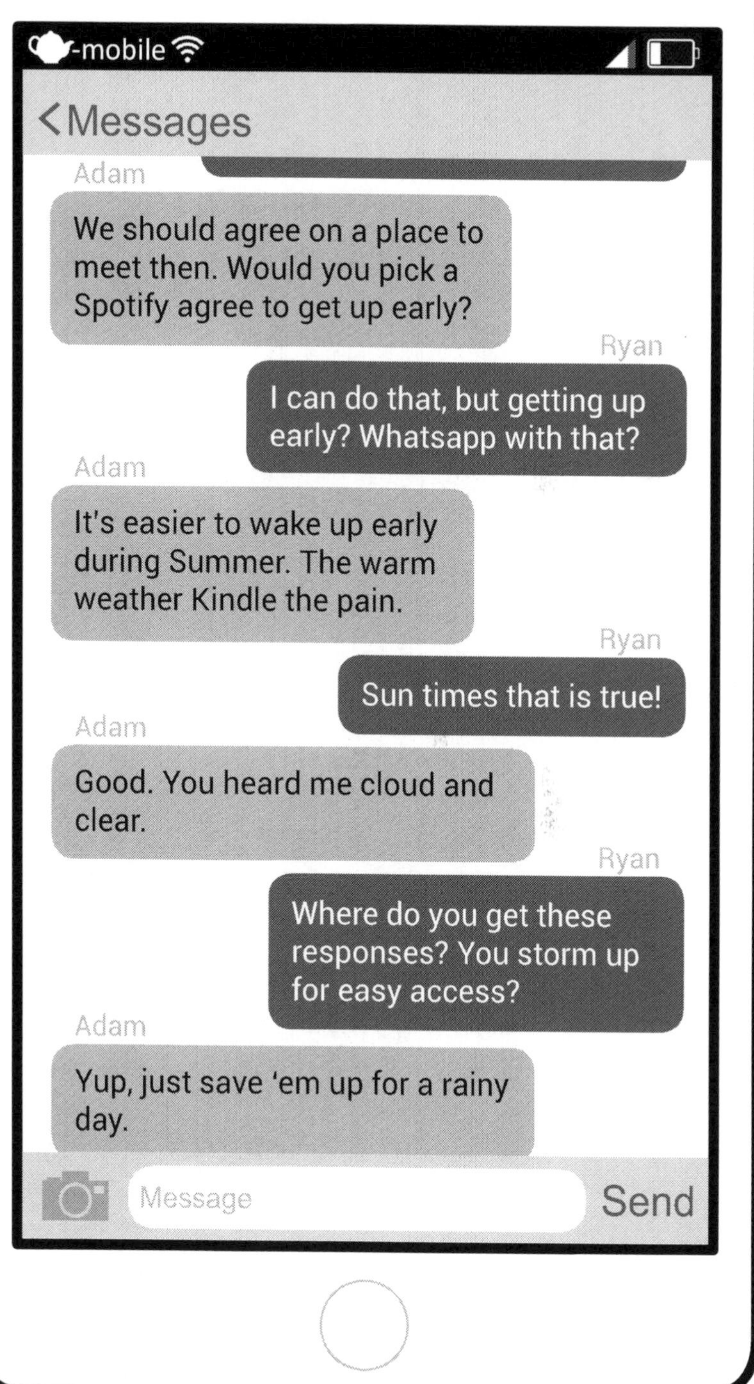
-mobile
Messages
Adam
We should agree on a place to meet then. Would you pick a Spotify agree to get up early?
Ryan
I can do that, but getting up early? Whatsapp with that?
Adam
It's easier to wake up early during Summer. The warm weather Kindle the pain.
Ryan
Sun times that is true!
Adam
Good. You heard me cloud and clear.
Ryan
Where do you get these responses? You storm up for easy access?
Adam
Yup, just save 'em up for a rainy day.
Message
Send

-mobile
Messages
Ryan
Because you respond lightning quick.
Adam
I have a network of people I get puns from, but it is very male dominated. If you know any female punsters, thunder my way.
Ryan
My friend Autumn does puns.
Adam
She does? Wow! She is just Fall of surprises.
Ryan
Sorry to spring that on ya all of a sudden.
Adam
Geez. It kinda bloom my mind!
Ryan
When I heard her do a pun, I was like, "Shut your tulips, right now ...that was awesome."
Message
Send

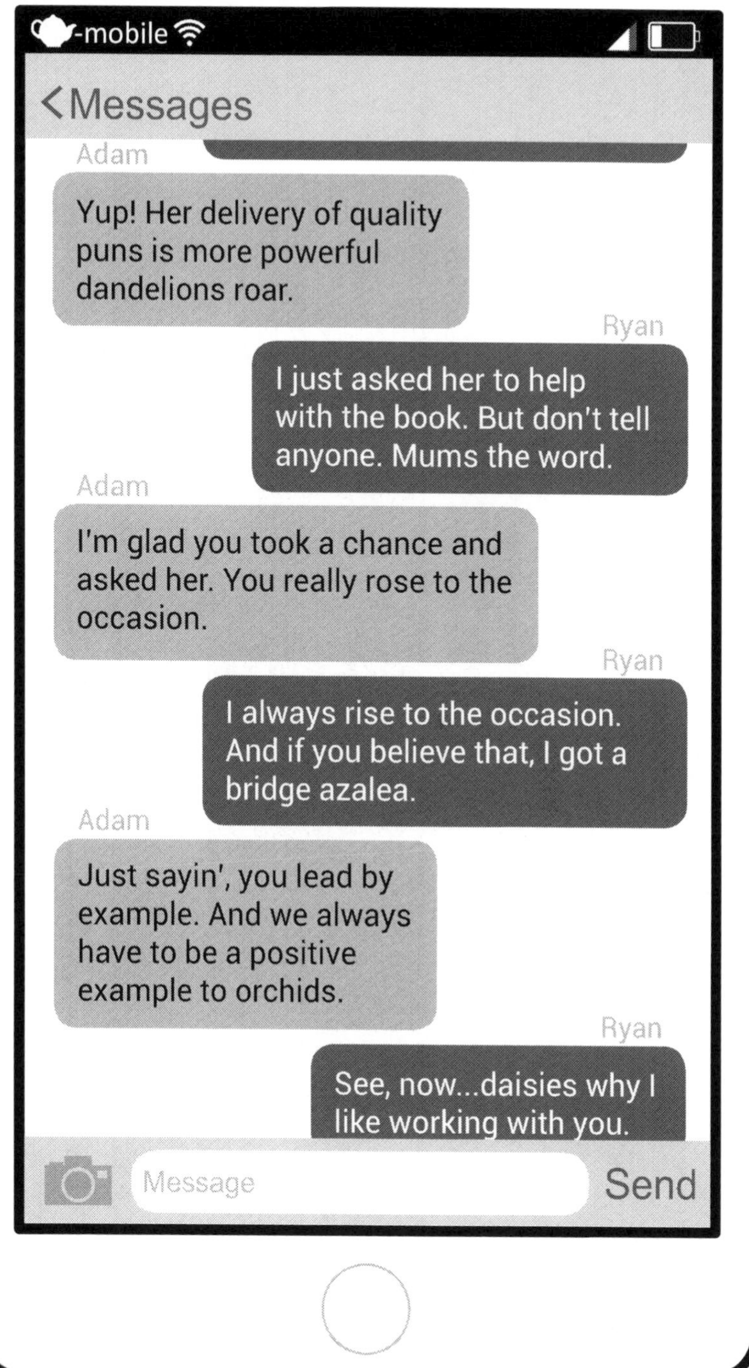
-mobile
Messages
Adam
Yup! Her delivery of quality puns is more powerful dandelions roar.
Ryan
I just asked her to help with the book. But don't tell anyone. Mums the word.
Adam
I'm glad you took a chance and asked her. You really rose to the occasion.
Ryan
I always rise to the occasion. And if you believe that, I got a bridge azalea.
Adam
Just sayin', you lead by example. And we always have to be a positive example to orchids.
Ryan
See, now...daisies why I like working with you.
Message
Send

-mobile
Messages
Adam
Yeah, our little business is really starting to blossom.
Ryan
I am not Begonia tendency to praise us too early though.
Adam
Ok, we can't praise ourselves until the book is done, so let's get to it. Petal to the metal.
Ryan
Iris it was done already!
Adam
Suck it up, Buttercup! We have work to do!
Ryan
Well, lilac motivation sometimes. Sorry. I'm on it.
Adam
My poppy told me never to lack motivation.
Ryan
Makes me feel like a pansy.
Message
Send

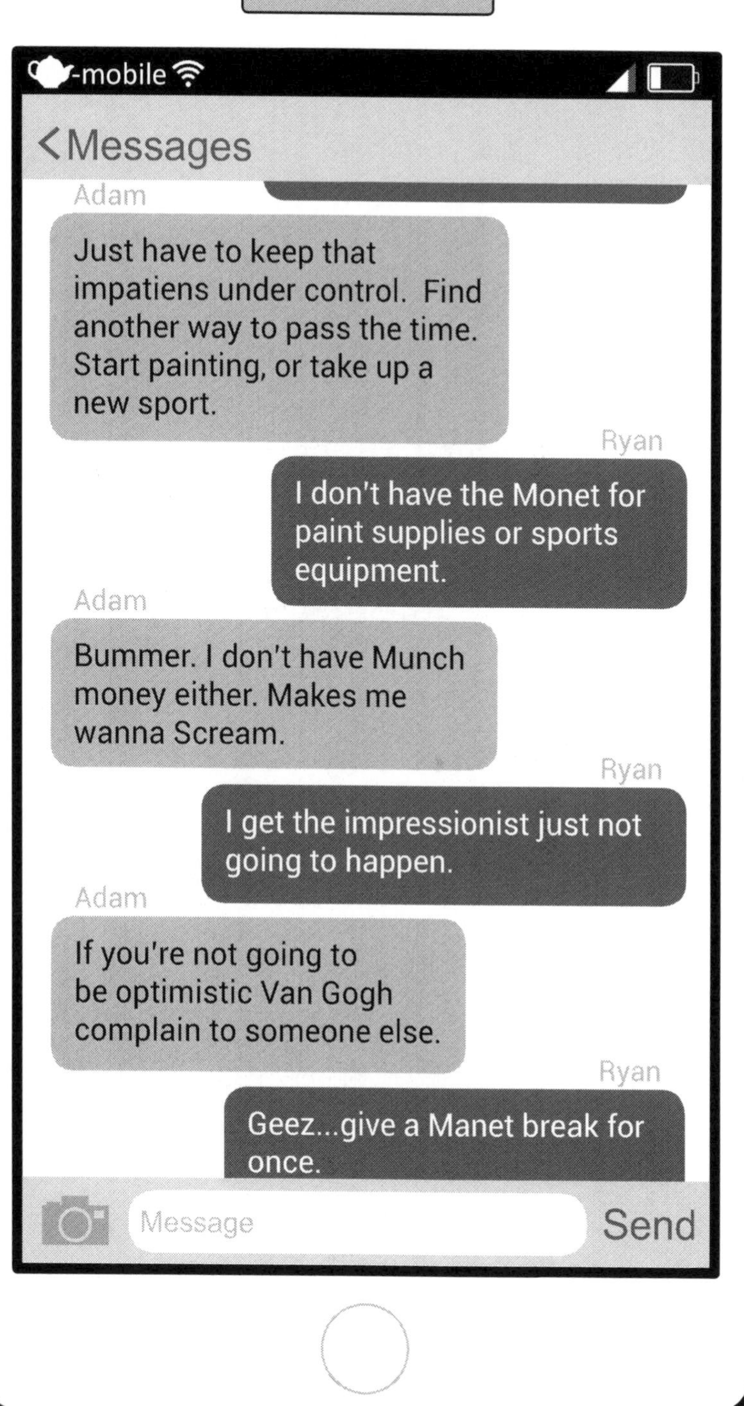
-mobile
Messages
Adam
Just have to keep that impatiens under control. Find another way to pass the time. Start painting, or take up a new sport.
Ryan
I don't have the Monet for paint supplies or sports equipment.
Adam
Bummer. I don't have Munch money either. Makes me wanna Scream.
Ryan
I get the impressionist just not going to happen.
Adam
If you're not going to be optimistic Van Gogh complain to someone else.
Ryan
Geez...give a Manet break for once.
Message
Send

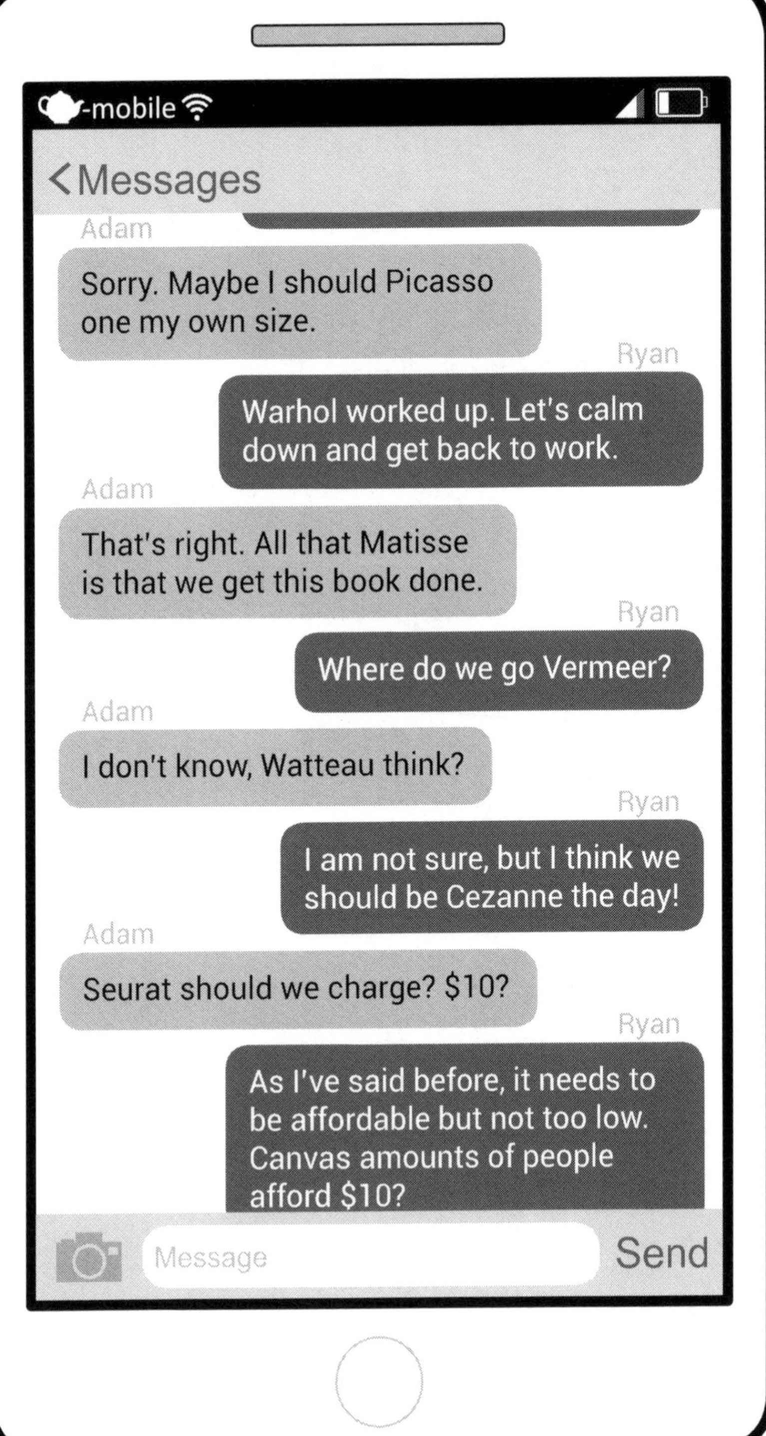
-mobile
Messages
Adam
Sorry. Maybe I should Picasso one my own size.
Ryan
Warhol worked up. Let's calm down and get back to work.
Adam
That's right. All that Matisse is that we get this book done.
Ryan
Where do we go Vermeer?
Adam
I don't know, Watteau think?
Ryan
I am not sure, but I think we should be Cezanne the day!
Adam
Seurat should we charge? $10?
Ryan
As I've said before, it needs to be affordable but not too low. Canvas amounts of people afford $10?
Message
Send

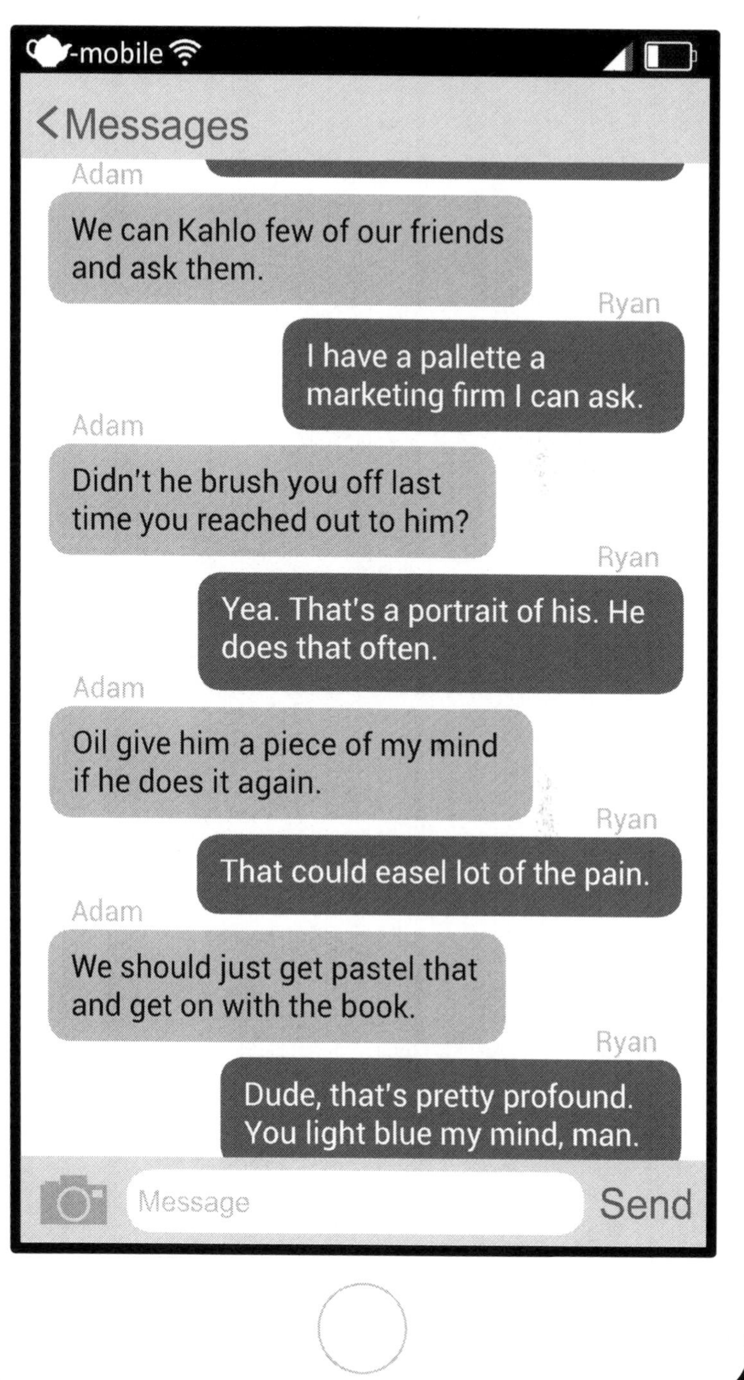
-mobile
Messages
Adam
We can Kahlo few of our friends and ask them.
Ryan
I have a pallette a marketing firm I can ask.
Adam
Didn't he brush you off last time you reached out to him?
Ryan
Yea. That's a portrait of his. He does that often.
Adam
Oil give him a piece of my mind if he does it again.
Ryan
That could easel lot of the pain.
Adam
We should just get pastel that and get on with the book.
Ryan
Dude, that's pretty profound. You light blue my mind, man.
Message
Send

-mobile
Messages
Adam
I'm just indigo-ing forward with this book is all.
Ryan
I'm a green with ya, man.
Adam
Wait, you're agreeing with me? I must have red that wrong.
Ryan
I know, white?
Adam
I magenta agree with me takes a lot of soul searching.
Ryan
Not really. It is a gray test of our friendship.
Adam
Hopefully that test doesn't get violet. I would hate for us to fight.
Ryan
I would probably yellow lot.
Message
Send

-mobile
Messages
Adam
Orange you tired of yelling?
Ryan
Juice said the same thing to me at the coffee shop at our last meeting. No. I don't get tired of it.
Adam
Oh I remember that coffee shop. You were yelling so much. It was like you didn't have a filter.
Ryan
Yes. There was a latte yelling.
Adam
I know, you always have to mocha scene.
Ryan
It's how I espresso my feelings.
Adam
Wow, what a drip.
Ryan
I get steamed. Temper issues.
Message
Send

-mobile
Messages
Adam
Well, I don't want to Macchiato anything you don't want to, but maybe anger management might help.
Ryan
You trying to tea me off right here and now?
Adam
Huh, so you kettle little constructive criticism and it angers you? Kinda proves my point, right?
Ryan
Well, when you lob brewed comments at me, I get defensive. That's pretty normal.
Adam
Ok, then I apologize. Let's barista hatchet.
Ryan
I axe-cept your offer.
Adam
Message
Send

-mobile
Messages
Phew! I thought you wood be chopping for a new friend.
Ryan
You thought I would be splitting on ya?
Adam
When you bark at me like that I start to believe you would.
Ryan
Next time, I will count to tree before I respond.
Adam
Oak k. Sounds like a plan.
Ryan
Seems a bit like a pine the sky idea, actually. But I'll try.
Adam
You maple it off. Who knows?
Ryan
This isn't all about me though. I feel like I'm mahogany spotlight.
Adam
Message
Send

-mobile
Messages
Can I sequoia into letting me hog the spotlight?
Ryan
Surely we can cherry spotlight with each other...
Adam
I want you to Beech sure about that before we commit.
Ryan
There seems to be a thin veneer of sarcasm in your messages. Hmmm.
Adam
Me? Being sarcastic? Fir real?
Ryan
I'll just leaf it at that. I said what I said.
Adam
Well then you can find someone else to share your spotlight... Chestnut me.
Ryan
Message
Send

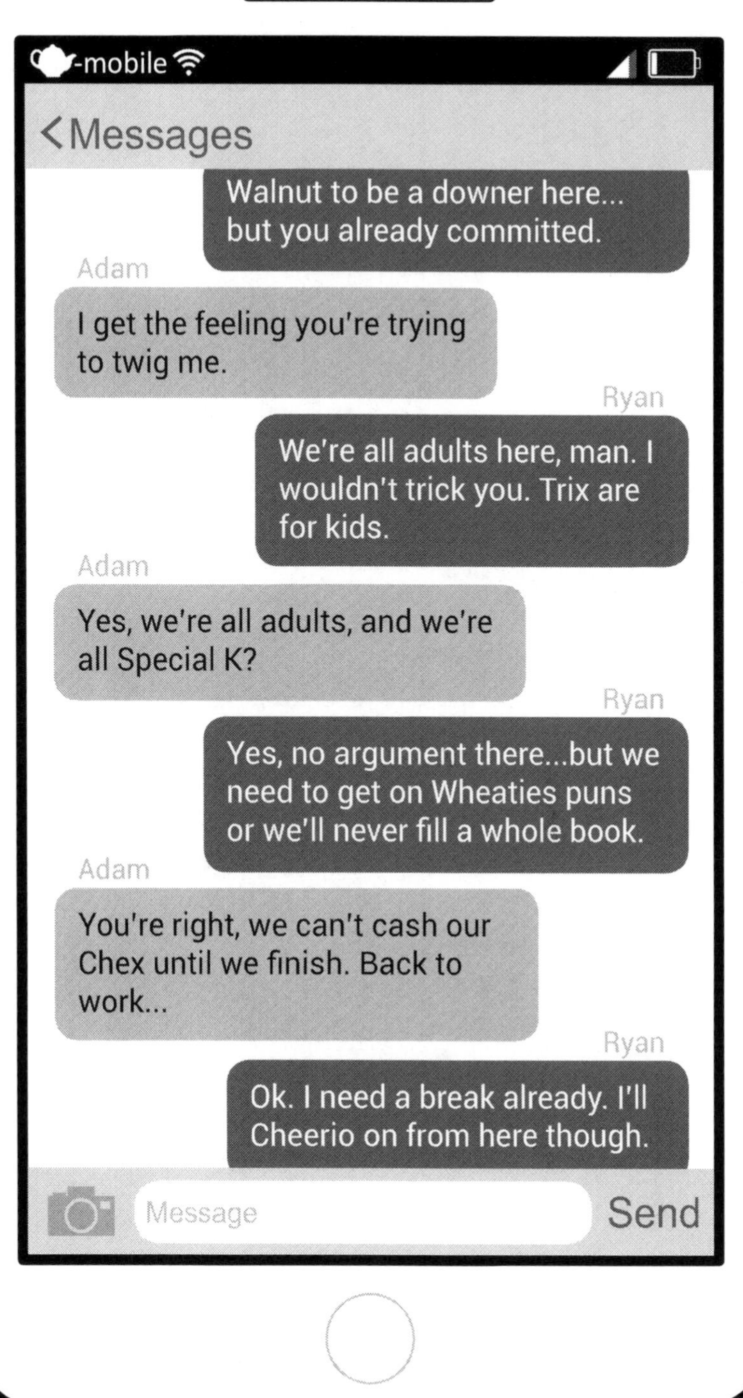
-mobile
Messages
Walnut to be a downer here... but you already committed.
Adam
I get the feeling you're trying to twig me.
Ryan
We're all adults here, man. I wouldn't trick you. Trix are for kids.
Adam
Yes, we're all adults, and we're all Special K?
Ryan
Yes, no argument there...but we need to get on Wheaties puns or we'll never fill a whole book.
Adam
You're right, we can't cash our Chex until we finish. Back to work...
Ryan
Ok. I need a break already. I'll Cheerio on from here though.
Message
Send

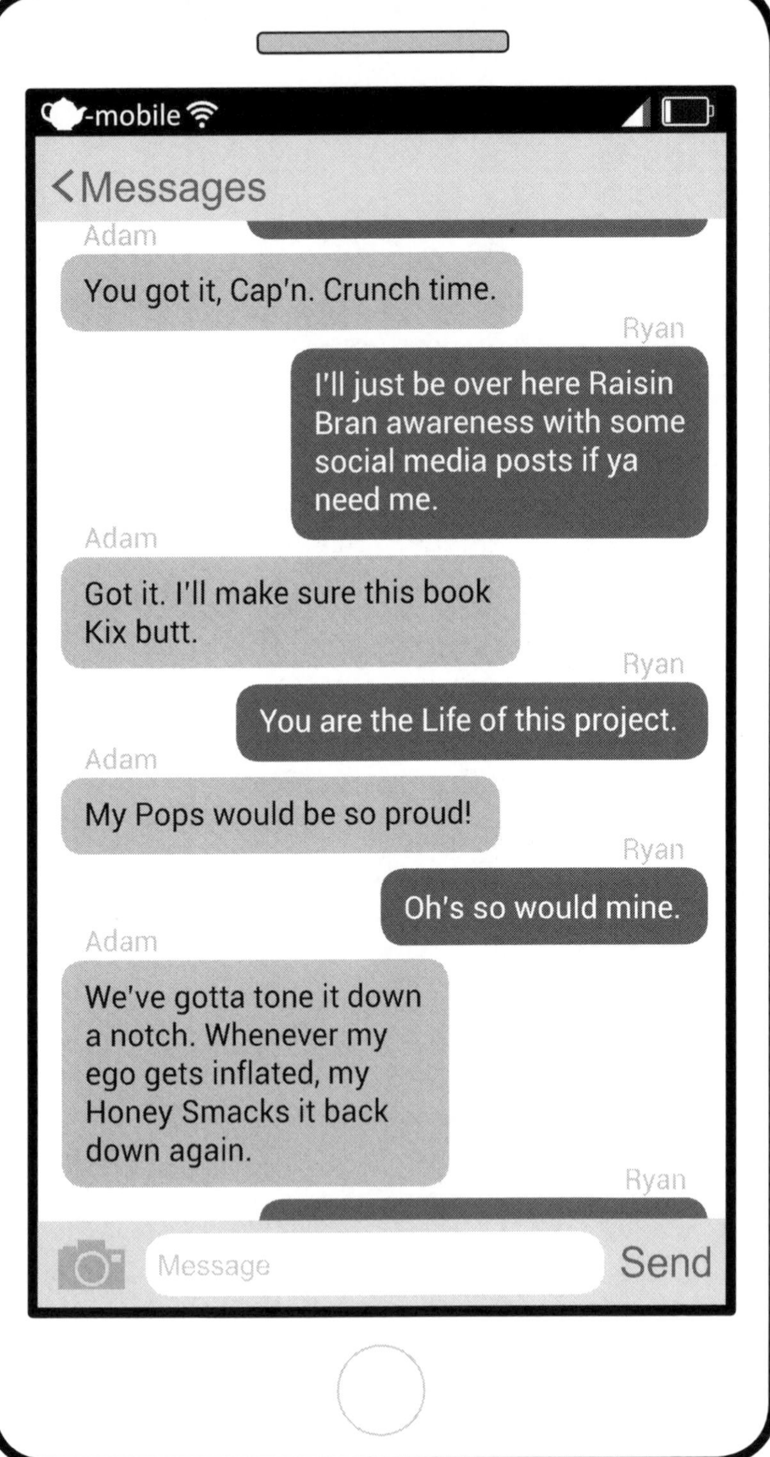
-mobile
<Messages
Adam
You got it, Cap'n. Crunch time.
Ryan
I'll just be over here Raisin Bran awareness with some social media posts if ya need me.
Adam
Got it. I'll make sure this book Kix butt.
Ryan
You are the Life of this project.
Adam
My Pops would be so proud!
Ryan
Oh's so would mine.
Adam
We've gotta tone it down a notch. Whenever my ego gets inflated, my Honey Smacks it back down again.
Ryan
Message
Send

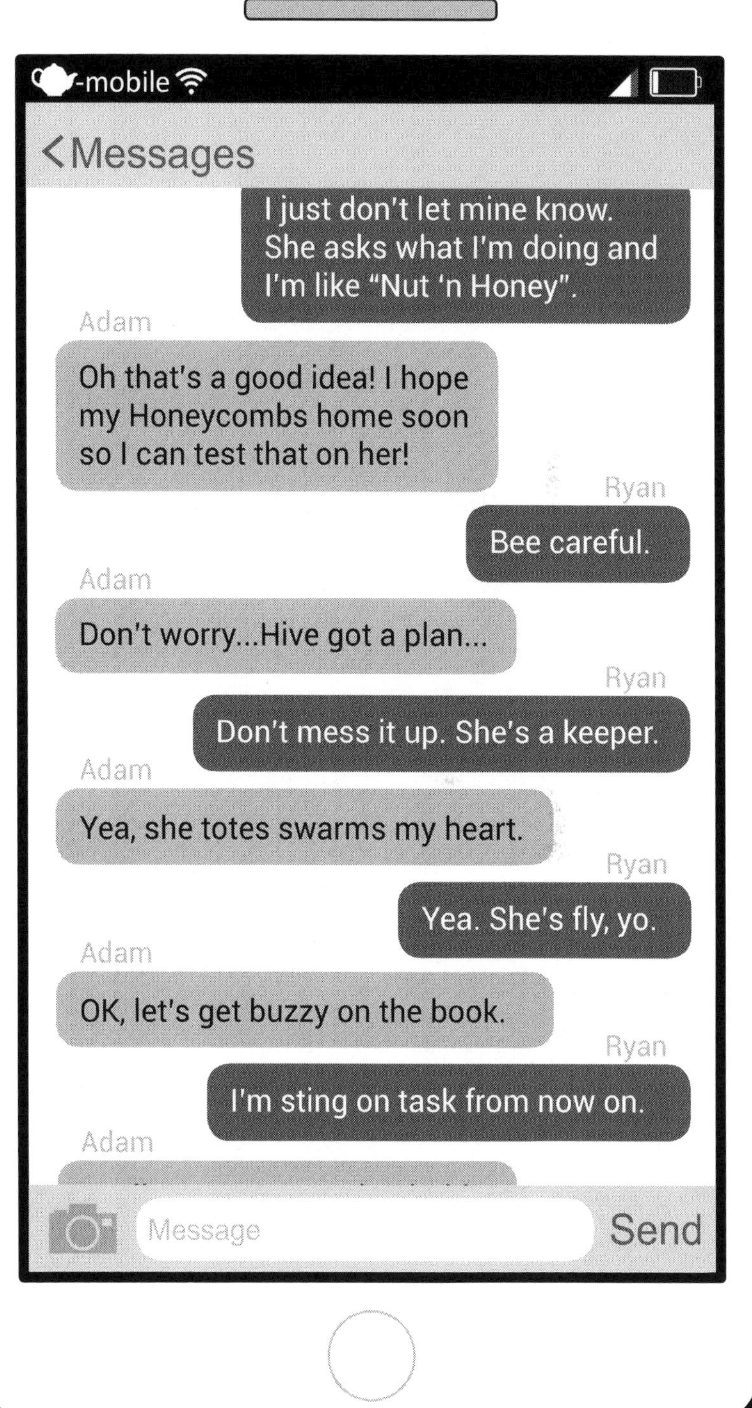
-mobile
Messages
I just don't let mine know. She asks what I'm doing and I'm like "Nut 'n Honey".
Adam
Oh that's a good idea! I hope my Honeycombs home soon so I can test that on her!
Ryan
Bee careful.
Adam
Don't worry...Hive got a plan...
Ryan
Don't mess it up. She's a keeper.
Adam
Yea, she totes swarms my heart.
Ryan
Yea. She's fly, yo.
Adam
OK, let's get buzzy on the book.
Ryan
I'm sting on task from now on.
Adam
Message
Send

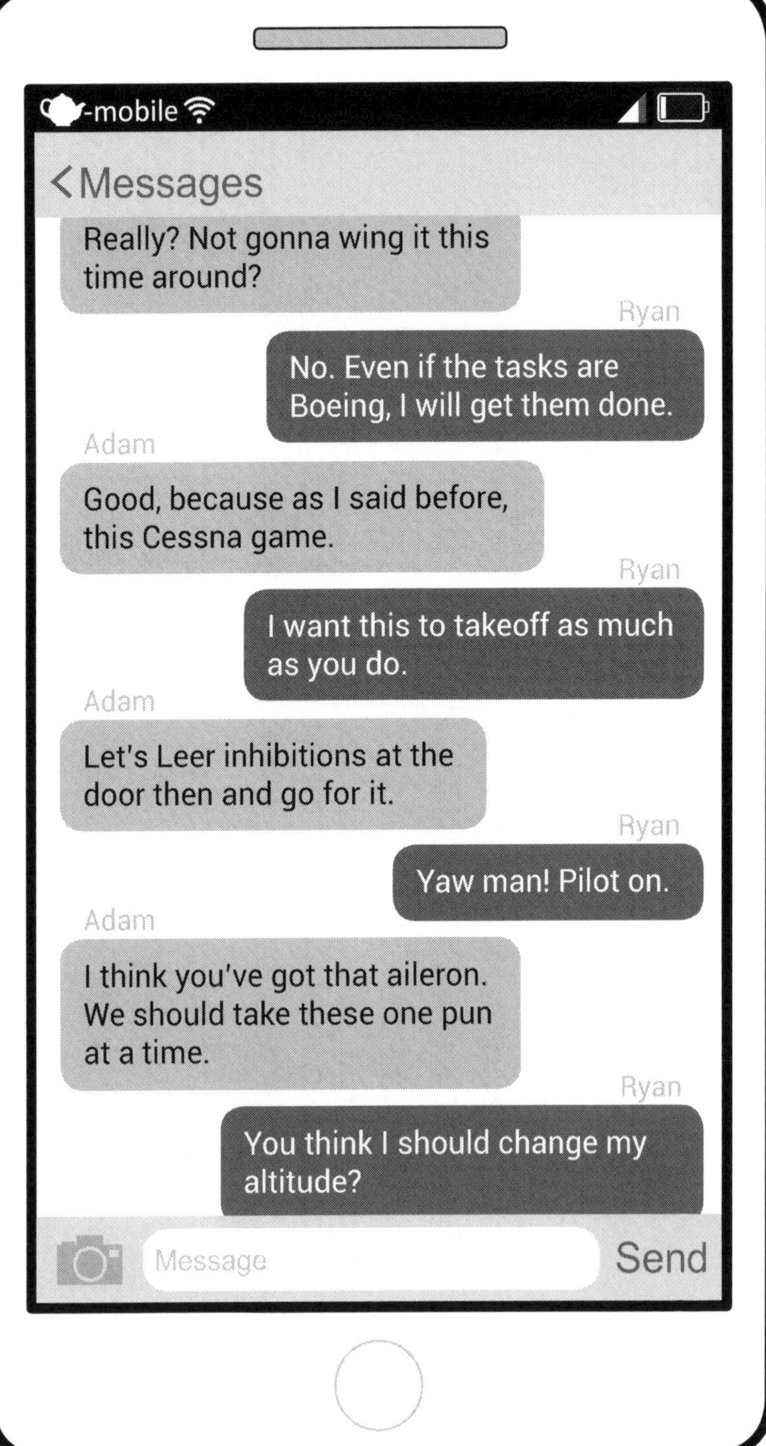
-mobile
Messages
Really? Not gonna wing it this time around?
Ryan
No. Even if the tasks are Boeing, I will get them done.
Adam
Good, because as I said before, this Cessna game.
Ryan
I want this to takeoff as much as you do.
Adam
Let's Leer inhibitions at the door then and go for it.
Ryan
Yaw man! Pilot on.
Adam
I think you've got that aileron. We should take these one pun at a time.
Ryan
You think I should change my altitude?
Message
Send

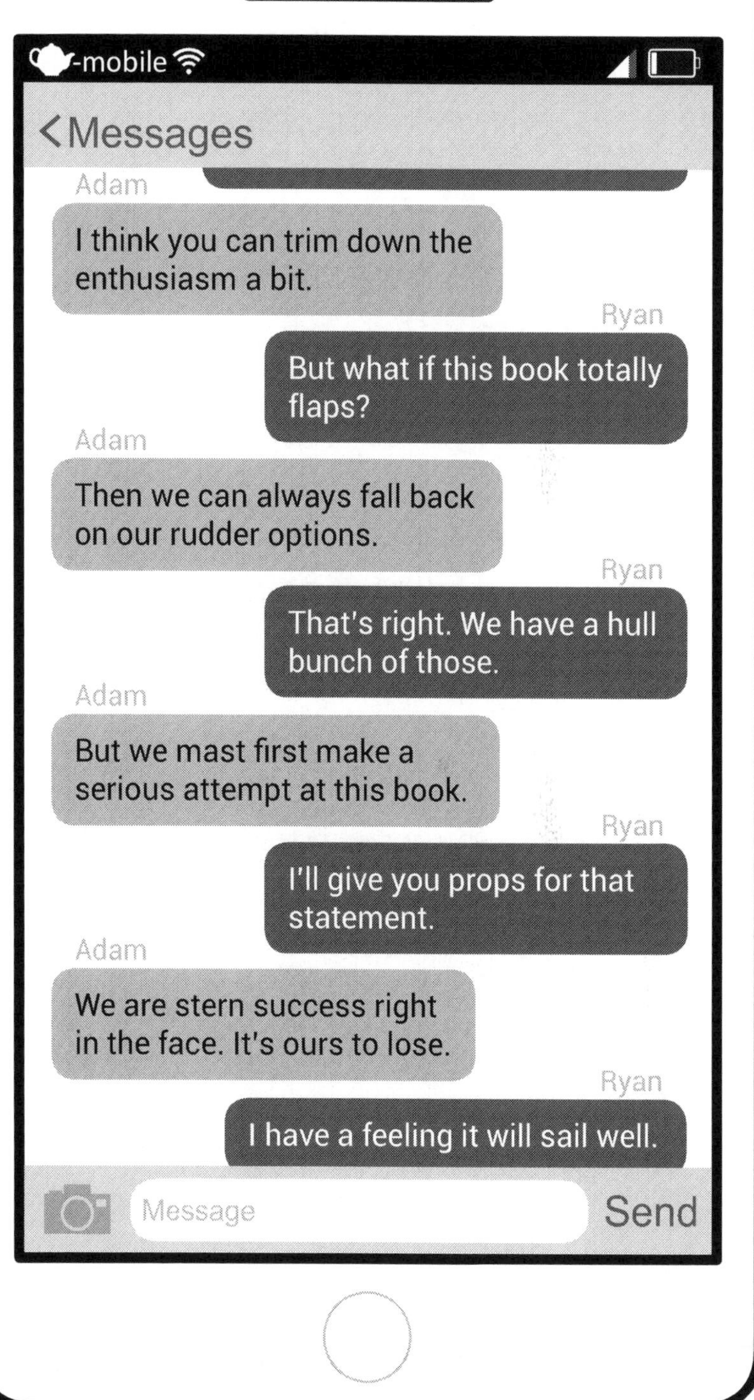
-mobile
Messages
Adam
I think you can trim down the enthusiasm a bit.
Ryan
But what if this book totally flaps?
Adam
Then we can always fall back on our rudder options.
Ryan
That's right. We have a hull bunch of those.
Adam
But we mast first make a serious attempt at this book.
Ryan
I'll give you props for that statement.
Adam
We are stern success right in the face. It's ours to lose.
Ryan
I have a feeling it will sail well.
Message
Send

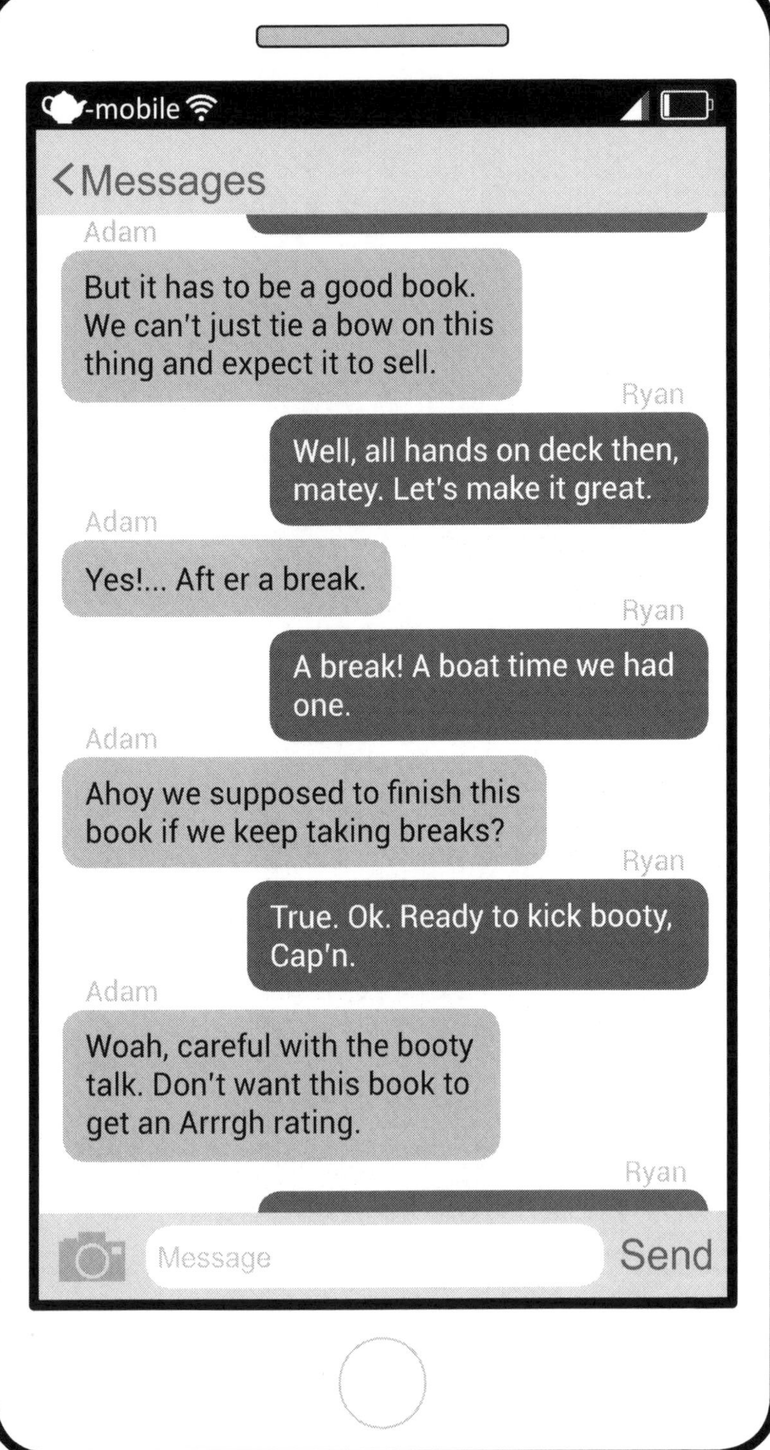
-mobile
Messages
Adam
But it has to be a good book. We can't just tie a bow on this thing and expect it to sell.
Ryan
Well, all hands on deck then, matey. Let's make it great.
Adam
Yes!... Aft er a break.
Ryan
A break! A boat time we had one.
Adam
Ahoy we supposed to finish this book if we keep taking breaks?
Ryan
True. Ok. Ready to kick booty, Cap'n.
Adam
Woah, careful with the booty talk. Don't want this book to get an Arrrgh rating.
Ryan
Message
Send

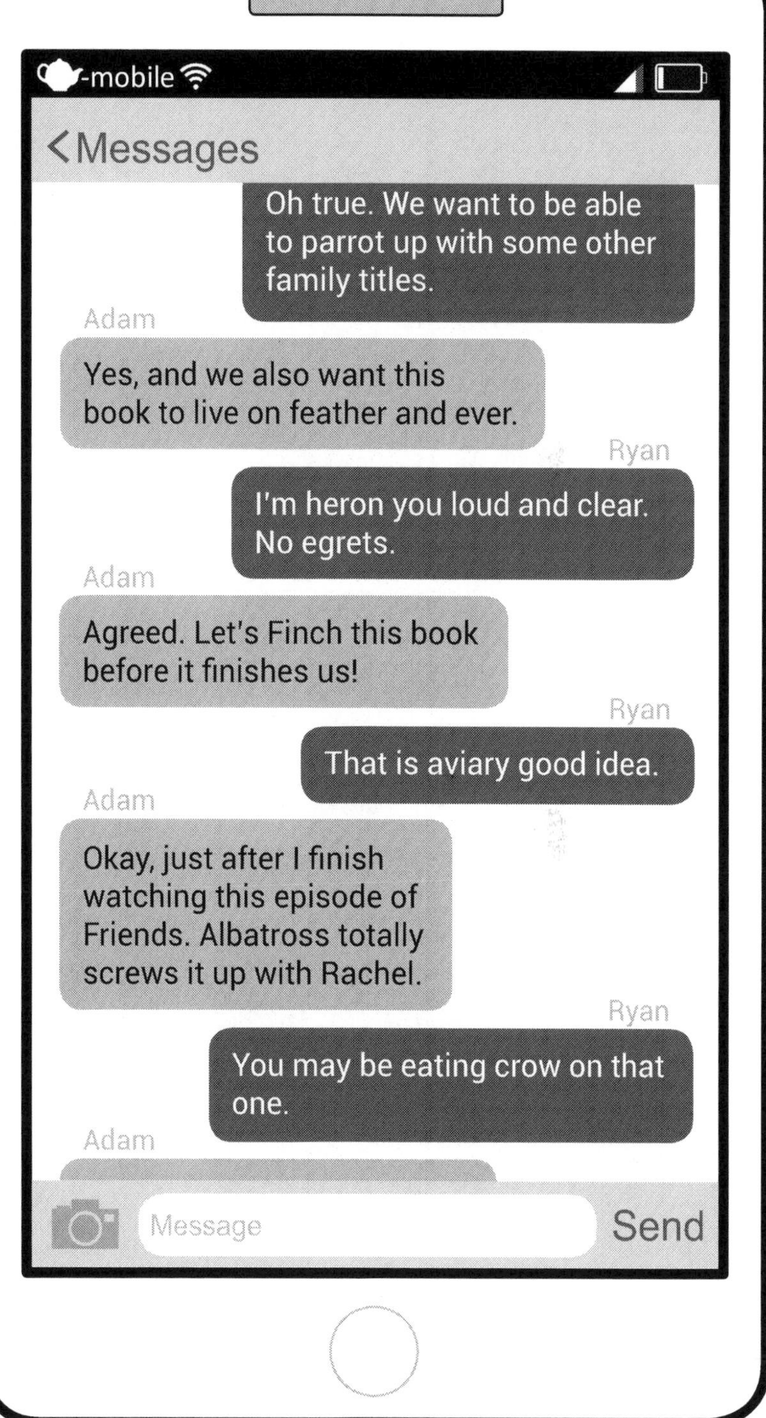
-mobile
Messages
Oh true. We want to be able to parrot up with some other family titles.
Adam
Yes, and we also want this book to live on feather and ever.
Ryan
I'm heron you loud and clear. No egrets.
Adam
Agreed. Let's Finch this book before it finishes us!
Ryan
That is aviary good idea.
Adam
Okay, just after I finish watching this episode of Friends. Albatross totally screws it up with Rachel.
Ryan
You may be eating crow on that one.
Adam
Message
Send

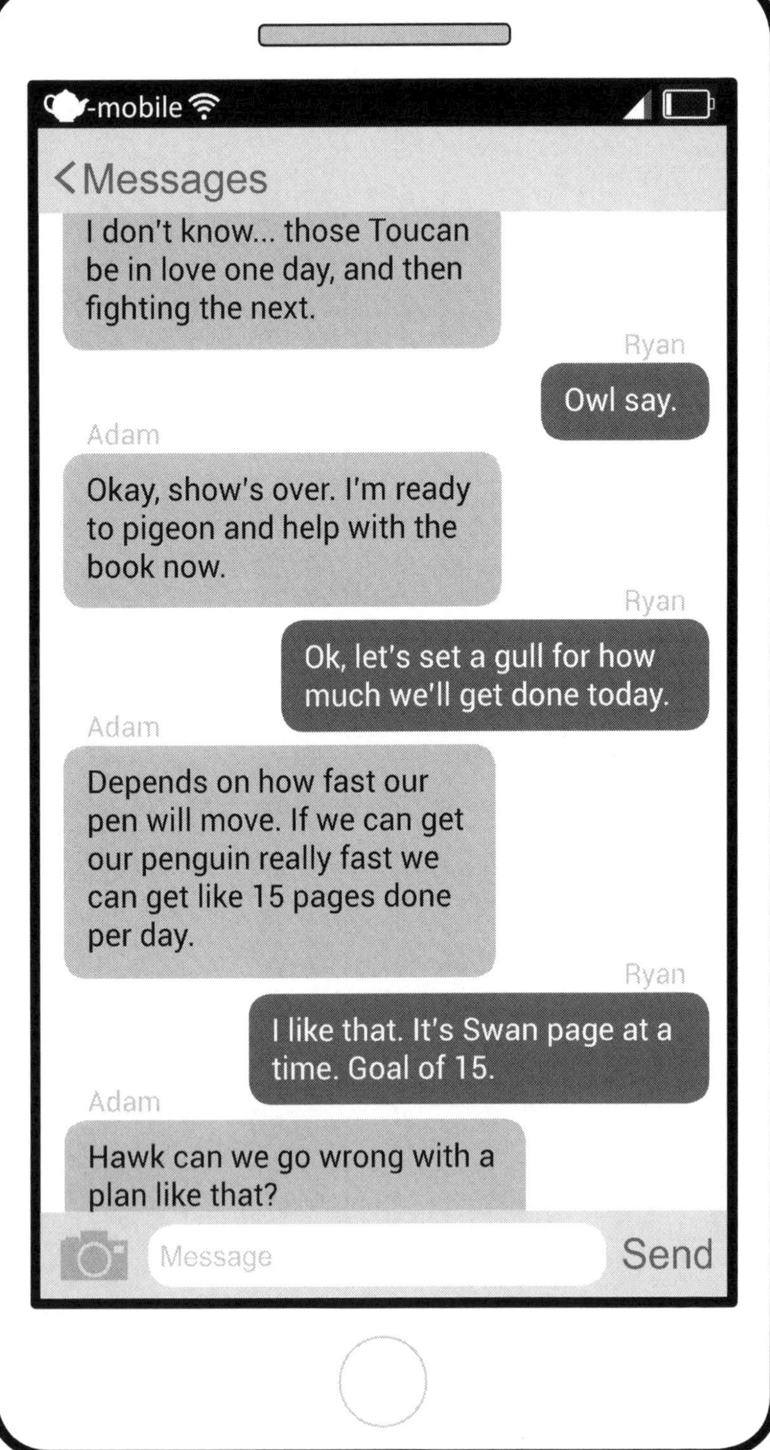
-mobile
Messages
I don't know... those Toucan be in love one day, and then fighting the next.
Ryan
Owl say.
Adam
Okay, show's over. I'm ready to pigeon and help with the book now.
Ryan
Ok, let's set a gull for how much we'll get done today.
Adam
Depends on how fast our pen will move. If we can get our penguin really fast we can get like 15 pages done per day.
Ryan
I like that. It's Swan page at a time. Goal of 15.
Adam
Hawk can we go wrong with a plan like that?
Message
Send

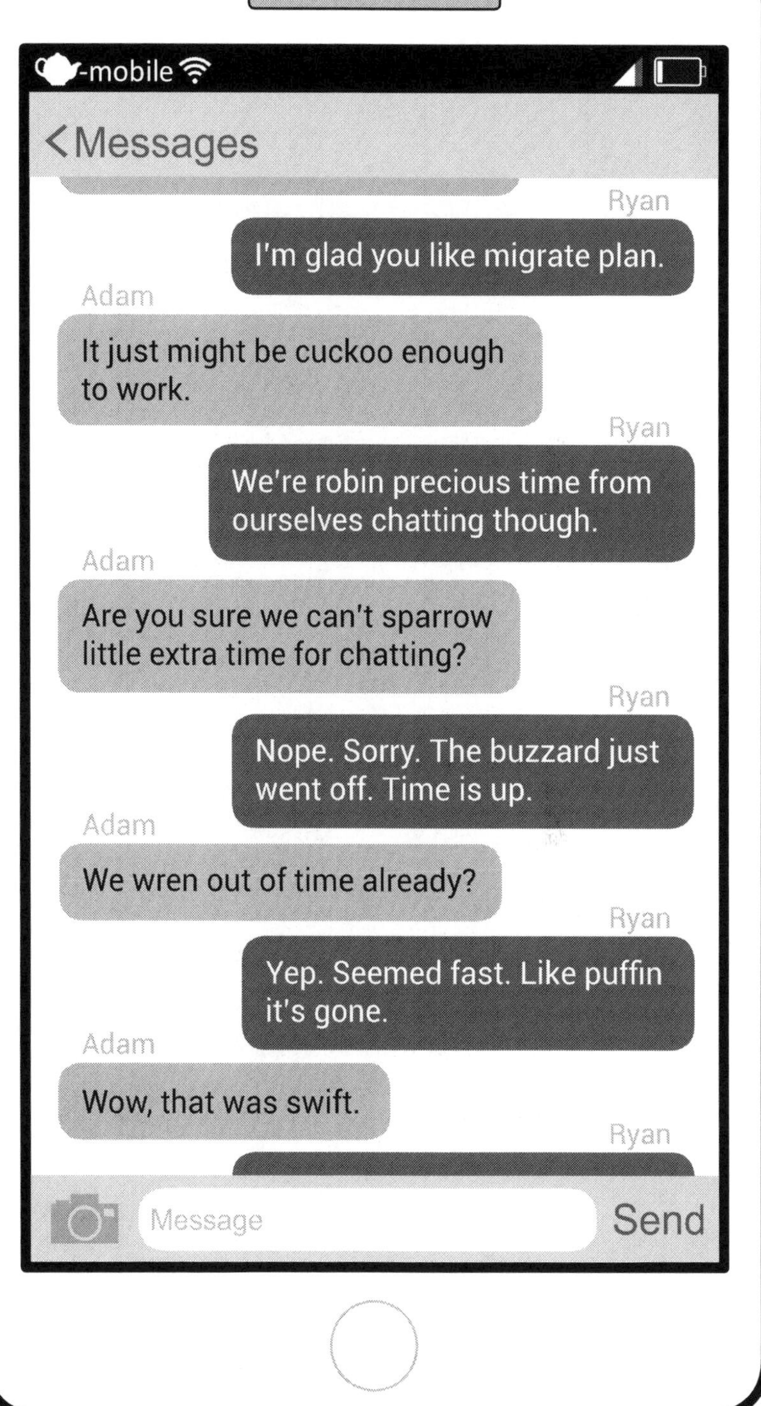
-mobile
Messages
Ryan
I'm glad you like migrate plan.
Adam
It just might be cuckoo enough to work.
Ryan
We're robin precious time from ourselves chatting though.
Adam
Are you sure we can't sparrow little extra time for chatting?
Ryan
Nope. Sorry. The buzzard just went off. Time is up.
Adam
We wren out of time already?
Ryan
Yep. Seemed fast. Like puffin it's gone.
Adam
Wow, that was swift.
Ryan
Message
Send

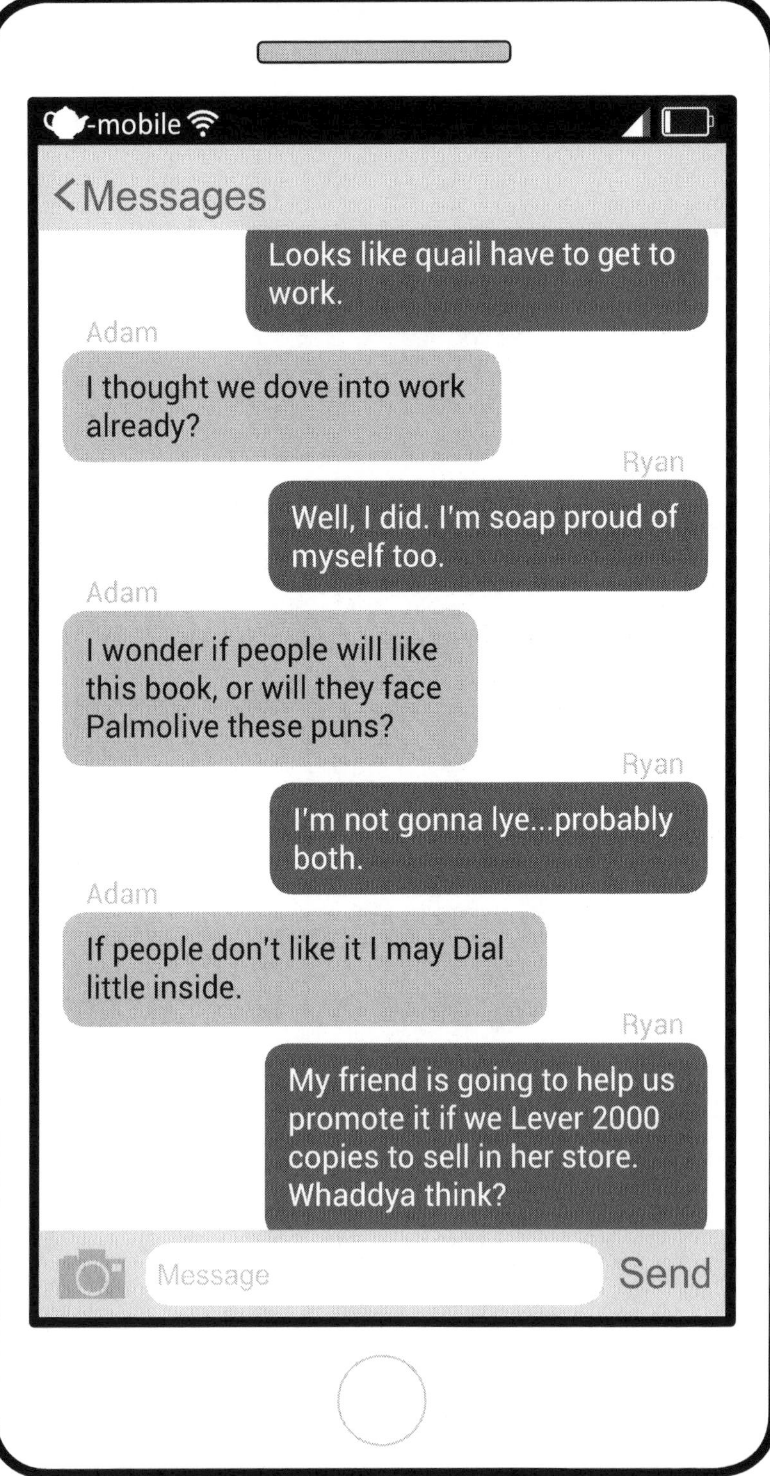
-mobile
Messages
Looks like quail have to get to work.
Adam
I thought we dove into work already?
Ryan
Well, I did. I'm soap proud of myself too.
Adam
I wonder if people will like this book, or will they face Palmolive these puns?
Ryan
I'm not gonna lye...probably both.
Adam
If people don't like it I may Dial little inside.
Ryan
My friend is going to help us promote it if we Lever 2000 copies to sell in her store. Whaddya think?
Message
Send

-mobile
Messages
Adam
I guess we'd have to give some copies away sooner or lather.
Ryan
We do need to wash our budget though.
Adam
That didn't Dawn on me.
Ryan
Well, either way. We need to get to work. Ivory started. Back to the book!
Adam
I had hoped we'd be done by May. Irish Spring were here so we could be finished already!
Ryan
Ah spring and the beautiful trees. Which reminds me of an idea I just had. Maybe we should make people paper pun rather than per book.
Adam
Message
Send

-mobile
Messages
Man, they would page gillions of dollars for that.
Ryan
Yea, TOC about exciting, huh?
Adam
Well, then I guess it's time for you to pour that glossary good wine and start writing.
Ryan
All write, I'll write, alright!
Oh shoot, man...I think my battery is dying. I guess that is my queue to get to work...
Send
Q W E R T Y U I O P
A S D F G H J K L
Z X C V B N M
123
space
return

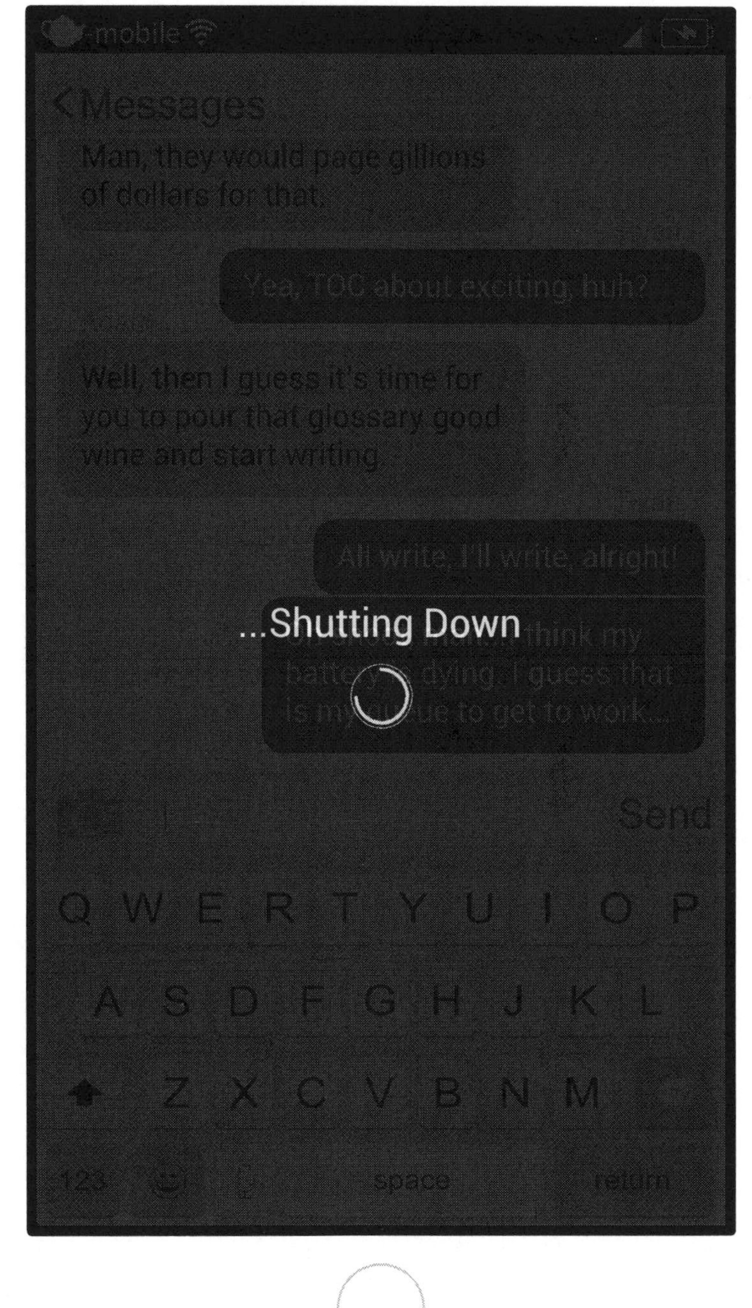
mobile
Messages
Man, they would page gillions of dollars for that.
Yea, TOC about exciting, huh?
Well, then I guess it's time for you to pour that glossary good wine and start writing.
All write, I'll write, alright!
...Shutting Down
think my
dying. I guess that
ue to get to work...
Send
Q W E R T Y U I O P
A S D F G H J K L
Z X C V B N M
123
space
return

Will Ryan and Adam find that PR firm to promote their book?

Will they ever agree on a price?

Will they remember to charge their phone batteries?

Will they ever stop talking about useless garbage and actually get around to writing the book?

Find out in the next installment of the series.
*actual existence of next book subject to change without notice.

Made in the USA
San Bernardino, CA
21 June 2019